Approaches to Teaching
the Works of C. P. Cavafy

Approaches to Teaching the Works of C. P. Cavafy

Edited by

Peter Jeffreys

and

Demetres P. Tryphonopoulos

The Modern Language Association of America
New York   2025

© 2025 by The Modern Language Association of America
85 Broad Street, New York, New York 10004
www.mla.org

All rights reserved. MLA and the MODERN LANGUAGE ASSOCIATION are trademarks owned by the Modern Language Association of America. To request permission to reprint material from MLA book publications, please inquire at permissions@mla.org.

To order MLA publications, visit www.mla.org/books. For wholesale and international orders, see www.mla.org/bookstore-orders. The EU-based Responsible Person for MLA products is the Mare Nostrum Group, which can be reached at gpsr@mare-nostrum.co.uk or the Mare Nostrum Group BV, Mauritskade 21D, 1091 GC Amsterdam, Netherlands. For a copy of the MLA's risk assessment document, write to scholcomm@mla.org.

The MLA office is located on the island known as Mannahatta (Manhattan) in Lenapehoking, the homeland of the Lenape people. The MLA pays respect to the original stewards of this land and to the diverse and vibrant Native communities that continue to thrive in New York City.

Approaches to Teaching World Literature 175
ISSN 1059-1133

Library of Congress Cataloging-in-Publication Data

Names: Jeffreys, Peter, editor. | Tryphonopoulos, Demetres P., 1956- editor.
Title: Approaches to teaching the works of C. P. Cavafy / edited by
    Peter Jeffreys and Demetres P. Tryphonopoulos.
Description: New York : The Modern Language Association of America, 2025.
Series: Approaches to teaching world literature, 1059-1133 ; 175 | Includes
    bibliographical references.
Identifiers: LCCN 2024046457 (print) | LCCN 2024046458 (ebook) | ISBN 9781603296502
    (hardcover) | ISBN 9781603296519 (paperback) | ISBN 9781603296526 (EPUB)
Subjects: LCSH: Cavafy, Constantine, 1863-1933—Criticism and interpretation. | Cavafy,
    Constantine, 1863-1933—Study and teaching. | Greek poetry—Study and teaching.
Classification: LCC PA5610.K2 Z566 2025 (print) | LCC PA5610.K2 (ebook) |
    DDC 889.1/32—dc23/eng/20250118
LC record available at https://lccn.loc.gov/2024046457
LC ebook record available at https://lccn.loc.gov/2024046458

To the memory of the poet and scholar George Economou:
μεγάλως θ' αγαπήθη

CONTENTS

Acknowledgments ix
Preface xi

PART ONE: MATERIALS

Editions and Translations 3
Critical Reception 7
Biographical Resources 12
Other Primary Sources 13
Background Reading, Reference Materials, and Teaching Guides 15
Multimedia Resources and Visual Art 16
Websites 18
Teaching Resources 20
The Digitized Cavafy Archive as a Teaching and Research Resource 24
  Angeliki Mousiou

PART TWO: APPROACHES

Introduction 33
  Peter Jeffreys and Demetres P. Tryphonopoulos

Theoretical, Cultural, and Historical Contexts

Teaching Cavafy with Queer Theory 37
  Cat Lambert

Bringing Cavafy the Egyptiote into the Classroom 44
  Hala Halim

Cavafy and History: An Interdisciplinary Approach 54
  Kelly Polychroniou and Loren J. Samons

Cavafy in Comparison: The Politics of Time 64
  Natalie Melas

Why Cavafy? Why Postcolonial? Teaching the Postcolonial Cavafy 72
  Martin McKinsey

Translating, Discovering, and Interpreting Cavafy

Cavafy Constructed: Archive, Editions, Translations 82
  Karen Emmerich

Which Cavafy? Selecting the Right Translation — 91
Sarah Ekdawi

The Poetics of Liminality: Anti-Economy and Cultural Politics in Cavafy — 101
Panagiotis Roilos

Intertextual Approaches

Cavafy's *Iliad* in the Classroom — 111
Stamatia Dova

Cavafy's Decadent Aesthetic — 120
Peter Jeffreys

Conversing with Cavafy through Music — 126
Vassilis Lambropoulos

Digital Cavafy: Teaching Poetry through Connective Media — 135
Foteini Dimirouli

Digital Intertextuality and the Cavafy Archive — 145
Takis Kayalis

Classroom Contexts

Teaching Cavafy to the *Instagram* Generation — 154
Gregory Jusdanis

"Dangerous Things"? Cavafy in the Modern Greek Language Classroom — 163
Elsa Amanatidou

Cavafy as a Bridge from Classics to Modern Greek Studies — 171
Johanna Hanink

Notes on Contributors — 181

Survey Respondents — 185

Works Cited — 187

ACKNOWLEDGMENTS

For a project as multifaceted and wide-ranging as this volume on teaching the works of C. P. Cavafy, we must begin by thanking Cavafy translators, literary critics, and textual scholars worldwide. These Cavafy specialists have spearheaded the scholarship, criticism, and textual study of Cavafy and have contributed not only to his rise as the most prominent modern Greek poet but also to his expansive global reputation.

Our seventeen contributors to this volume reflect a diversity of approaches to reading and studying Cavafy and share their distinctive experiences teaching the poet in the classroom, primarily in English translation. We are deeply grateful to them for sharing their pedagogical expertise and for their fortitude in sticking with this project for over several years.

This volume is dedicated to the late George Economou, in recognition of his life in poetry and his passion for translating Cavafy. At the time of his passing, he was in the process of composing an essay for inclusion in this volume. Even without that essay, his involvement proved inspirational, and he enlightened us (and so many others) with his poetic talents and deep knowledge of Cavafy.

The editors are grateful to the editorial staff and production team at the MLA, in particular James Hatch, Michael Simon, Erika Suffern, and Susan Doose. Their assistance has been vital in overseeing this project from its inception. This volume has benefited greatly from the advice, criticism, and suggestions of at least seven anonymous reviewers as well as from the work of the MLA Publications Committee, whose members reviewed, evaluated, and commented on the proposal and manuscript on three occasions. To all these readers who contributed to the progress of the manuscript, many thanks are due.

We wish to acknowledge those who responded to the questionnaire that was circulated as we were drafting our proposal. Special thanks go to Gregory Jusdanis, who assisted with the original prospectus and has written a wonderful essay in this volume.

A special thanks goes to Sara Dunton, our incredibly supportive editorial assistant, who has been a model of responsiveness and clarity and who efficiently managed and edited contributors' submissions and helped compile the works-cited list.

Demetres thanks Litsa, Panayiota, and Panayiotes for their encouragement and support of his work as a scholar and for making it possible for him to complete another scholarly project. He would also like to thank the research officers and the library staff of the two institutions where he worked during the preparation of this volume (Brandon University and University of Alberta, Augustana) for their support. While working on this book, Demetres held grants from the Social Sciences and Humanities Research Council in Canada, and he would like to acknowledge the council's important contribution to this and other projects.

PREFACE

In Matthew Lopez's 2016 play *The Inheritance*—a queer reframing of E. M. Forster's *Howards End* that problematizes the current reception of gay literary culture—one of the young protagonists (a sensitive street hustler) pulls from his backpack a copy of C. P. Cavafy's poems along with three other gay classics: James Baldwin's *Giovanni's Room*, André Aciman's *Call Me by Your Name*, and Alan Hollinghurst's *The Swimming-Pool Library*. The play's engagement with the Greek poet is further confirmed by its use of Cavafy's poem "Hidden," which serves as the epigraph for the play's published script and lends the drama a decidedly Cavafian tone. Forster appears in the play as a central character who interacts intergenerationally and intertextually with millennials, who defer to his literary fame but censure his refusal to come out fully during his lifetime. Lopez makes the point that there is a queer literary inheritance that must be acknowledged and embraced, however problematic it might be; his choice to have a collection of Cavafy's poems pop out of a hustler's backpack enforces the poet's relevance in queer and popular culture in the twenty-first century.

Cavafy's relevance is also evident in *Find Me*, the 2019 sequel to André Aciman's best-selling novel and movie adaptation *Call Me by Your Name*. In the final chapter of *Find Me*, the novel's two thwarted lovers, Elio and Oliver, reconnect in Alexandria and visit the home of Cavafy. The novel concludes with a quasi-romantic recasting of the Cavafy poem "Poseidonians" that comments on the dangers of forgetting. Similarly, Cavafy's poem "One of Their Gods" features in a chapter of the 2021 novel *Alec*—William di Canzio's reimagined sequel to Forster's *Maurice*—although, curiously, Cavafy's name appears neither in connection with the poem nor within the novel, the implication being that the poet's identity is self-evident given his global fame. In these three notable twenty-first-century literary contexts, Cavafy holds a place of cultural prominence. Taken in tandem with the moment when his poetic fame reached its zenith—the reading of "Ithaka" at the funeral of Jacqueline Kennedy Onassis—these texts manifest the indisputable phenomenon of Cavafy as a global cultural commodity, something a once-marginal poet writing in Alexandria at the turn of the twentieth century could hardly have imagined.

Cavafy and his early translator George Valassopoulo were introduced to the English-speaking world in 1919 through the efforts of Forster. By 1930, only a dozen or so of Cavafy's poems had appeared in English translation, in journals like *The Athenaeum* and *The Criterion*, but as of 2023, more than twenty-five translations of his poems are available in English. The translations, along with the growing critical attention to Cavafy's works, testify to the irresistible quality of his poems, the allure of their subject matter, and the poet's inimitable tone and voice. The essays in this volume have been selected with the view to exploring and demonstrating the power and attraction Cavafy's poems hold in anglophone classrooms throughout the world.

Anyone wishing to teach Cavafy's poems encounters not only the abundance of translations but also the challenges of choosing among them. So too do they encounter the lucid glimpses that Cavafy offers us through the window of art, allowing us to delve into the complex realms of beauty, ambitious dreams gone wrong, old age, human hopes dashed by fate, and the workings of passions and desires. Many of these themes are presented against the background of the city of Alexandria with its bustling cafés and shops. This modernist urban ethos is one of the characteristics Cavafy shares with many high-modernist Anglo-American poets. Yet his distinct marginality continues to distinguish him from many of his contemporaries.

Cavafy's relatively small creative corpus has drawn considerable scholarly interest, both in Greek and in English, and research on him and his work continues apace. Cavafy regularly generates more critical attention in English than do the two Greek Nobelists (George Seferis and Odysseus Elytis) and at least as much as the novelist Nikos Kazantzakis does. There are a handful of Cavafy poems known and celebrated by a wider public: "Waiting for the Barbarians," "Ithaka," "Thermopylae," "Candles," "Desires," and "Walls." Indeed, Cavafy is the writer of astonishing poems that combine his innovative style with a subtle appreciation for Greek prosody.

Nor is it surprising that Cavafy's private life and homosexuality attracted interest from readers early on. Cavafy often gives voice to the erotic, especially the suppressed longings of queer desire. In "He Asked about the Quality," a shop assistant and an office clerk fix their eyes on each other. The clerk enters the store and asks about the quality of the handkerchiefs, though the real purpose of his visit is to brush hands with the shop assistant under the pile of wares, which hide their activity from the shop owner's watchful eye. Similarly, in "Theater of Sidon (A.D. 400)," the speaker, a handsome young man of the theater, occasionally composes exceedingly daring verses in the Greek tongue, "verses about an exceptional kind of sexual pleasure, / the kind that leads toward a condemned, a barren love" (*Collected Poems* [Barnstone] 126).

Cavafy offers glimpses into the fortunes of a Hellenism existing within the cauldron of ancient empires and peoples. He seems spellbound by the idea of the decisive moment and even more so by fatal choices. He is particularly interested in history's often inconsequential moments: a Spartan king's disappointment over advising an enemy, knowing all along that the noble things desired are no longer attainable; Mark Antony's anguish in bidding farewell to his beloved Alexandria; the terrible crisis leading to the demise of the Trojans; the wretched Lares trembling as they sense the footsteps of the Furies approaching the slumbering Nero; Ephialtes's betrayal at Thermopylae; the dissolution of Demetrios Soter's dreams for the former glory of his Syrian motherland. Cavafy's poetry is a mosaic, a pattern of peoples and races, of hellenized so-called barbarians—Jews, pagans, and Christians who form a complex world brought together by their

Greek education and shared Greek language. He rescues from history those minor moments in the ethnic, religious, cultural, and racial blending of the Hellenistic kingdoms and the Roman Empire. He is especially attuned to the tensions of such conflicts and sees in them the opportunity for social critique and self-examination. Cavafy is the poet for whom success comes to resemble splendid failure—and failure ruinous success—and who finds that moments of defeat are also occasions for awareness and epiphany.

One of the goals of this volume is to bring Cavafy's oeuvre closer to instructors and students by providing pedagogically sound examples of how the work may be taught. Cavafy's personal history (moving from Alexandria to Liverpool, London, Istanbul, and back to Alexandria) is rife with enigmas and meaningful gaps. Learning about Cavafy involves a sharpened attentiveness to important twentieth-century aesthetic ideas and perspectives. Like the Anglo-American modernists, but working independently of them from his Alexandrian periphery, the Greek poet modernized himself all on his own. By grappling with the pedagogical issues of teaching Cavafy and approaching his work from a variety of transnational, intertextual, and interdisciplinary modalities, the contributors to this volume present a rich variety of ways to teach his complex poems and appreciate his rich poetics. Their essays offer a wide range of approaches and topics dealing with a compelling poet whose extraordinary poems inevitably lead to an ultimate insight, a final verse line that, like the climax of an ancient tragedy, keeps surprising the reader even though the story and its familiar ending were well-known all along.

Part One

MATERIALS

Editions and Translations

Upon publishing one of his earliest compositions—Κτίσται ("Ktistai"; "Builders")—in the Athens journal Αττικόν Μουσείον (*Attikon Mousion; Attic Museum*) in 1891, Cavafy arranged to have broadsheets of the poem typeset at a printery in Alexandria, inaugurating a lifelong process whereby he would distribute his poems privately to a select readership. From the outset of his poetic career, he was intent on targeting readers beyond those who encountered him in the newspapers, periodicals, and literary journals that featured his work. This handpicked audience formed the foundation on which his subsequent global reputation would be built, a prospect about which an obscure poet writing in Greek in a Mediterranean commercial city could only have dreamed. The publication of this early poem signaled Cavafy's arrival as a poet in the Athenian literary world. Cavafy would proceed to build his poetic body of work one poem at a time, but remarkably, he never published an edition of poems during his lifetime, at least not in the conventional sense. Rather he would circulate various versions of his privately printed work, either as broadsheets, pamphlets, bound volumes, clipped batches, or sewn notebooks. Through this unique means of dissemination, he created curiosity about his work while entrusting it to a largely sympathetic audience. Given how unconventional his poetry was, distinguished by its mixed linguistic idiom (both purist and demotic Greek), its increasingly daring forays into homoerotic subject matter, and its unapologetic sensuality, this particular manner of distribution proved to be an ingenious if demanding modus operandi. Indeed, the labor-intensive task of producing and circulating these privately printed texts consumed a large portion of his time, but then so did his work placing poems in literary and journalistic venues. Cavafy certainly had a long-term strategy in mind: he was determined to be recognized as a bona fide poet, the profession by which he officially designated himself on his final passport. But more important, he was aiming for posthumous fame while building up a contemporary readership.

Shortly after his death in 1933 at the age of seventy—he died on 29 April, the day of his birth—his literary executor, Alekos Sengopoulos, along with Alekos's wife, Rika, oversaw the publication of the first edition of the 154 so-called canonical poems. Ever since the appearance of this volume in 1935 (Cavafy, *Piimata*), a debate has raged about the arrangement and categorization of Cavafy's poems. Cavafy's first academic editor, George Savidis, who acquired the poet's archive in 1969, employed a systematic editing strategy and classification of all the extant poetic material, bringing out his own edition of the canon in 1963 (Cavafy, *Piimata, A'* and *Piimata, B'*, revised in 1984 and 1991). These publications constituted the standard versions of the Cavafy canon in Greece up until quite recently. Savidis subsequently edited and published the noncanonical material, which he grouped into various categories—unpublished, repudiated, hidden, and unfinished—labels that, while attempting to organize the remainder of the poetic corpus for a wider audience, have proved equally problematic.

The challenge of arranging and classifying this poetic corpus stems largely from the refusal by Cavafy to oversee and authorize a definitive edition of poetry during his lifetime. Many editorial dilemmas have ensued from the poet's sui generis publishing methods and revising practices. His reluctance to issue a conventional collection of poems also extended to his refusal to authorize an edition of English translations. His brother John (an aspiring poet) and his friend George Valassopoulo (an Alexandrian lawyer) made the most headway in this regard as his first committed and stalwart English translators. But Cavafy was loath to sign off on the efforts of either of them, and thus no volume of English translations appeared during his lifetime. Various explanations for these equivocations have been put forth. One is that Cavafy was unwilling to cease revising his poems, never being content with his finished drafts. Another attributes this hesitation to an aristocratic predisposition that viewed the release of a commercial volume as déclassé. While both explanations hold some degree of truth, there was also a certain neurosis at play in the poet's obsessive revising of his poems and frenetic distributing of his printed material. It is no coincidence that he had a room set aside in his flat for producing and assembling pages of his work, a veritable scriptorium where he would ceaselessly correct, collect, and emend offprints. He was fastidious about keeping lists of the recipients of his poetic offerings, which document the staggering fact that during his lifetime he managed to distribute some 2,200 handmade collections in one form or another (Emmerich 136). This is an almost unprecedented publishing procedure for a twentieth-century poet and one that has greatly contributed to the challenges of collecting, arranging, and editing his poetry (see Emmerich's essay in this volume).

The publication history of Cavafy's work remains a complex and fascinating subject, and anyone teaching the material would benefit from a basic overview of the attendant controversies and debates that have raged among scholars, editors, and translators. The first contentious matter involves the arrangement of the 154 canonical poems—whether they should be presented thematically or chronologically. Cavafy once divided his poems into three broad thematic categories: philosophical, historical, and hedonistic. When he first distributed his volume editions in 1904 and 1910, he arranged the poems thematically. Later batches were organized both thematically and chronologically, indicating that the poet was open to and experimenting with both options. When Alekos and Rika published the first edition of the poems, they followed a strictly chronological order,[1] although this sequencing was complicated by their method of dating the poems, which could be by either the year of their composition, their printing date, or their date of publication in literary or journalistic venues. Savidis, after conducting a systematic study of the poet's publishing and distribution practices—his Οι Καβαφικές εκδόσεις, 1891–1932 (*I Kavafikes ekdosis, 1891–1932*; *Cavafian Editions, 1891–1932*) remains the standard resource on the topic—followed a mixed template when he brought out his two-volume edition of the canon in

1963. In an effort to reflect Cavafy's own evolution in arranging the compilations of poems, the first volume adhered to a thematic arrangement and the second to a chronological one. This presentation of the canon has remained standard and has served as the organizing basis for many subsequent translations.

Savidis's editorial practices for selecting the final textual versions of the poems and standardization of Cavafy's spelling, punctuation, and accentuation went relatively unchallenged until a series of critical articles effectively contested the editor's choices, methods, and procedures (Hirst and Ekdawi; Hirst, "Philosophical"). This critique, initially led by Sarah Ekdawi and Anthony Hirst, also extended to the organization of the noncanonical material,[2] which was gradually released in a series of volumes presented under the following categories: *Unpublished Poems, 1882–1923*, *Repudiated Poems and Translations, 1886–1898*, and *Hidden Poems, 1877?–1923*. Capping these off is *Unfinished Poems, 1918–1932*, edited by Renata Lavagnini (Cavafy, *Ateli piimata*). Scholars further lament the lack of critical editions of both the canonical and uncanonical poems documenting all known textual variations and revisions. Subsequent Greek editions of note include those by Renos, Irkos, and Stantis Apostolidis (Cavafy, *Apanta ta dimosieumena piimata*); Sonia Ilinskagia (Cavafy, *Apanta ta piimata*); and Dimitris Eleftherakis (Cavafy, *Piimata*).[3] In 2015, a scholarly edition of the entire poetic corpus, edited by Dimitris Dimiroulis, was published: Κ.Π. Καβάφης: Τα ποιήματα δημοσιευμένα και αδημοσίευτα (*K. P. Kavafis: Ta piimata dimosieumena kai adimosieuta*; *C. P. Cavafy: The Published and Unpublished Poems*); this 813-page edition, which arranges the canonical poems chronologically, contains an extensive introduction, a chronology of Cavafy's life, and copious annotations, and it includes Cavafy's translations, literary prose, and selected comments and notes on the poetry.

Since the acquisition of the Cavafy archive by the Onassis Foundation in 2012 and its full digitization in 2019, many of these editorial and textual debates have entered a new phase. The recent scholarly work of Karen Emmerich and William Stroebel has reshaped the discussion on redacting the poems by expanding it to take into account the "fundamental instability" of Cavafy's texts (Emmerich 158 and, on this subject, 131–59) and the existence of new digital ways by which readers may experience and assemble them (Stroebel 305). For Stroebel, Cavafy's final intentions remain "an open workshop" since a Cavafy poem "evolved *while* it was being shared and read" (280, 281).[4] The future editing of Cavafy's work surely depends on how the archival material will be approached digitally and on how new reading and editing strategies will be applied to this public archival platform. Indeed, the digitized archive holds exciting pedagogical potential. We have included one additional essay as an addendum to "Materials": Angeliki Mousiou's "The Digitized Cavafy Archive as a Teaching and Research Resource." Mousiou's work as an archivist at the Onassis Foundation Cavafy Archive informs the essay, which constitutes a dive into the riches of the archive and the possibilities it offers to researchers, teachers, and students. The digital collection, Mousiou notes, is a vast and exciting repository that facilitates open access, archival research, and the use of primary resources in the classroom.

To date, there exist over twenty-five full-length English translations of Cavafy's poems. Based on the survey conducted at the outset of planning this volume, the choice of a particular text varies according to the nature of the class and the approach of the instructor. The older translations by Rae Dalven and by Edmund Keeley and Philip Sherrard remain popular since general readers tend to be more familiar with them; they also have a foundational status by virtue of having appeared in the earliest critical work done on the poet. Yet there are important differences that distinguish these many translations and that justify a preference for one translation over another. Instructors looking for a text with ample footnotes and a solid critical apparatus may wish to opt for Daniel Mendelsohn's *Complete Poems* (Cavafy, *Complete Poems* [Mendelsohn]). Most respondents and contributors use a single edition of the available translations, but others (especially in comparative literature classes and classes dealing with translation theory and practice or creative writing) use more than one edition, for purposes of comparison. And there are those instructors who use their own translations. Besides Keeley and Sherrard's bilingual *Collected Poems* (Cavafy, *Collected Poems* [Keeley and Sherrard, 1992]), Dalven's *The Complete Poems of Cavafy* (Cavafy, *Complete Poems* [Dalven]), and Mendelsohn's *Complete Poems*, other collections mentioned by survey respondents include Evangelos Sachperoglou's *Collected Poems* (Cavafy, *Collected Poems* [Sachperoglou]), Aliki Barnstone's *The Collected Poems of C. P. Cavafy* (Cavafy, *Collected Poems* [Barnstone]), Theoharis Theoharis's *Before Time Could Change Them: The Complete Poems of Constantine P. Cavafy* (Cavafy, *Before Time*), and George Economou's *Complete Plus* (Cavafy, *Complete Plus*).

A few of our respondents prefer discussing a single poem in several of the translations listed above in order to illustrate to their students the nature and process of translation itself. For instance, in focusing on particular versification practices, one respondent's teaching strategy involves examining three different translations of two Cavafy poems. When considering tone of voice, the same instructor uses passages from Dalven's translation. One instructor uses the Keeley and Sherrard translation but also turns to Lawrence Durrell's idiomatic versions and points to W. H. Auden's endorsement of the early translation by Dalven. Finally, one respondent, a comparatist, references an anxiety about translation that is overcome by providing at least two translations of any given poem. Relying largely on Mendelsohn's *Complete Poems*, this instructor also uses Keeley and Sherrard's translation as well as Barnstone's. Indeed, there are several scholar-translators who have published complete collections of the poems in English, all of them providing opportunities for readers to experience Cavafy's complexities, including the fact that, as George Seferis observed, Cavafy wrote "in his own language" (*Poet's Journal* 138). This insight into Cavafy's language contains both criticism and praise; his mixture of purist and demotic Greek is something that many of his readers and critics focus on and that many instructors strive to explore and appreciate in their classes.

Critical Reception

The early critical view of Auden, one of Cavafy's most astute readers, still serves as an insightful point of departure when exploring the distinctive allure of Cavafy's work: "What, then, is it in Cavafy's poems that survives translation and excites? Something I can only call, most inadequately, a tone of voice, a personal speech. I have read translations of Cavafy made by many different hands, but every one of them was immediately recognizable as a poem by Cavafy; nobody else could possibly have written it. . . . A unique tone of voice cannot be described; it can only be imitated, that is to say, either parodied or quoted" (Introduction xvi–xvii). This assessment effectively frames the first stage of Cavafy's reception both in Greece and throughout the Greek-speaking diaspora, when, during the final decades of his life and immediately following his death, derisive parody gradually gave way to zealous imitation. Among the Greek Athenian critics and poets, adulation of his verse had been present early on, but the poet's detractors became increasingly vocal and intent on denigrating the Alexandrian threat to the then reigning national poet of Greece, Kostis Palamas.[5]

In Alexandria, the work of Cavafy appeared regularly in three literary venues—Νέα Τέχνη (*Nea Techni*; *New Art*), Γράμματα (*Grammata*; *Letters*), and Αλεξανδρινή Τέχνη (*Alexandrini Techni*; *Alexandrian Art*)[6]—as well as in numerous other diasporic newspapers and journals. His rise to fame in Greece, however, was a much more protracted and complicated affair, and it was in Athens where the real battle for his literary reputation was effectively waged. Major moments in this critical reception during his lifetime include a 1903 laudatory essay by Grigoris Xenopoulos in the Athenian literary journal Παναθήναια (*Panathinea*; *Panathenian*) as well as the dedication of special volumes on Cavafy's work: in 1924, Νέα Τέχνη (*Nea Techni*; *New Art*), and in 1932, Κύκλος (*Kyklos*; *Circle*).[7] In due course, Cavafy would win over the more progressive elements of the Greek literati. Yet there was a persistent faction that remained opposed to all things Cavafy, an αντικαβαφησμός (*antikavafismos*; "anti-Cavafism"), as it were. In his illuminating study of Cavafy's reputation in Greece, Η Αθηναϊκή κριτική και ο Καβάφης, 1918–1924 (*I Athinaiki kritiki kai o Kavafis, 1918–1924*; *Athenian Criticism and Cavafy, 1918–1924*), Ch. L. Karaoglou identifies the basic critical faults of the poet that were identified by many of his Athenian detractors. In contrast to Palamas's lyrical and metrically conventional verse, Cavafy's poetry was derided as being too cerebral, unpoetically prosaic, and lacking in both emotion and description. His supporters however, chief among them Marios Vaianos and Napoleon Lapathiotis,[8] recognized in the Alexandrian a fresh modern voice whose pessimism in particular appealed to Greek poets and writers during the difficult interwar years. Gradually, an appreciation for Cavafy's inward focus on isolation, impasse, futility, and self-analysis would win out over the folkloric and nationalist narratives favored by the Palamas coterie (Karaoglou, *Athinaiki kritiki* 45, 63).

The phenomenon of Cavafian parody, quotation, and imitation that Auden perceptively identified has been documented in three important critical anthologies by the Greek scholars Dimitiris Daskalopoulos and Nasos Vagenas that chronicle Cavafy's gradual rise to fame. Daskalopoulos offers an insightful delineation of Cavafy's eventual ascendency in the world of Greek poetry in Παρωδίες καβαφηκών ποιημάτων, 1917–1997 (*Parodies Kavafikon piimaton, 1917–1997; Parodies of Cavafy Poems, 1917–1997*) and Ελληνικά καβαφογενή ποιήματα, 1909–2001 (*Ellinika Kavafogeni piimata, 1909–2001; Greek Cavafian Poems, 1909–2001*). Parodies of Cavafy's verse by detractors began as early as 1917 and increased throughout the 1920s, continuing well beyond the death of the poet. These perverse homages took aim at a number of the poet's personal attributes: his idiosyncratic behavior and perceived vulnerabilities, his alleged paranoia and sensitivity, his excessive obsequiousness toward his supporters, his speech and linguistic peculiarities, and above all else, his homoerotic aesthetic and his sexual orientation (Daskalopoulos, Introduction). Imitation and praise soon outpaced and replaced this parodic reception, first in Greece and later internationally. Greek poets not only began imitating Cavafy's prosody and style (writing *à la manière de* Cavafy) but also dedicated poems to him, composed thematically related verse, emulated his tone, copied his topics, dramatized his life, and even incorporated his name into their work. Poets outside of Greece soon replicated these mimetic dynamics; included in Vagenas's anthology Συνομιλώντας με τον Καβάφη: Ανθολογία ξένων καβαφογενών ποιημάτων (*Snomilontas me ton Kavafi: Anthologia xenon kavafogenon piimaton; Conversing with Cavafy: An Anthology of Foreign Cavafian Poems*) are poets from over thirty countries, a number that has been greatly surpassed in the two decades since the volume was published.

Cavafy's reception by Greek literary critics and philologists followed a similar trajectory. After his death, his legacy was defined by two vociferous and uncompromisingly opposed critics: Timos Malanos and Stratis Tsirkas. Malanos was initially a friend of the poet who soon turned into one of his harshest detractors. His book, Ο ποιητής Κ.Π. Καβάφης (*O piitis K. P. Kavafis; The Poet C. P. Cavafy*), published in 1933, just three months after the poet's death, is a Freudian biocritical reading of the life and work of Cavafy that set the tone for much of the negative criticism that would plague the poet's reputation after his death, focusing as it does on Cavafy's character flaws and perceived weaknesses (his egocentrism, cowardice, vanity, inconsistencies, and psychoses, among other alleged traits). Malanos's withering critique was countered in turn by Tsirkas's Marxist rehabilitation of Cavafy in two books: Ο Καβάφης και η εποχή του (*O Kavafis kai i epochi tou; Cavafy and His Times*) and Ο πολιτικός

Καβάφης (*O politikos Kavafis*; *The Political Cavafy*), where, in an equally reductive reading,[9] he refashions the poet into a political and reactionary artist whose work he decodes for its inherent critique of British colonial exploits in Egypt. These two critics effectively dominated Cavafy criticism for decades and succeeded in both illuminating and distorting their subject. Also entering into this fray was the Greek poet and Nobel laureate George Seferis, whose 1944 lecture "Cavafy and Eliot: A Comparison" attempted to align Cavafy with other trends in modernism, all the while charting out Seferis's own path as the successor to Palamas as the new national Greek poet and, in the process, attempting to unseat Cavafy (Lambropoulos, *Literature* 197–200).

Outside of Greece and the Greek diaspora, E. M. Forster may be credited with doing the most to launch Cavafy's global reputation. His essay "The Poetry of C. P. Cavafy" in *Pharos and Pharillon*, along with his tireless promotion of Cavafy's poetry in anglophone venues, established one of the most important literary trajectories in the poet's life. The relationship between the novelist and the poet is documented in *The Forster-Cavafy Letters: Friends at a Slight Angle*, as is the history of Forster's failed attempt to persuade Cavafy to sanction a publication of an English translation of the poems by the Hogarth Press (Jeffreys, *Forster-Cavafy Letters*). Other studies that shed light on this important connection are Jane Lagoudis Pinchin's *Alexandria Still: Forster, Durrell, and Cavafy*; Michael Haag's *Alexandria: City of Memory*; and Peter Jeffreys's *Eastern Questions: Hellenism and Orientalism in the Writings of E. M. Forster and C. P. Cavafy*.

Important anglophone monographs on Cavafy began appearing in the latter half of the twentieth century. Peter Bien's early informative essay *Constantine Cavafy*, part of the Columbia Essays on Modern Writers series, stands as a foundational academic introduction. Keeley's *Cavafy's Alexandria: Study of a Myth in Progress* explores the centrality of Alexandria as an informing idea that attains a universal perspective in the poetic corpus. C. Capri-Karka's *Love and the Symbolic Journey in the Poetry of Cavafy, Eliot, and Seferis* offers a humanist reading of the journey as a metaphor for love and includes a generous sampling of the critical views of major Greek Cavafy critics in addition to a detailed poem-by-poem analysis of key texts. An important collection of essays, *The Mind and Art of C. P. Cavafy: Essays on his Life and Work*, edited by Denise Harvey, was published in 1983; it includes essays by Forster, Stephen Spender, Patrick Leigh Fermor, Renato Poggioli, and Vagenas, as well as a translation of Seferis's lecture on Cavafy and Eliot.

The year 1983 marked the fiftieth anniversary of the poet's death, and numerous dedicatory volumes appeared both in Greece[10] and abroad. *Grand Street* devoted much of its 1983 spring issue to Cavafy (vol. 2, no. 3), with notable essays by G. W. Bowersock and Keeley, a translation of Cavafy's short story "In Broad Daylight" by James Merrill, and translations of articles by the Greek scholars J. A. Saregiannis and C. Th. Dimaras, along with photos of the poet, his family, and his dwelling. The next year, Marguerite Yourcenar reprinted her influential essay "A Critical Introduction to Cavafy"[11] in her collection of translated articles, *"The Dark Brain of Piranesi" and Other Essays*.

In reaction to decades of traditional philological readings by Greek scholars, new poststructuralist critiques of Cavafy's works appeared in the 1980s. Significant in this regard is the spring-summer 1983 issue of the *Journal of the Hellenic Diaspora* (Alexiou, C. P. Cavafy), which includes groundbreaking essays by Margaret Alexiou and Vassilis Lambropoulos that signaled a major shift in Cavafy studies. In contrast to what the editor of the volume terms the "ethnocentric romanticism" and "philological pedantry" (Alexiou, Introduction 7) that she felt characterized much of the critical work on Cavafy to date, the volume proposes to open "new strategies of interpretation" and to "encourage a vigorous debate among adherents of conflicting viewpoints ranging from traditional literary criticism to post-structuralism" (8). Supplementing this is another significant volume with essays on Cavafy and Greek literature: *The Text and Its Margins: Post-structuralist Approaches to Twentieth-Century Greek Literature* (Alexiou and Lambropoulos). Important monographs would follow in the wake of these theory-oriented publications. Gregory Jusdanis's *The Poetics of Cavafy: Textuality, Eroticism, History* offers a reading of Cavafy's poetics based on Roman Jakobson's model of verbal communication that frames Cavafy within the European literary movements of the late nineteenth and early twentieth centuries. Christopher Robinson's *C. P. Cavafy* includes an informative exploration of Cavafy's prosody and poetic technique. David Ricks's *The Shade of Homer: A Study in Modern Greek Poetry* traces Cavafy's use of Homeric lore; in his three chapters on Cavafy (85–118), particular attention is paid to the poet's mode of misquotation and adaptation of Homer into history. Mat Crispin's *Cavafy: Anatomy of a Soul* explores the poet's creative phases and inner odyssey. John P. Anton's *The Poetry and Poetics of Constantine P. Cavafy: Aesthetic Visions of Sensual Reality* is a biocritical study that endeavors to reconstruct the poet's axiological world and show how Cavafy's aesthetic attainments transform experience into a work in progress. The poet's signature prosaic poetics are the focus of Panagiotis Roilos's *C. P. Cavafy: The Economics of Metonymy*, where Roilos examines what he identifies as Cavafy's main discursive modality—metonymy—and how it defines the poet's recurrent deviation from the established socioaesthetic expectations of the time.

In terms of Cavafy's inspiration of other creative writers, it would not be an exaggeration to say that imitating and translating Cavafy have become rites of passage for many poets, particularly queer poets. Mark Doty traces what he terms a "lineational" lineage and notes that "practically every gay and lesbian writer in English has a poem called 'Days of Something-or-Other'" (Hennessy 87). Cavafy's current global appeal is due in large part to the poet's powerful and seductive exploration of the queer male gaze. While Cavafy's verses are not sexually explicit by today's standards, queer readings have shown that in their time they were groundbreaking in their suggestive and complicated understanding of desire. Cavafy was working out of the tradition of decadent aestheticism that paved the way for the work of modern gay writers. His writings evolved from this cultural milieu, and the gradual queering of critical studies of his poetry, abetted by the unflagging loyalty of his expanding queer readership, remains linked to this decadent aesthetic legacy, a topic explored in Jeffreys's book *Reframing Decadence: C. P. Cavafy's Imaginary Portraits*. Cavafy's ability to portray the gay cruising culture of his day and the courageous manner in which he problematizes same-sex desire are factors that have generated queer-theory-based critiques of his work. Such readings of the poet's sexuality aver that Cavafy was indeed one of the first modern gay poets. Important in this regard is the work of Dimitris Papanikolaou, whose Greek monograph Σαν κ' εμένα καμωμένοι: Ο ομοφυλόφιλος Καβάφης και η ποιητική της σεξουαλικότητας (*San k' emena kamomenoi: O omofylofilos Kavafis kai i piitiki tis sexoualikotitas*; *Created Like Me: Gay Cavafy and Sexual Poetics*), remains foundational for any discussion of Cavafy's queer poetics (for an overview in English, see Papanikolaou, "Days"). Notable as well is the recent special issue of the *Journal of Greek Media and Culture*, which focuses on the poet's queerness along with more intertextual topics, such as Cavafy's influence on popular culture, photography, comics, animation, and film (Papanikolaou and Papargyriou, *Pop Cavafy*).

Cavafy's poetic interests extended beyond the aesthetic-hedonistic realm to include various explorations of history and empire. The years Cavafy spent in England as a youth gave him a definitive metropolitan perspective, as did his employment in what amounted to a British ministry in Egypt—a country that was, for most of Cavafy's lifetime, essentially a British protectorate. This postcolonial dimension is examined by Martin McKinsey in his *Hellenism and the Postcolonial Imagination: Yeats, Cavafy, Walcott. Alexandria, Real and Imagined*, edited by Anthony Hirst and Michael Silk, contains numerous essays that consider Cavafy's relationship to Alexandria as both a city and a construct. Cavafy's complex relation to the Arab world and the problematic cosmopolitanism of Alexandria's literati are taken up by Hala Halim in *Alexandrian Cosmopolitanism: An Archive*, which features chapters on Cavafy, Forster, and Durrell; her reading of Cavafy reconsiders the poet's relation to Egyptian culture and politics. Other transnational perspectives on Cavafy are offered by Konstantina Georganta in *Conversing Identities: Encounters between British, Irish and Greek Poetry, 1922–1952*, Joanna Kruczkowska in *Irish Poets and Modern Greece: Heaney, Mahon, Cavafy, Seferis*, and Paschalis Nikolaou in *The Return of Pytheas: Scenes from British and Greek Poetry in Dialogue*, which includes a chapter on translations of Cavafy's work. Michelle Zerba's *Modern Odysseys: Cavafy, Woolf, Césaire and a Poetics of Indirection* examines the Odyssean tropes of diffusion, isolation, passage, and return in a receptionist reading of the poetics of indirection in Cavafy's lyrical homoeroticism. Foteini Dimirouli's *Authorising the Other: C. P. Cavafy in the English and American Literary Scene* explores the writings and activities of famous authors in England and America who were key in securing Cavafy's worldwide recognition. Takis Kayalis's *Cavafy's Hellenistic Antiquities: History, Archaeology, Empire* is a reappraisal of Cavafy's historical poetics contextualized and discursively framed within late-nineteenth- and early-twentieth-century historical, archaeological, and imperial redactions of Hellenistic antiquity. And Maria Boletsi's *Specters of Cavafy* offers a reading of the spectral and its presence in Cavafy's work, spectrality being the continuation of and haunting by the past in the present.

A number of special editions and collections of essays are available for consultation. The fall 2003 issue of *Classical and Modern Literature* presents papers from the conference Greek at a Slight Angle: Cavafy and Classical Poetry, held at the University of Michigan. In *"What These Ithakas Mean": Readings in Cavafy*, Artemis Leontis, Lauren Talalay, and Keith Taylor gather together commentaries on poems and paired artifacts based on the exhibit *Cavafy's World*, held at the Kelsey Museum of Archaeology at the University of Michigan; the website *Cavafy's World* documents the exhibit. *Modern Greek Studies (Australia and New Zealand)* devoted part of its 2003 volume to Cavafy, with major essays and translations of his commentaries on his poems and translations of his prose poems (Karalis and Tsianikas). Roilos's edited volume *Imagination and Logos: Essays on C. P. Cavafy* includes essays on diverse cross-disciplinary approaches to the poetics, intertexts, and impact of Cavafy's work, with contributions from Eve Kosofsky Sedgwick, Helen Vendler, Richard Dellamora, and Mark Doty. A special issue of *Studies in the Literary Imagination* edited by Louis Ruprecht includes an essay by Orhan Pamuk titled "Other Countries, Other Shores." The seminars of the 2019 Cavafy International Summer School, which focused on the poet's orientations, were published in *Boundary 2* (Gourgouris, *Cavafy Dossier*). A rich array of essays is available at the C. P. Cavafy forum on the University of Michigan website ("C. P. Cavafy Forum"). Among many noteworthy projects posted on the forum is "Greek Diaspora Intellectuals on 'The Meaning of Cavafy Today,'" a sequence of brief essays and notes by approximately fifty intellectuals from Greek diaspora communities around the world.

Biographical Resources

Given Cavafy's global stature, it is rather astonishing that, to date, only two conventional biographies of the poet have been written: Michalis Peridis's Ο βίος και το έργο του Κωνσταντίνου Καβάφη (*O vios kai to ergo tou Konstantinou Kavafi; The Life and Work of Constantine Cavafy*) in 1947 and Robert Liddell's *Cavafy: A Biography* in 1974. This might have less to do with the fact that the poet led a rather unremarkable life than it does with the less exalted status of biographies in Greece. Malanos and Tsirkas, as noted above, produced studies heavily weighted with biographical material. While biographical intentionalism abounds in Greek critical work on Cavafy, life studies are less in demand in

Greece. Jusdanis and Jeffreys's *Constantine Cavafy: A New Biography* will be published in 2025. And there are various linear timelines, such as those compiled by Tsirkas in 1963 (published in adapted form in Χάρτης [*Chartis*; *Map*] in 1983 ["Chronologio"]) and the substantial chronological assemblage by Daskalopoulos and Maria Stasinopoulou, Ο βίος και το έργο του Κ.Π. Καβάφη (*O vios kai to ergo tou K. P. Kavafi*; *The Life and Work of C. P. Cavafy*).[12]

For those interested in exploring the poet's life, the digitization of much of the poet's archive affords great possibilities.[13] Primary and secondary documents are available for casual and protracted study. In addition, print resources that shed light on Cavafy's life exist, although the majority are in Greek. Lena Savidis's Λεύκωμα Καβάφη, 1893–1910 (*Leykoma Kavafi, 1893–1910*; *Cavafy Album, 1863–1910*) reproduces important primary documents from the poet's archive. Useful English resources include Memas Kolaitis's *Cavafy As I Knew Him*, an intimate portrait of the poet from one of his close literary acquaintances. Manolis Savidis's Κ.Π. Καβάφης: Κατάλογος εκθεμάτων (*K. P. Kavafis: Katalogos ekthematon*; *C. P. Cavafy: Exhibit Catalogue*) offers a bilingual account of the poet's life illustrated with rich archival documents. Manolis Savidis's CD-ROM Κ.Π. Καβάφης: Ο ανθρωπος και η εποχή του (*K. P. Kavafis: O anthropos kai i epochi tou*; *C. P. Cavafy: The Man and His Epoch*) features a thorough timeline of the significant moments in the poet's life aligned with parallel events in Alexandria, Greece, and the world at large. Haag's *Alexandria: City of Memory* is a composite biography of Cavafy, Forster, and Durrell set within the historical context of cosmopolitan Alexandria.

A number of biographical sketches and notes are available online, mostly as part of literary sites that also present several of Cavafy's poems in translation. The *Onassis Cavafy Archive* offers a brief biography written by Daskalopoulos and translated by Emmerich (Daskalopoulos, "C. P. Cavafy"). Keeley's brief "C. P. Cavafy's Biography" is accurate and informative, and the even briefer biographies on the websites *Poetry Foundation* and *Academy of American Poets* are good starting points for students interested in having a general overview of the poet's life ("C. P. Cavafy" [*Poetry Foundation*]; "C. P. Cavafy" [*Academy*]).

Other Primary Sources

Published and edited writings that fall outside the poetic corpus are available in print; in addition, many of them are accessible on the Onassis Foundation Cavafy Archive website. Cavafy's prose essays were first published and edited by George Papoutsakis, in Πεζά (*Peza*; *Prose*), and more recently by Michalis Pieris, in Τα Πεζά, 1882–1931 (*Ta peza, 1882–1931*; *The Prose Works, 1882–1931*). Selected English translations are available in two editions: *Selected Prose Works*, translated by Jeffreys, includes published and unpublished essays, book reviews, notes by Cavafy on poetics and ethics, and his comments on other poets and writers. Martin McKinsey's *Clearing the Ground: C. P. Cavafy: Poetry and Prose, 1902–1911* presents a parallel reading of poems, personal notes, and essays spanning the crucial ten-year period of 1902–11 (Cavafy, *Clearing*). McKinsey's afterword, "The Aesthetics of Pleasure," surveys Cavafy's sexuality, offering insights into the writer's subsequent poetic breakthrough and artistic maturing. Selections of Cavafy's commentaries on his poems, prose poems, and reflections are also included in the 2003 volume of *Modern Greek Studies (Australia and New Zealand)* (Karalis and Tsianikas 7–39).

Other important documents by Cavafy that might be of use in the classroom include the poet's marginalia and notes on Gibbon (Haas, "Cavafy's Reading Notes") and Ruskin (Tsirkas, *Political Cavafy* 223–65);[14] his early work "Constantinopoliad an Epic"; his Ριμάριο ("Rimario"; "Dictionary of Rhymes"; Karaoglou, "K. P. Kavafi"); his diaries and journals on the death of his mother (Pieris, "Simiomata"; Cavafy, *Poesie* 1662–705) and his good friend Mikès Ralli (Cavafy, *Peza* 253–58); his diary of his trip to Athens in 1901 (Cavafy, *Peza* 259–300); his genealogical notes (Karagiannis); his Ανέκδοτα σημειώματα ποιητικής και ηθικής (*Anekdota simiomata piitikis kai ithikis*; *Unpublished Notes on Poetics and Ethics*), a collection of his previously unpublished notes; and his Το λεξικό παραθεμάτων (*To lexiko parathematon*; *Dictionary of Citations*), compiled and completed by Michalis Pieris in 2015. Useful primary material may be found in the two volumes titled Μικρά Καβαφικά (*Mikra Kavafika*; *Small Cavafy Works*; see Savidis, *Mikra Kavafika A* and *Mikra Kavafika B*), which contain unpublished archival matter with commentaries by George Savidis. Seventeen of Cavafy's comments on the poems, written in shorthand and edited by Diana Haas, were published in Κύκλος Καβάφη (*Kyklos Kavafi*; *Cavafy's Circle*; see Cavafy, "Scholia"). A few others have been published in the Greek periodicals *Logeion* and Κονδυλοφόρος (*Kondylophoros*; *Penholder*).[15] The remainder of these comments have not yet been edited or published.

Edited editions of Cavafy's letters include *The Forster-Cavafy Letters: Friends at a Slight Angle* and Κ.Π. Καβάφη: Επιστολές στον Μάριο Βαιάνο (*K. P. Kavafi: Epistoles ston Mario Baiano*; *C. P. Cavafy: Letters to Marios Vaianos*). Transcriptions of the poet's Greek letters to Alekos Sengopoulos (written between 1918 and 1919) are available in *Poesie e prose*, edited by Lavagnini and Christiano Luciani (Cavafy, *Poesie* 2298–393).

Cavafy's personal library has been amply documented by Michaela Karampini-Iatrou in Η βιβλιοθήκη Κ.Π. Καβάφη (*I bibliothiki K. P. Kavafi*; *C. P. Cavafy's Library*), a catalogue consisting of 964 printed items that also appears in digital form (in Greek and English) in the *Onassis Cavafy Archive* ("Cavafy Library"). Supplementing this is Katerina Ghika's "Ideal Library," which includes an additional 870 printed items that Cavafy either owned or read but that, for a variety of reasons, did not survive as part of his library.

Background Reading, Reference Materials, and Teaching Guides

Roderick Beaton's *An Introduction to Modern Greek Literature* provides a good starting point for exploring the place of Cavafy's work in the context of Greece's literary, social, and cultural developments over the past two centuries, from the time of national independence in 1821 to the 1990s. Other noteworthy introductions to Greek literature are C. Th. Dimaras's *A History of Modern Greek Literature* and Linos Politis's *A History of Modern Greek Literature*. Those wishing to explore modern Greek poetry will find the bilingual volume *A Century of Greek Poetry, 1900–2000* most useful (Bien et al.), and they may also wish to consult Nanos Valaoritis and Thanasis Maskaleris's *An Anthology of Modern Greek Poetry* and Kimon Friar's *Modern Greek Poetry*. For informative essays and monographs on modern Greece and Greek culture, the following volumes offer fine perspectives: Katerina Zacharia's *Hellenisms: Culture, Identity, and Ethnicity from Antiquity to Modernity*; Dimitris Tziovas's *Greek Modernism and Beyond*; Vangelis Calotychos's *Modern Greece: A Cultural Poetics*; Lambropoulos's *Literature as National Institution: Studies in the Politics of Modern Greek Criticism*; Stathis Gourgouris's *Dream Nation: Enlightenment, Colonization and the Institution of Modern Greece*; Richard Clogg's *A Concise History of Greece*; Thomas W. Gallant's *The Edinburgh History of the Greeks, 1768 to 1913: The Long Nineteenth Century*; and Beaton's *Greece: Biography of a Modern Nation*. The Greek language controversy and the conflict between demoticists and purists have been thoroughly explored by Peter Mackridge in his *Language and National Identity in Greece, 1766–1976*. Michael Herzfeld's *Ours Once More: Folklore, Ideology, and the Making of Modern Greece* offers an illuminating study of the overwhelming presence of λαογραφία (*laographia*; folklore) in modern Greek culture.

Alexander Kitroeff's *The Greeks and the Making of Modern Egypt* traces the fortunes of the Greeks and their communities in Egypt from the early nineteenth century, beginning with the reign of Muhammad Ali, and proceeding through the 1960s and the reforms of Gamal Abdel Nasser. Mary N. Layoun's edited volume *Modernism in Greece? Essays on the Critical and Literary Margins of a Movement* includes essays on Seferis, Yiannis Ritsos, Kostas Karyotakis, Melpo Axioti, and Cavafy. Of the seventeen essays by Bowersock in *From Gibbon to Auden: Essays on the Classical Tradition*, three deal with Cavafy ("Cavafy and Apollonius" [151–59], "Julian Poems" [136–50], and "New Cavafy" [160–74]). Haag's *Vintage Alexandria: Photographs of the City, 1860–1960* is a paean to the vanished cosmopolitan city that Cavafy knew and celebrated in his poetry. Robert Ilbert and Ilios Yannakakis's *Alexandria, 1860–1960: The Brief Life of a Cosmopolitan Community* offers an informative collection of essays that contextualize the city's multinational identity.

As an avid reader of Greek authors and writings representing diverse periods and places, Cavafy was especially drawn to the Greek and Palatine Anthologies.[16] Peter Brown's *The World of Late Antiquity, AD 150–750* is a study of the history and culture of an era that, like the Hellenistic and Byzantine periods, fed the poet's imagination. Peter Green's *The Hellenistic Age* presents a brief introduction to an era Cavafy used as a setting for many of his poems. Bowersock's *Julian the Apostate* is a concise portrait of a historical figure who captivated Cavafy's imagination. Forster's *Alexandria: A History and a Guide* is a guidebook to the Alexandria of Cavafy's era, and Forster's *Pharos and Pharillon* contains important essays on Hellenistic and contemporary Egypt. And the four novels in Durrell's *Alexandria Quartet* bring to life Cavafy's Alexandria in a fictional mode (*Justine, Balthazar, Mountolive,* and *Clea*).

Multimedia Resources and Visual Art

Recommended multimedia resources include two biopics, both from the 1990s. Constantine Giannaris's *Trojans: A Life of C. P. Cavafy* is a thirty-five-minute film, circulating in both Greek and English versions (*Trojans* / Τρώες; *Trojans*), that follows the techniques of New Queer Cinema to present the poet's life as a "radical identity quest" and positions the poet "in a queer genealogy" (Papanikolaou, "Pensive Spectator" 279, 285). Yannis Smaragdis's eighty-five-minute film *Kavafis* (with English subtitles) features several popular Greek actors and has a soundtrack by the composer Vangelis. Cavafy's short story "In Broad Daylight" was made into a short film by Takis Spetsiotis, Εις το φως της ημέρας (*Is to fos tis imeras; In Broad Daylight*). Another film of interest is Τη Νύχτα που ο Φερνάντο Πεσσόα συνάντησε τον Κωνσταντίνο Καβάφη (*Ti nychta pou o Fernando Pessoa synantise ton Konstantino Kavafi; The Night Fernando Pessoa Met Constantine Cavafy*), in Greek with Portuguese and English subtitles. Written and directed by Stelios Charalambopoulos, it is based on the fictional premise of a meeting between Cavafy and the Portuguese poet Fernando Pessoa aboard a ship that carries immigrants from Mediterranean ports to America. Additionally, Κ.Π. Καβάφης, Η Πόλις (Όπου Το Μάτι Μου Γυρίσω) (*K. P. Kavafis, i polis (Opou to mati mou gyriso); C. P. Cavafy, The City (Wherever I Turn My Eye)*) is a recent, brief experimental film directed by Panayiotis Kountouras and Aristarchos Papadaniel.

Several documentaries and films have been made for Greek television. Η Παγκοσμιότητα του Κωνσταντίνου Καβάφη (*I pangkosmiotita tou Konstantinou Kavafi; Constantine Cavafy's Universalism*), directed by Tasos Psarras, in the series Εποχές και Συγγραφείς (*Epoches kai Syngrafis; Epochs and Writers*), was produced in 2013 by ERT1 in Greek without English subtitles. Κ.Π. Καβάφης—50 Χρόνια από τον θάνατό του (*K. P. Kavafis—50 xronia apo to thanato tou; C. P.*

Cavafy—Fifty Years after His Death) is a fine Greek documentary that includes interviews with Malanos, Polys Modinos, Kyveli Sengopoulou, Savidis, and Yourcenar. In Έλληνες του πνεύματος και της τέχνης: Κωνσταντίνος Καβάφης (*Ellines tou pneumatos kai tis technis: Konstantinos Kavafis*; *Greeks of the Life of the Spirit and Art: Constantine Cavafy*), a fifty-five minute documentary televised by SKAI in 2012, the actor and director Dimitris Lignadis traces the steps of Cavafy in his beloved Alexandria.

A Tribute to C. P. Cavafy, produced by PEN America and sponsored by the Stavros Niarchos Foundation, is a ninety-minute celebration of the 150th anniversary of the poet's birth that brings together distinguished writers, actors, performers, translators, and artists who engage with some of the best-known poems and offer personal and scholarly reflections on the poet. Participants include André Aciman, Michael Cunningham, Mark Doty, Olympia Dukakis, Craig Dykers, Keeley, Mendelsohn, Orhan Pamuk, Dimitris Papaioannou, and Kathleen Turner.

When it comes to multimedia resources, the *Onassis Cavafy Archive* offers a rich array of perspectives on the poet. The foundation's *YouTube* channel archives numerous videos that comprise a valuable and multidisciplinary collection, from readings of the poems to performances, lectures, educational workshops, and explorations of material artifacts (www.youtube.com/@Onassis FoundationChannel).

Greek visual artists have long been fascinated and inspired by Cavafy's work: the cubist painter Nikos Hadjikyriakos-Ghikas illustrated the landmark publication of Cavafy's poems Ποιήματα, 1896–1933 (*Piimata, 1896–1933*; *Poems, 1896–1933*), published by Ikaros Press in 1966. Several illustrators were featured in a later deluxe edition, Κ.Π. Καβάφης: Ποιήματα (*K. P. Kavafis: Poiemata*; *C. P. Cavafy: Poems*), published by Kastaniotis in 2005. And in 2013, a major exhibition at the European Cultural Centre of Delphi featured more than "one hundred paintings, sculptures, engravings, drawing and art illustrations by distinguished Greek artists" ("Exhibition").

Instructors often point their students to visual materials such as those by the English artist David Hockney and the Egyptian painter Anna Boghiguian. Among many other visual responses to Cavafy and his work are the *Visual Dialogues*, a series of original artworks on six themes produced over three years. The artists involved in this series use contemporary media such as video, electronic images and photographs, sound installations, animation, and other interactive works.

Several key photographic projects based on Cavafy's poetry have been exhibited and published. Notable among these is the work of Duane Michals, who published *Homage to Cavafy* in 1978, a photobook that he went back to three decades later and reissued as *The Adventures of Constantine Cavafy*. Other photographic works include Stathis Orphanos's *My Cavafy: Chance Encounters*, with a preface by Gore Vidal, and Dimitris Yeros's *Shades of Love: Photographs Inspired by the Poems of C. P. Cavafy*. In his nearly seventy photographic illustrations in this book, Yeros has used as subjects an assortment of models and artists, including Gore Vidal, Clive Barker, and Jeff Koons. The book also presents new translations of Cavafy by David Connolly.

There is no shortage of online recordings of people reciting Cavafy's work in English translation and performing musical renditions or adaptations of his poems. For instance, students are likely to find a reading of "Ithaka" by Sean Connery of interest ("'Ithaca' by C. P. Cavafy"). Recitations of the poems in Greek at the Center for Neo-Hellenic Studies can be found online ("C. P. Cavafy: Anthology"). Equally interesting and accessible is Leonard Cohen's song "Alexandra Leaving," which is based on Cavafy's poem "The God Abandons Antony."[17] Readings of Cavafy's poetry in Greek have been recorded by distinguished Greek artists and literary scholars, among them the actor Karyofyllia Karambeti, who for one album selected and read twenty-one poems (Karambeti). A song cycle of thirteen poems by Cavafy was created in 2010 by Lena Platonos and performed that year at the Pallas Theater in Athens. The design and staging were done by Dimitris Papaioannou. In 2013, Kyriacos Karseras produced the website *Cavafy Thirteen* (cavafy13.com), which has the video of the live concert.

When it comes to Cavafy's presence in popular culture and various media, including websites with interactive artwork, comics, animation, and the like, Lilia Diamantopoulou and Zyranna Stoikou's summary of where the poet is featured these days is most instructive: "Cavafy's poems have appeared in TV-spots, advertising cat food and cars. We have seen them on the London Underground, on buses and underground stations in Athens, and on walls in South America. We have listened to them being read and recorded, sung and performed on the stage and in film. We have also encountered his poems in newspaper comic strips or even transformed into Japanese animations" (299). For an example, see the comic "Ithaka: A Poem by Constantine P. Cavafy" in *Zen Pencils*. The author and illustrator, Gav, explains that "[m]y hero in the comic is NOT meant to be Odysseus. I used Cavafy's words and drew upon my childhood diet of comic books and Ray Harryhausen movies to tell a different story."

Websites

Of several important Cavafy websites, the *Onassis Cavafy Archive* has a digital collection that is indispensable and accessible. It is designed to support open access and experiential and experimental research, and it offers resources for digital teaching and learning both inside and outside the classroom. With Greek and English user platforms, it now includes in digitized form a large collection of Cavafy's texts. A rich array of essays, notes, and responses to various Cavafy topics and happenings are available on the C. P. Cavafy forum on the University of Michigan website ("C. P. Cavafy Forum"). These include "The Typography of Desire," six essays along with introductory notes that constitute the final papers from Karen Van Dyck's 2009 course on Cavafy at Columbia University; the essays all deal with some aspect of Cavafy and translation. The forum also features the *C. P. Cavafy Music Resource Guide*, a resource on musical settings of Cavafy's poetry that lists more than one hundred bibliographic entries for compositions, performances, recordings, and printed scores in every imaginable musical genre and style. The composer and conductor Dimitri Mitropoulos, who corresponded with Cavafy in the 1920s, was the first to set the poems to music. In his essay "Conversing with Cavafy through Music," included in this volume, Vassilis Lambropoulos notes that more than ninety Greek and more than forty non-Greek composers have written "some four hundred pieces of music based on [Cavafy's] poetry."

Worth visiting in Alexandria—in person or virtually—are the Cavafy House and the Bibliotheca Alexandrina. The Cavafy House occupies the apartment where the poet spent the last twenty-six years of his life. It has been renovated and reappointed as an exhibit space by the Onassis Foundation and now offers visitors a rich interaction with the poet's life, personal effects, and Alexandrian connections. The Bibliotheca Alexandrina is dedicated to recapturing "the spirit of openness and scholarship" of the original Library of Alexandria ("About"). Its website features various contributions to Cavafy studies, including the library's international symposia, poetry celebrations, musical concerts, and the activities of the Alexandria Center for Hellenistic Studies, which organizes lectures, seminars, courses, and conferences.

Several websites and web pages highlight critical events and exhibits focused on Cavafy. The Cavafy Symposium *Facebook* page ("Kavafia"), for one, is a treasure trove of documents and information; the page is dedicated to capturing the highlights of the Fifteenth International Cavafy Symposium 2019, which took place in Cairo and Alexandria in October 2019 and was organized by the Hellenic Foundation for Culture. An excellent online exhibition, *Cavafy's World*, features an overview of the poet's life in Alexandria and pairs individual poems with an array of artifacts (from Egypt, Greece, and Rome) housed in the Kelsey Museum at the University of Michigan. The exhibit *Cavafy's World: Hidden Things* includes etchings by Hockney that deal with notions of sexuality and memory in the poet's work ("Cavafy's World: Hidden Things"), and *Cavafy's World: Ancient Passions* is an a exhibit of period photographs of Cavafy and his Alexandria set among objects that came from the worlds that inspired him and that now belong to the Kelsey Museum's classical, Hellenic, and Byzantine collection ("Cavafy's World: Ancient Passions").

Finally, it might be useful not only to consider Cavafy's presence in academia but also to think about how the poet's global presence and reputation have spread. Thoughts on this are offered by Foteini Dimirouli in her 2021 lecture at the British School in Athens, "C. P. Cavafy in the World: Origins, Trajectories and the Diasporic Poet." Instructors may wish to consider the poet's place in the digital humanities and the ways in which Cavafy will be fashioned, presented, and disseminated in new discursive networks. Similarly, in "Cavafy's

Web Legacy: C. P. Cavafy in the Public Sphere of the Web 2.0.," Anna-Maria Sichani considers "how the social web and digital networking technologies could remodel literary sociality, in which the Cavafian oeuvre and scholarship are submerged, within the digital era" (321).

Teaching Resources

Cavafy's poetry is taught widely in translation in English-speaking universities, mostly at the undergraduate level and less often at the graduate level. However, a few respondents to our questionnaire indicated that they teach graduate-level courses such as Cavafy and the Writing of Homosexuality, Cavafy and Translation, and creative writing courses—and one of them pointed to a graduate course called Cavafoucault. Taught at the few institutions that offer Greek studies programs, Cavafy's work receives considerable attention in courses covering twentieth-century and modern Greek poetry. In addition, Cavafy often fits onto syllabi dealing with a variety of topics and involving several writers; in such cases, instructors devote only a portion of the course, often one to two weeks, to his poetry. One case would be devoting a class to the ways Cavafy's rendering of queer sensuality persisted throughout the twentieth century, making it possible for poets of the AIDS crisis to imagine the Greek poet's tragic vision as a way of understanding their own losses. Another case would be a literature class in which Cavafy is introduced along with selections of poems (and often novels), such as Mark Doty's *My Alexandria*, Richard McCann's *Nights of 1990*, the Irish poet Cathal Ó Searcaigh's *Out in the Open* and *Out of the Wilderness*, Robert Liddell's *Unreal City*, Ibrahim Abdel Meguid's *No One Sleeps in Alexandria*, Lawrence Durrell's *Justine*, and Edwar al-Kharrat's *Girls of Alexandria* and *City of Saffron*.

Resources in Greek

Cavafy was first included in Greek school textbooks in 1930, when "Trojans" and "Thermopylae" appeared in the grade 11 textbook Νεοελληνικά Αναγνώσματα (*Neohellinika anagnosmata*; *Modern Greek Readings*). The same publication for grade twelve students included "Candles" and "Waiting for the Barbarians." With some notable exceptions when his poetry disappeared from the educational literary canon (between 1938, when it was censored, and 1950, when it was reestablished), Cavafy continues to be taught extensively at all educational levels, often as the author responsible for introducing modernism into Greek literary circles. As Sotiria Kalasaridou writes, during the past eighty years, "C. P. Cavafy is found in thirty-five anthologies, teachers' textbooks and curricula . . . ; 'Ithaka' is the most anthologized poem" (103). There are several guides to the poetry and a number of books that present pedagogical perspectives and strategies on teaching Cavafy. A seminal text is Theseas Tsiastikas's Ο Σχολικός

Καβάφης (*O scholikos Kavafis; The Teaching Guide to Cavafy*), a book whose 408 pages include an introduction to the poetry and commentaries on individual poems along with teaching instructions and a brief anthology.

Equally valuable for teaching Cavafy are several bibliographic guides: Haas and Michael Pieris's standard Βιβλιογραφικός Οδηγός στα 154 Ποιήματα του Καβάφη (*Bibliografikos odigos sta 154 piimata tou Kavafi; Bibliographic Guide to the 154 Poems of C. P. Cavafy*); Dimitris Daskalopoulos's important Βιβλιογραφία Κ.Π. Καβάφη, 1886–2000 (*Bibliografia K. P. Kavafi, 1886–2000; Bibliography of C. P. Cavafy, 1886–2000*); and the addendum to this bibliography that was published in Κονδυλοφόρος (*Kondylophoros; Penholder*) and that covers the years 2001–10: Προσθήκες στη βιβλιογραφία Κ.Π. Καβάφη ("Prosthikes sti bibliografia K. P. Kavafi"; "Addendum to the Bibliography of C. P. Cavafy"). Additional material has been gathered by Lefteris Papaleontiou in Προσθήκες στη βιβλιογραφία Κ.Π. Καβάφη, 1907–2000 ("Prosthikes sti bibliografia K. P. Kavafi, 1907–2000"; "Supplements to the C. P. Cavafy Bibliography, 1907–2000").

Programs such as Cavafy Goes to School ("Cavafy Goes"), organized by the Onassis Foundation Cavafy Archive, and other pedagogical workshops have been offered since 2013 to educators, university and high school students, and the general public at the Onassis Foundation but also across Greece. Using multimedia and experimental approaches, these programs familiarize participants with a variety of interpretive approaches to Cavafy's poems as well as to the digitized treasures in the Cavafy Archive.

Various editions of the poems present pedagogical perspectives and strategies on teaching Cavafy. These include Renos, Irkos, and Stantis Apostolidis's Άπαντα τα δημοσιευμένα ποιήματα (*Apanta ta dimosieumena piimata; Complete Published Poems*), an idiosyncratic edition of all the poems with commentaries that incorporate literary, historical, and aesthetic teaching approaches (Cavafy, *Apanta ta dimosieumena piimata*), and Margarita A. Papadopoulou's Η διδακτική του Καβάφη: Διδακτική προσέγγιση ποιημάτων με βάση γλωσσοπαιδαγωγικά πρότυπα ανάλυσης (*I didaktiki tou Kavafi: Didaktiki proseggisi piimaton me basi glossopaidagogika protypa analysis; Methods of Teaching Cavafy: An Approach to the Poems Based on Glosso-Pedagogical Models Analysis*), which demonstrates how to read several poems using what the author proposes is a model for linguistic-pedagogical analysis. Finally, many elementary and high school Greek literature anthologies published by the Greek Οργανισμός Εκδόσεως Διδακτίκων Βιβλίων (Organismos Ekdoseos Didaktikon Biblion; Digital Books Publication Organization) are designed for teaching modern Greek literature, include sections on Cavafy, print some of his best-known poems, and offer approaches to teaching his poetry.

Resources in English

Although no English teaching guides for Cavafy exist per se, readers can consult special editions of periodicals and journals that offer readings of the poetry—including the aforementioned special edition of the *Journal of the Hellenic Diaspora* (Alexiou, *C. P. Cavafy*) and the fall 2023 issue of *Classical and Modern Literature*—collected commentaries such as *"What These Ithakas Mean": Readings in Cavafy* (Leontis et al.), and the web page "C. P. Cavafy Forum." Instructors can draw on the digitized archival material on the Onassis Foundation Cavafy Archive website, presented in both Greek and English, and several activities organized around the theme of teaching Cavafy, which offer strategies on how to make effective use of the material in the classroom. For a useful discussion on this topic, see Takis Kayalis's essay in this volume.

The only study guide to Cavafy's poetry available in English is *A Study Guide for C. P. Cavafy's "Ithaca."* This brief guide (eighteen pages long), published in 2017, uses an effective conventional approach: plot summary, character analysis, author biography, study questions, historical context, and suggestions for further reading.[18] Though not conceived in pedagogical terms, many other texts are useful for teachers, including J. Phillipson's *Historical Poems*, which offers extensive commentaries on seventy-two of Cavafy's poems (Cavafy, *Historical Poems*).[19] Daniel Mendelsohn's *Collected Poems* offers a "Notes" section that contains informed and easily adaptable commentary on all the poems (Cavafy, *Collected Poems* [Mendelsohn] 355–536). Instructors are likely to benefit from the website *Census of Modern Greek Literature*, which provides a comprehensive bibliography with references, according to the home page, "to *all* the English-language translations of modern Greek literature and to *all* the critical studies in English that relate to modern Greek literature" (*Census*). This site constitutes an expanded edition of Dia M. L. Philippides's 1990 monograph, *Check-list of English-Language Sources Useful in the Study of Modern Greek Literature, 1824–1987*.

NOTES

1. Hirst argues compellingly about the intended meaning generated by the thematic arrangement of the poems and the "mutually disruptive way" they comment on each other ("Philosophical" 50).

2. Ekdawi and Hirst take issue with Savidis's presentation and categorization of the noncanonical material.

3. The Apostolidis edition includes all the published poems, divided and sequenced on the idiosyncratic basis of merit, along with a few unpublished poems and copious annotations (Cavafy, *Apanta ta dimosieumena piimata*); Ilinskagia's edition, arranged along the lines of Savidis's edition (e.g., Ilinskagia places "Poems 1904" first, not last), presents the canonical poems, followed by the disowned, unpublished, and unfinished poems, along with ample annotations (Cavafy, *Apanta ta piimata*); Eleftherakis's edition features only the canonical poems, arranged chronologically with annotated commentaries (Cavafy, *Piimata*).

4. Stroebel notes the evolution of publication terms: *collections*, used by Cavafy; *editions*, used by Savidis; and *assemblages*, used by Stroebel (Stroebel 280, 281, 305).

5. Palamas, a founder of the New Athenian School, was noted for his ethnocentric and folkloric lyrical poetry as well as his longer narrative works written strictly in demotic Greek.

6. *Alexandrian Art* was Cavafy's own literary venue, over which the poet maintained strict editorial control.

7. In 1929, *Le semaine Égyptienne* (Cairo) dedicated a special issue to Cavafy, and shortly after his death, special dedicatory volumes were published by Νέα Εστία (*Nea Estia*; *New Hearth*) in Athens in 1933 and by Παναιγύπτια (*Panaigyptia*; *Panegyptian*) in Alexandria in 1933. See Cavafy, K. P. *Kavafis: Ta piimata* 769.

8. Vaianos was an intellectual and journal editor who became the publisher of Νέα Τέχνη (*Nea Techni*). Lapathiotis, a poet and critic, founded the literary magazine Ἠγησώ (*Igiso*) in 1907.

9. Lambropoulos identifies Tsirkas's reading as an ideological version of Malanos's psychological mode of "biographical intentionalism" (*Literature* 194). Lambropoulos is known for interrogating the humanistic presuppositions underlying Greek criticism, in particular its patriotic moralism, biographical intentionalism, and symbolist formalism; see *Literature* 204.

10. Greek special editions were published by the following journals: Διαβάζω (*Diavaso*; *I Read*), Χάρτης (*Xartis*; *Map*), Σύγχρονοι Καιροί (*Synchroni Kairi*; *Modern Times*), Οδός Πανός (*Odos Panos*; *Panos Road*), Το Δένδρο (*To Dendro*; *The Tree*), Η Λέξη (*I Lexi*; *The Word*), Διαγώνιος (*Diagonios*; *Diagonal*), Νέα Σύνορα (*Nea Synora*; *New Boundaries*), Ο Πολίτης (*O Politis*; *The Citizen*), Τετράδια Ευθύνης (*Tetradia Eythynis*; *Notebooks of Responsibility*), Γράμματα και Τέχνες (*Grammata kai Technes*; *Letters and Arts*), and Σημειώσεις (*Simiosis*; *Notes*).

11. This 1939 essay served as the introduction to the 1958 French translations by George Papoutsakis.

12. This invaluable resource is replete with citations from critics, contemporaries, and Cavafy himself, functioning as a veritable compendium of quotations, events, and dates.

13. Other undigitized archival material exists at ELIA (Hellenic Literary and Historical Archive) and at the Benaki Museum. ELIA houses a plethora of archival material, including archives from Alekos and Rika Sengopoulos, Timos Malanos, Michalis Peridis, and Stratis Tsirkas.

14. The notes on Ruskin were more recently published in the bilingual Greek-Italian edition Cavafy, *Poesie* 1797–865.

15. Haas, "Anekdoto autoscholio sto piima 'I naumachia,'" "Anekdoto autoscholio sto piima 'Ta d'alla,'" "K. P. Kavafi: Anekdoto autoscholio," "K. P. Kavafi: Autoscholia sta piimata 'Dimitriou Sotiros,'" and "K. P. Kavafi: Autoscholia sta piimata 'I synodia.'"

16. A bilingual edition of *The Greek Anthology* in five volumes, with an English translation by W. R. Paton, published between 1916 and 1918, is available on the *Perseus Digital Library* as part of the Greek and Roman Materials collection (www.perseus.tufts.edu/hopper).

17. The lyrics are composed by Sharon Robinson and Leonard Cohen.

18. See encyclopedia.com/arts/educational-magazines/ithaka.

19. For more on Phillipson's edition, see the essay in this volume by Kelly Polychroniou and Loren J. Samons.

The Digitized Cavafy Archive as a Teaching and Research Resource

Angeliki Mousiou

Back in 1963, in his first report on the Cavafy archive, George P. Savidis compared the poet C. P. Cavafy to an iceberg: one that remains largely hidden underwater, waiting to be discovered ("Archio K. P. Kavafi" 35). In the same article, Savidis also describes his own first encounter with the archive, shown to him by Alekos Sengopoulos—the heir to the poet. The archive was presented to Savidis in μια μεγάλη βαλίτσα γεμάτη χειρόγραφα, φωτογραφίες, και έντυπα—τα οποία κοιτάξαμε μαζί, επί πολλές, αλησμόνητες μέρες ("a big suitcase full of manuscripts, pictures, and documents—which we then inspected together for many unforgettable days"; 39; my trans.). Fast-forward to March 2019, following the acquisition of the archive by the Onassis Foundation in late 2012, when the publication of the digital collection of the Onassis Foundation Cavafy Archive was announced, opening up Savidis's suitcase and rendering the entirety of the poet's archive accessible online. The Cavafy archive—along with the correlated Aleco and Rica Singopoulo fonds[1]—consists of more than two thousand items belonging or related to the celebrated poet.

A Short History of the Archive

Savidis's description of the suitcase and its contents might be the first comprehensive depiction of the Cavafy archive. Prior to Savidis, another Cavafy scholar, Michalis Peridis, who had also worked with materials from the archive, was the first to confirm the collection's existence and to employ documents from the archive extensively, in his 1948 study Ο βίος και το έργο του Κωνσταντίνου Καβάφη (*O vios kai to ergo tou Konstantinou Kavafi*; *The Life and Work of Constantine Cavafy*). However, Peridis was not interested in giving details on the documents he consulted and cited. Instead, he describes the place of Cavafy's life and work—namely, Cavafy's bedroom, which also functioned as the poet's study (Peridis 97). Included in the Singopoulo fonds in the digitized archive is an image that captures the poet's bedroom and study, where one may notice stacks of papers and books, hastily piled on Cavafy's desk (Ververis).[2]

Savidis's first account of the collection signifies the beginning of an important phase in the archive's history. In 1963, following K. Th. Dimaras's advice and with the help of V. P. Panagiotopoulos of the National Hellenic Research Foundation, Savidis documented the archive for the first time in 146 microfilms of thirty shots each (G. Savidis, "Archio K. P. Kavafi" 40). The same year, Alekos Sengopoulos entrusted the study and publication of the archive to Savidis; the Sengopoulos family would keep ownership of the archive until 1969, when, following Alekos's death, his widow, Kyveli Sengopoulou, would officially pass the archive over to Savidis (G. Savidis, "Archio K. P. Kavafi" 52). Later on, the microfilms, which constitute the first reproduction of the collection, would function as a basis for the first cataloguing of the archive, as is evident in the surviving G. P. Savidis Historical Catalogue, now hosted in the digital collection of the Onassis Foundation Cavafy Archive.

In late 2012, the Onassis Foundation acquired the Cavafy archive, preventing a potential fragmentation of the collection and ensuring that it remained in Greece. Since 2017, the coordination of activities undertaken by the Onassis Foundation Cavafy Archive has been entrusted to a nine-member international academic committee. That same year, the digitization of archival material was completed, producing 11,086 high-definition pictures and 4,741 copies of the microfilms containing the 1963 reproduction of the archive. The digitization provided the basis for documenting and disseminating the archive's contents while also fortifying the safety and long-term preservation of the original items ("Archive of Incalculable Value").

The archive's documentation was another major step toward creating a digital collection. Amalia Pappa, deputy director of the General State Archives of Greece, supervised the documentation process, while the professors Michalis Chryssanthopoulos and Takis Kayalis supervised its literary documentation.[3] At this time, the archive was catalogued, described, and subsequently arranged de novo; descriptions were completed on an item level, according to the General International Standard Archival Description. During the documentation process, it was observed that the original collection also contained a number of documents pertaining to Alekos and Rika Sengopoulos. This material was arranged as a second, separate set of fonds under the title Singopoulo, Alekos / Singopoulo, Rica fonds. The collection Cavafy C. P. Fonds contains the poet's papers and was further classified into three sub-fonds: Work (by C. P. Cavafy), Personal Papers (of C. P. Cavafy), and Post-2012 Acquisitions. The first sub-fonds contains documents pertaining to Cavafy's work, the second contains the poet's personal archive including his correspondence, and the third hosts archival materials that were added to the collection after its acquisition by the Onassis Foundation.

Concurrently, the process of enriching the documentation of the archive with literary and critical annotations resulted in the creation of two additional description fields: Related Works by C. P. Cavafy and Additional Comments. These were also completed on an item level. The first field was used to link individual archival items to works of Cavafy's that are directly referenced, quoted in, or related to these documents. The titles of Cavafy's works were also linked to the number of their respective entries in Dimitris Daskalopoulos's Βιβλιογραφία Κ.Π. Καβάφη, 1886–2000 (*Bibliografia K. P. Kavafi, 1886–2000; Bibliography of C. P. Cavafy, 1886–2000*) in order to assist readers in their research on the publication history of those works. The description field Additional Comments was created to offer readers useful literary or critical avenues to explore as they study the material.

The thorough documentation and classification of the archive established the conditions needed for presenting the material digitally. Concurrently, the decision to render the archive digitally accessible shaped the documentation process. As an example of this dynamic relationship, the archival and literary documentation of the material produced 5,500 access points: that is, keywords that allow for targeted content searches within the digital collection. Access points were grouped as follows: (names of) persons, (names of) corporate bodies, families, places, and subjects. Access points in the last category, subjects, relate to the genre of the items (i.e., keywords like *letters, certificates,* and *records*). Additionally, subjects were subdivided into the following categories that pertain to the literary documentation of the archive: works by Cavafy, literary and other characters (historical, mythological, and invented by the poet), works by other authors, journals, newspapers, and works by Cavafy in translation ("Index"). In short, this set of keywords, with its distinct categories, functions as an additional digital index to the archival materials, allowing for searches that include items from both archives (Cavafy and Singopoulo fonds).

The Archive as a Teaching and Research Resource

To think about how one can use the digital collection as a teaching or research resource, we should begin by considering what the collection is and what it is meant to do. The digital collection is a Greek-English bilingual online repository that invites readers from different parts of the world to discover the Cavafy archive, digitized and documented in its entirety. In other words, it is a collection that aspires to find its place among the well-known digital archives of global literary figures while rendering the Cavafy archive accessible to everyone. Toward this goal, the digitized archival materials are accompanied by a body of digital materials, such as the description and documentation of the archive and its classification scheme, which are also available in Greek and English and are intended to be accessible to users of all backgrounds. The digital collection suggests different ways of navigating the materials in order to target different research needs. For instance, the "Index" page facilitates content-specific searches and is suitable for students, instructors, and researchers who are exploring the archive with a set of specialized preexisting inquiries in mind. On the other hand, the main menu offers a quick glimpse at the collection's contents and is convenient for readers who want to access larger groups of items at once, while the general search field offers quick but less specific results, including partial matches in its search results. Finally, through the classification scheme of the Cavafy and Singopoulo fonds, one can examine the complete arrangement of the fonds and thoroughly inspect the contents of every archival folder.

Whether we picture the Cavafy archive as the precious contents of a suitcase, a mountain of documents piled up on the poet's desk, or—most recently—a body of images and digital materials constituting an online collection, it is the richness of the archive itself that captures the imaginations of explorers of Cavafy's papers. As Amalia Pappa observes, literary archives διαφέρουν μεταξύ τους, όσο και τα πρόσωπα που τα δημιούργησαν ("differ from each other, as much as the persons that created them"; 378; my trans.). Naturally, the contents of literary archives diverge depending on the personalities, relationships, and activities of their creators, while—like all archives—they carry traces not only of their creators but also of the people that consulted their archival materials (378). Cavafy's work and personal life are thoroughly represented in the archive, whose corresponding sub-fonds contain documents relating to most aspects of Cavafy's activities. While the Cavafy archive is undoubtedly an invaluable resource for the literary scholar looking to work on the poet's manuscripts, it also contains remnants of the poet's everyday life. This synthesis produces a collection where important manuscripts coexist with personal notes, bills and receipts, and even handwritten recipes and lists of household chores.

Archival items strictly related to Cavafy's work as a poet are included in the archive's first sub-fonds (Work). There we can find drafts, manuscripts, and printings of Cavafy's works as well as so-called printer copies, namely handwritten manuscripts of poems intended as prototypes for Cavafy's collections of broadsheets. In these, we can sometimes observe the poet's emendations, handwritten indications of the page on which each poem should be printed or even notes on the publication date and the name of the printing company. Handwritten notes and fragments of verses or variations on published verses are accompanied by copies of Cavafy's finished collections and various translations of the poet's work. This way, the archive allows both researchers and instructors to detect different stages of the creation of a Cavafy poem as it progressed from the drawer to the printer and, subsequently, to the hands of the recipients of his handmade collections. In this sense, the digital collection positions us inside the poet's workshop, allowing the researcher (or the literature classroom) to witness parts of Cavafy's creative process. At the same time, the archival materials also help us visualize the various networks around the poet and detect archival remnants of the sociohistorical context of his time. Cavafy's broadsheet collections are closely associated with the poet's famous distribution catalogues, which, in turn, are in dialogue with his correspondence. The archive includes drafts and copies of Cavafy's letters that document his well-known epistolary friendship with E. M. Forster as well as with other, less famous addressees, and it also includes a large amount of correspondence addressed to the poet.

The digital collection functions as a fundamental source of both firsthand and secondary information on Cavafy's life story, extending from the poet's rich family correspondence and everyday personal notes—both part of the Cavafy archive's second sub-fonds (Personal Papers)—to secondhand biographical descriptions included in the Singopoulo fonds. Rika Sengopoulos's biographical notes on the poet, along with scraps of Cavafy's genealogical endeavors and numerous other relevant items, can inspire hands-on approaches to biography inside the literature classroom. At the same time, different pictorial portrayals of Cavafy, varying from photographs and sketches to caricatures, not only present us with the many faces of the poet but can also inspire comparative interpretations of Cavafy's public image that engage with multiple readings of his work.

The versatility of the digital environment, allowing for the juxtaposition of different documents, is especially appropriate for interactive teaching approaches, where students are invited to carry out original research, compare and critically combine information, or even reuse the digitized items to produce original material beyond the field of research, thus giving the items another form of materiality. On a practical level, these uses of the digital collection are in line with the Onassis Foundation's commitment to provide free and open access to the archive. Users are allowed to "download and reproduce the digital objects and descriptions of the Cavafy archive, solely under the condition that they refer to their source, namely the Onassis Foundation Cavafy Archive," and that they provide open access "to any derivative works they produce" ("Copyright"). This decision promotes the materials' use (both the digital objects themselves and their descriptions) and their redistribution for all purposes, including educational, creative, and research uses, while also supporting open access in practice.

Since the Onassis Foundation's acquisition of the archival collection in 2012, the Onassis Foundation Cavafy Archive has supported "a range of educational programs directed at the Greek and international academic community and the general public with an emphasis on young people" ("Archive of Incalculable Value"). It is only natural that these programs adhere to the same values as the digital collection itself, always looking to engage with different audiences and communities that share an interest in Cavafy's life and work. The numerous initiatives that are undertaken by the foundation and presented on the Onassis Foundation website constitute a rich parallel archive ("Cavafy Archive"). They include, along with open calls and announcements of new programs, a series of short blog posts on Cavafy written by renowned academics, Cavafy's poems, and materials on the organization and activities of the archive. These materials, along with a continuously updated array of recorded events, serve as valuable educational materials in their own right while also offering a framework for audiences first approaching Cavafy's work and the archive.

Since 2021, the digital collection's users have also been able to download the metadata that derives from the documentation of the archive in machine-readable format (i.e., EAD XML). This option facilitates further utilization of the archive in research and educational digital humanities projects, so that research communities around the world can be introduced to Cavafy's collection. In the spring of 2023, the Onassis Foundation in New York presented a week-long festival inspired by the life of Cavafy, under the title "Archive of Desire," featuring an array of "performances, digital art presentations, short film screenings, poetry readings, literary discussions," and more live events ("'Archive of Desire'"). In November of 2023, the Onassis Foundation inaugurated a new space for the Cavafy Archive, located in the heart of Athens; the space, "dedicated to the poet's archive," houses not only his papers and books but also personal items and furniture along with artworks belonging or related to Cavafy ("New Cavafy Archive Building").

The next steps for the Cavafy Archive include working on further developing the collection's contents and digital function, while educational initiatives will continue exploring the potential of the digital collection as a research and educational resource. A new initiative involves the publication of a series of open, online lessons and learning material dossiers dedicated to the Cavafy Archive. The series consists of ten lessons pertaining to different subjects drawn from the archive and will include original learning materials as well as self-assessment exercises, critical and creative activities, and detailed educational scenarios addressed to educators, students, and others ("Digital Material"). At the same time, the Onassis Foundation has been coordinating the project of documenting and digitizing the poet's library, aiming to make Cavafy's book collection available online in the years to come.

The digital collection of the Cavafy Archive aspires to be a dynamic repository facilitating open access, archival research, and the further incorporation of primary resources in education. But the digital archive intends to do more than just allow researchers to read Cavafy's papers remotely; it aims to become a valuable resource for teaching Cavafy and a platform for creative uses that explore new and unexpected research and teaching avenues.

NOTES

1. The term *fonds* stands for the records "organically created and/or accumulated and used by a particular person, family, or corporate body in the course of that creator's activities and functions" (*General International Standard Archival Description* 10).

2. The picture, taken by Apostolos Ververis, belongs to a series of images of Cavafy's house, recorded with the care of Alekos and Rika Sengopoulos after the death of the poet in 1933.

3. For more information, see the "Literary Documentation" page of the Onassis Foundation Cavafy Archive website. For a full list of the many contributors to this project, see the website's "Credits" and "Acknowledgements" pages.

Part Two

APPROACHES

Introduction

Peter Jeffreys and Demetres P. Tryphonopoulos

The volume's sixteen essays have been chosen on the basis of their diverse approaches—both thematic and methodological—to teaching Cavafy's poetry. They are meant to fill a void: although Cavafy is translated, read, and taught in English, the pedagogy surrounding the teaching of his work has not received the attention it deserves. Cavafy himself suggested that his poems fell into three categories: philosophical, historical, and hedonistic. Useful and practical as this categorization is for teachers, it does not begin to define Cavafy's nuanced poetic output. The essays in this volume focus on the complexities, difficulties, and challenges posed by the poetry, since the goal of this collection is to emphasize the richness of Cavafy's oeuvre rather than place it into simplistic groupings.

It is not difficult to make the case for Cavafy more definitively as a poet of the Greek diaspora living far from the cultural center of Athens, for the expediency of reading him through the lenses of postcolonial or queer theory, or for framing his work in various theoretical, cultural, and historical contexts. Living his entire mature life in Alexandria, Cavafy was especially sensitive to unremarkable and peripheral places, individuals, and epochs. Indeed, it is his marginal status that shaped his multifaceted and comparative approaches to so many topics. The five essays included in the section "Theoretical, Cultural, and Historical Contexts" focus on Cavafy as a poet of the periphery and pose historical, cultural, and theoretical questions about his work, underscoring his cosmopolitanism, modernism, and transnationalism.

By including a module on Cavafy in an upper-level undergraduate seminar called Queer Classics: Desire, Embodiment, Backward Glances, Cat Lambert invites students to apply queer theory in considering how contemporary discourses of homosexuality helped shape the poet's work. In "Teaching Cavafy with Queer Theory," Lambert explores the possibilities that queer theory offers in engaging with Cavafy's poetics from perspectives beyond those of the poet's own biography and identity, since the poems often probe and imagine the confluences and junctures between "queerness, temporality, embodiment, and desire." In "Bringing Cavafy the Egyptiote into the Classroom," Hala Halim challenges accounts in which Cavafy has been claimed as part of an Alexandrian cosmopolitanism that was the successor to the Hellenic diaspora and Western hegemonic culture. Halim counters anglophone perspectives that have long projected Cavafy as mostly uninterested in things Egyptian; in doing this, she problematizes traditional readings of Cavafy within an exclusively European canon. "Cavafy and History: An Interdisciplinary Approach" is based on a course taught at Boston University by Kelly Polychroniou and Loren J. Samons in which the instructors combine source-driven and linguistic approaches to help students achieve a better understanding of Cavafy's treatment of particular historical periods. In "Cavafy in Comparison: The Politics of Time," Natalie Melas discusses her collaboration with students in approaching modern poetics transnationally and comparatively as a worldly force; in so doing, she develops an understanding of those theoretical and historical dynamics that underlie discourses of modernism. Martin McKinsey, in "Why Cavafy? Why Postcolonial? Teaching the Postcolonial Cavafy," makes the biographical case for Cavafy as a postcolonial writer. Despite postcolonial literature and its study being predicated on the use of a major colonial language, McKinsey adds the Greek poet to a mix of postcolonial writers such as J. M. Coetzee, Chinua Achebe, Salman Rushdie, and Derek Walcott.

The three essays in the section "Translating, Discovering, and Interpreting Cavafy" address the persistent and imaginative reinterpretation of Cavafy and the commitment successive generations of translators demonstrate in retranslating his work. They also focus on how the Cavafy taught in the classroom cuts an odd figure whose ironic voice offers opportunities for exploring a world of lexical subtlety found either in his sources or created by the poet's imagination. Much has been written about his distinctive, inimitable tone of voice. W. H. Auden's observation that Cavafy's poetry survives translation is often taken as a self-evident fact. We might even argue that there is an embarrassment of riches when it comes to the number of English translations and that there is no definitive way of capturing his voice or translating his poems. The essays in this section confirm another truth: Cavafy has always been (and continues to be) read in a modified, mediated form that endures and produces diverse interpretations with each new reading, translation, and editorial intervention.

Karen Emmerich's essay, "Cavafy Constructed: Archive, Editions, Translations," examines the risks of referring to original or source texts, especially when it comes to a poet who chose not to publish a single volume of poems during his lifetime. Whether in the original or in translation, reading Cavafy, Emmerich contends, is a matter of reading him in adapted, modified, mediated forms. In "Which Cavafy? Selecting the Right Translation," Sarah Ekdawi begins by pointing out that there are two opposing strands in translation appreciation, broadly summarized by Willis Barnstone in *The Poetics of Translation*: one that strives to remain faithful to the spirit of the original or source text, including its formal aspects, and one that provides a crib for readers who need help following the source text. Ekdawi argues that, for pedagogical purposes, it seems wise to choose translations of Cavafy that mirror his Greek as closely as possible. Readers of Cavafy's poetry are often drawn into the interactions of various revolutionary discursive choices that are made within the poet's subversive socioeconomic critique, and in "The Poetics of Liminality: Anti-Economy and Cultural Politics in Cavafy," Panagiotis Roilos examines Cavafy's challenge to dominant European rhetorical tropes, primarily metaphor. Using examples from the poetry, Roilos encourages his students to discover Cavafy's gradual development of a new, inimitable idiom through which the poet destabilized conventional synchronic conceptualizations of modernist poeticity.

In the section "Intertextual Approaches," five contributors offer a variety of intertextual perspectives, including Cavafy's treatment of the Homeric and Hellenic past and classical aesthetics in several poems focusing on the myths of the Trojan cycle. Essays in this section address Cavafy's relation to literary decadence, his representation in musical scores of all types and genres, and his multidisciplinary footprint on the web. In "Cavafy's *Iliad* in the Classroom," Stamatia Dova discusses Cavafy's reception of Homer's *Iliad* and examines the dynamics of poetic inspiration against the backdrop of the multiformity of the Homeric tradition. By juxtaposing Cavafy's poems with the Homeric passages that inspired them, Dova's class engages in an aesthetic, literary, and historical search for Cavafy's Homer. In "Cavafy's Decadent Aesthetic," Peter Jeffreys positions Cavafy within the context of the broader transnational literary tradition of decadence, inviting students to appreciate more fully the poet's current worldwide reputation by locating him in the decadent European movements of his time. In "Conversing with Cavafy through Music," Vassilis Lambropoulos discusses the use of musical settings of Cavafy's poetry for teaching purposes, especially as examples of the modern dialectic between poetry and music that emerged with the German lied and became a major artistic and philosophical issue. In "Digital Cavafy: Teaching Poetry through Connective Media," Foteini Dimirouli focuses on optimal ways of integrating digital resources into the classroom. Given the influx of new tools and the current, radical transformation of the literary project, the essay provides suggestions about how to balance traditional and innovative methods in teaching Cavafy's poetry in the digital age. In "Digital Intertextuality and the Cavafy Archive," Takis Kayalis takes into account current theoretical and pedagogical challenges that teachers face when teaching with a digital archive and points to the new tools and opportunities available in the Cavafy archive's digital collection. Kayalis demonstrates the possibilities for meaningful readings, responses, and experiences that emerged from Cavafy Goes to College, the experimental extracurricular workshop offered in March 2019 at the University of Ioannina in Greece.

Finally, the three essays in the section "Classroom Contexts" should help students and readers appreciate Cavafy's unique poetics from the perspective of aesthetics, form, and subject matter, allowing the instructor to enable students to hear Cavafy's speakers. Whether teaching courses in the general curriculum, Modern Greek language studies, or the classics, these contributors employ theoretical and pedagogical methodologies that support students in thinking textually, critically, and creatively. Although Cavafy may be one of the poets most translated into English and is certainly one of the most significant poets of the twentieth century, most students at American universities have never heard of him. If they have, it is because they have read "Ithaca" in high school or because someone has read it to them.

In "Teaching Cavafy to the *Instagram* Generation," Gregory Jusdanis notes that instructors have to assume that students possess little knowledge about Greece, let alone about Greek literature. In his large lecture course, Introduction to Classical Literature, Jusdanis includes works by Cavafy and organizes the texts thematically, focusing on empathy and our relationship to the other and arguing that literature encourages an empathic reaction that allows us to have vicarious experiences. Drawing from the mandate of the 2007 Modern Language Association report "Foreign Languages and Higher Education" (Ad Hoc Committee) and the scholarship of second language acquisition experts and linguists, Elsa Amanatidou, in "'Dangerous Things'? Cavafy in the Modern Greek Language Classroom," situates the study of Cavafy in the cross-cultural and translingual frames of a literacy-driven foreign language curriculum. This work involves examining content and language at every turn. Amanatidou argues for the necessity of reconceptualizing foreign language education, reinstating its role within the humanities as a tool for teaching analytical and interpretative skills, content acquisition, and aesthetic perception and for bringing students into contact with "cultural narratives that appear in every kind of expressive form," including poetry. In "Cavafy as a Bridge from Classics to Modern Greek Studies," Johanna Hanink points to Cavafy's significance as a meeting point for both the scholars and students of classics and Modern Greek studies. She considers the complex ways in which Cavafy was influenced by the "antiquity industrial complex," paying particular attention to his prose writings on the Parthenon marbles and his expansive Hellenism.

Cavafy's poetry presents many pedagogical hurdles, but it also offers rich opportunities for teachers to convince students that modern poetry in general and Cavafy's in particular need not intimidate. The essays in this volume illustrate how Cavafy's poems work in powerful and complex ways. The strategies they propose will surely help students appreciate Cavafy as a world poet and themselves as global readers.

THEORETICAL, CULTURAL, AND HISTORICAL CONTEXTS

Teaching Cavafy with Queer Theory

Cat Lambert

Cavafy often positioned himself as writing for the future, in his words, "a poet of the future generations" (*Selected Prose Works* 143). In a famous note from December 1905, he writes, "The wretched laws of society—neither the result of healthy or critical thinking—have diminished my work. They have inhibited my expressiveness; they have prevented me from imparting light and emotion to those made like me" (134). A similar sentiment motivates the poem "Hidden": lamenting that an "obstacle" has prevented him from expressing himself openly, the poet declares that "[a]fterwards—in some more perfect society— / someone else who's fashioned like me / will surely appear and be free to do as he pleases" (*Complete Poems* [Mendelsohn] 319). While Cavafy predates the mobilization of a queer lens as a theoretical analytic, his work seems to look ahead not just to those made like him but also to lively corners of queer theory today. Teaching Cavafy with queer theory invites students to situate the poet within the contemporary discourses of homosexuality that shaped his work. Cavafy lived during a historical juncture that transformed what had been forbidden, sodomitical acts into subjecthood: in Michel Foucault's famous terms, the homosexual was now "a species," a type of person, an identity (*Introduction* 43). Additionally, teaching Cavafy through the prism of queer theory enables students to engage with his poetics from angles that move beyond the topic of Cavafy's own identity, to consider how Cavafy's poems themselves theorize the intersections between queerness, temporality, embodiment, and desire.

    I include a module on Cavafy in the upper-level undergraduate seminar Queer Classics: Desire, Embodiment, Backward Glances. I designed and piloted this new course for the Classics Department at Columbia University, and it attracted eighteen students with a wide range of backgrounds and interests, mostly non-majors. In this course, students investigate classical antiquity through the prism of queer studies. In addition to analyzing ancient representations of homoeroticism and gender variance, students critique how scholars' methodologies, desires, or cultural prejudices shape (our knowledge of) the past and its queer possibility. Further, students compare how writers and artists beyond academia have engaged with the classical past to construct queer history and community and empower nonnormative and marginalized expressions of gender, sexuality, and identity. In this essay, I discuss how and why I teach Cavafy in the context of this course, and how I might expand my pedagogical approach to the queer Cavafy in the future.

Students encounter Cavafy midway through the course as a kind of hinge. Prior to reading Cavafy, students have focused on ancient, primary evidence for homoeroticism and gender variance and scholarly approaches to these sources. One theme that emerges here is that academic scholarship is a genre of writing that rarely theorizes or dares to speak of the desires that motivate its own backward glances, often because it seeks to maintain a pose of epistemological rigor and a claim of authority over the object of study. By contrast, Cavafy's poetry helps students imagine alternative modes of engaging with the classical past: Cavafy looks back to, even "cruises," the distant past to articulate homoerotic desire, constructing a community of those made like him who seep across and disturb linear temporal boundaries. While scholarly poses might strive to keep the object of study at a critical distance, Cavafy's poems find oblique ways to generate erotic relations between past and present: Cavafy's backward glances embody what the medievalist Carolyn Dinshaw identifies as a queer historical impulse "for partial affective connection, for community, for even a touch across time" (21). Reading Cavafy thus also primes my students for the second half of the course, which considers how contemporary queer communities have drawn on and mobilized classical antiquity.

We begin our unit on Cavafy by thinking about the closet, "the defining structure of gay oppression" in the twentieth century (Sedgwick, *Epistemology* 71). Students are assigned the poems "Walls," "Hidden," "One Night," and "In an Old Book—" (Cavafy, *Complete Poems* [Mendelsohn] 191, 319, 46, 114). In preparation, students also read Dimitris Papanikolaou's essay "'Words That Tell and Hide': Revisiting C. P. Cavafy's Closets." This essay helpfully orients students to Cavafy and homosexuality through key passages and arguments from Foucault's *History of Sexuality* and Eve Kosofsky Sedgwick's *Epistemology of the Closet*.[1] Papanikolaou advocates for a new understanding of Cavafy's relationship to sexuality: instead of treating Cavafy's homosexuality as something the writer largely suppressed and then unveiled only toward the end of his life, we ought to understand Cavafy as constructing (in Foucauldian fashion) homosexuality through a "dialectic of telling and hiding" across his entire poetic oeuvre ("'Words'" 236). For Papanikolaou, the trope of the closet figures this poetics of the homosexual self: Cavafy transforms the closet from a technology that represses and silences those who are homosexual into a platform for speech, "a positive space in which to forge queer identities" (238).[2]

In this session, students are most intrigued by "Walls," which Papanikolaou reads as especially programmatic for Cavafy's poetics of "telling and hiding." What might these walls symbolize? Who might these builders be, and why are they silent? What is the relationship between the walls in which the poet is enclosed and "Walls" the poem? To get students thinking about these questions in a focused, concrete way, I put them in small groups and ask them to compare Mendelsohn's translation of the poem and the translation by Edmund Keeley and Philip Sherrard (Cavafy, *Collected Poems* [2009] 3). Students point out formal differences between the two: for example, Mendelsohn's translation has an ABAB rhyme scheme, while Keeley and Sherrard's does not. (I read the original Greek poem aloud to them, so they can hear that it, too, has an ABAB rhyme scheme). Students observe the irony of a poem that describes a silent imprisonment yet resounds with echoes: does this echoing reinforce or disturb the concept of the closet?

In our next segment, students extend their analysis by considering poems that Papanikolaou leaves to the side, particularly poems set in (or about) the historical past. We focus in particular on "In the Month of Hathor" and "Caesarion" (Cavafy, *Complete Poems* [Mendelsohn] 70, 61). How might these poems relate to the trope of the closet and the forging of homosexual identity and eroticism? How might the distant past, and its fragmented, partial materiality, resonate with the "dialectic of telling and hiding"? In our discussion of "In the Month of Hathor," many students draw connections to Sappho, whose fragments we read earlier in the semester through Anne Carson's translation, *If Not, Winter*. Carson's translation typographically preserves the ancient Lesbian poet's fragmentary materiality and the modern critic's textual conjectures through brackets, spaces, and ellipses. Students thus compare Cavafy's typographic choices (e.g., the bracketed letters, the space slicing through the middle of a poem) and consider how such aspects, as in Sappho's work, both simulate and stimulate the reader's longings. I also invite students to consider "In the Month of Hathor" in the light of our previous discussion of "Walls," "Hidden," and other Cavafy poems. How does "In the Month of Hathor" play with speech and silence, presence and absence? What formal strategies does the poet use to (safely) give voice to Leucius's (and his own) desires?

Our discussion here of the erotics of reading the work of Cavafy and of reading in his work feeds naturally into our next topic, which is a recurring theme in the course: the backward glance or scholarly pose and its libidinal investments. Here, we focus on "Caesarion," whose title character is "the only historical figure from antiquity in Cavafy's poetry to be explicitly treated as an object of homoerotic desire" (Kayalis, "Cavafy's Historical Poetics" 61). In preparation for our discussion, I assign Takis Kayalis's essay "Cavafy's Historical Poetics in Context: 'Caesarion' as Palimpsest." Contrary to the assumption that Caesarion was a marginal, obsolete figure (as the poem itself suggests), this essay teaches students that Caesarion had long been mobilized as a symbol of homoerotic desire, whether by Frederick II of Prussia (in 1750) or Edward Carpenter (in 1906), and that symbol was in wide circulation during Cavafy's time, including in the cinema.

With this broader context in mind, students explore why Cavafy chooses to portray Caesarion as a marginal and elusive figure and how this choice might relate to the construction of queerness in particular. They start by assessing how the narrator's readerly pose shifts as the poem progresses. The poet begins by playing the historian, trying to "ascertain a certain date."[3] An affective shift occurs when the narrator suddenly encounters "a tiny, / insignificant reference to King Caesarion." Students situate Cavafy's imaginative treatment of Caesarion—"In history there are only a few / lines that can be found concerning you; / and so I could fashion you more freely in my mind" (*Complete Poems* [Mendelsohn] 61)—as part of his poetics of "hiding and telling." I have them closely compare the readerly subjects in "Caesarion" and "In an Old Book—," a poem in which the narrator, leafing through an old book, happens upon an anonymous watercolor portrait of an attractive young man. In comparing these poems, students are invited to consider how the historical past might provide distinct affordances for Cavafy to express homoerotic desire and practice a kind of queer historiography. By tracing the poem's shift from historicist certitude to "indefinite / charm," students consider how "Caesarion" might queer the figure of the scholar, insinuating that the scholar, too, is driven by libidinal investments.

If our discussion of "Caesarion" encourages students to think about Cavafy formulating his queer poetics while out at the movies (see Kayalis, "Cavafy's Historical Poetics" 61–63) rather than living as an isolated antiquarian in his room, our final segment on Cavafy gets students thinking about Cavafy at the museum. For the dreamy, weary figure of Caesarion enters the poet's dark room not just in a cinematic manner but also like a Greek sculpture, "fashion[ed]," a word Cavafy frequently uses as a sculptural metaphor. Here, students read the poems "In a City of Osrhoene" (*Complete Poems* [Mendelsohn] 68), "In the Presence of the Statue of Endymion" (57), "I've Gazed So Much—" (75), "In the Entrance of the Café" (45), and "Maker of Wine Bowls" (111). I give students the following guiding questions: How do classical and Hellenistic Greek sculpture shape Cavafy's poetics of desire and queerness? How does Cavafy refashion ancient Greek sculpture as a medium for expressing gay desire in the present and constructing queer community that cuts across time? How do recent theorizations of queer temporality help us understand Cavafy's poetic treatment of the ancient past?

To supplement our discussion, students read J. L. Watson's essay "Bodies Out of Time: Sculpting Queer Poetics and Queering Classical Sculpture in the Poetry of C. P. Cavafy." This essay models for students how one might frame Cavafy's sculptural poems through the lens of queer temporality, thus introducing students to one of the liveliest corners of queer theory in recent decades. Critics from a wide range of disciplinary backgrounds have attended to queer time,[4] such as José Esteban Muñoz, who harmonizes with Cavafy in *Cruising Utopia: The Then and There of Queer Futurity*. For Muñoz, "[q]ueerness is not yet here. . . . We have never been queer, yet queerness exists for us as an ideality that can be distilled from the past and used to imagine a future" (1). Thinking together with the essays by Muñoz and Watson, students assess how Cavafy draws on the past to challenge the linearity of time, "sculpting" homoerotic desire and erotic encounters that blur the boundaries between past and present. Cavafy's poetics of sculpture gives students a concrete, materialist hook into this difficult, sophisticated corpus of queer theory.

In our discussion of Cavafy, sculpture, and time, students note how often the bodies of male lovers are painted in sensuous yet vague brush strokes, like the "lovely body" in "In the Entrance of the Café" (*Complete Poems* [Mendelsohn] 45), or are summoned up as ghostly apparitions, like Caesarion, who died young. In future iterations of the course, I might help students probe these observations further by assigning Muñoz's chapter "Gesture, Ephemera, and Queer Feeling" from *Cruising Utopia* (65–81). Here, Muñoz muses on the "vexed relationship" between queerness and evidence: "Historically, evidence of queerness has been used to penalize and discipline queer desires, connections, and acts. . . . Queerness is rarely complemented by evidence, or at least by traditional understandings of the term. The key to queering evidence, and by that I mean the ways in which we prove queerness and read queerness, is by suturing it to the concept of ephemera" (65). The gesture, the gait, the glance, the lingering hand, the parenthetical remark: these form the lexicon of queer history, often illegible as real evidence to a homophobic society. Cavafy's poems abound in such features (examples include "The Window of the Tobacco Shop" [*Complete Poems* (Mendelsohn) 77], "In an Old Book—" [114], "On the Stairs" [314], "In the Theatre" [315], "He Asked about the Quality—" [166], "The Bandaged Shoulder" [333], and "Since Nine—" [55]). Muñoz's chapter provides students with a powerful theoretical lens for analyzing Cavafy's poetics of ephemerality, embodiment, and gesture as a distinctly queer poetics.

Further, Cavafy presents students an opportunity to consider the nexus between queerness and Muñozian ephemerality not only in terms of the poems' verbal and thematic content but also through their typographic and bibliographic materiality. Closely reading "The Art of Losing," by Elizabeth Bishop, Muñoz suggests that we might read Bishop's parenthetical asides as "a queer trace that lingers" (75). This argument chimes rather nicely with Papanikolaou's work on Cavafy's use of the hanging dash at the end of seven of the poet's titles: the "dash stands for the mark of the unsaid, symbolizing the homosexual subtext of the poem" ("'Words'" 258n5). Students might compare Cavafy's use of the hanging dash with other typographic moves, such as the brackets in "In the Month of Hathor," hanging dashes in "In an Old Book—" and other poems, or ellipses in "He Came to Read—." Further, students might compare how different translators and editors treat such typographic features: for example, Keeley and

Sherrard do away with the hanging dashes altogether. What effect does that editorial erasure have on our understanding of the poems and their queer potential? Instructors might also share with students a bit about how Cavafy originally circulated his poems:[5] how might the experience of handling an idiosyncratic pamphlet of Cavafy's poems compare to reading his poems as part of a complete, bound edition? How might such differences in materiality and the readerly experiences they afford relate specifically to queer gestures, ephemera, and feelings? Instructors might actively engage students in these considerations of queer materiality and affect: students could experiment with making and circulating their own zine-style pamphlets of Cavafy's works (and using the font Cavafy Script, available for download from the Cavafy Archive website ["Cavafy Script"]).

Finally, in the future I would supplement this heavily text-based approach to the queer Cavafy with visual materials. David Hockney's *Illustrations for Fourteen Poems from C. P. Cavafy* would generate lively discussion: How do the drawings in this series represent or supplement Cavafy's poetics of homosexual desire? Should we view them as translations of Cavafy's poems, and if so, what aspects of the poems (e.g., verbal content, tone, mood, or affect) do they translate? How does the materiality of line drawing relate to Cavafy's poetics of memory, desire, and fleeting experience? Students might then compare Hockney's drawings to photographs. For example, instructors might share images from Dimitris Yeros's *Shades of Love: Photographs Inspired by the Poems of C. P. Cavafy*. To connect this exercise back to earlier themes, students might consider these visual representations in the context of Cavafy's poetics of "telling and hiding": how does a homoerotic photograph or drawing tell and hide compared to a poem about a drawing or photograph (e.g., "In an Old Book—" and "The Bandaged Shoulder")?

Cavafy is now part of the gay canon, but this was not always the case. In 1983, the editors of the *Journal of the Hellenic Diaspora* stated, "Let it finally be said: Cavafy is neither 'perverse' nor 'obscene' nor 'obsessed' nor even 'erotic.' . . . Cavafy articulates a *specifically* homosexual strategy of liberation and historical consciousness. And if we distort this, most central, aspect of Cavafy's *perception* of human society, we have decimated him beyond recognition" (Alexiou, *C. P. Cavafy* 6). Papanikolaou's Σαν κ' εμένα καμωμένοι: Ο ομοφυλόφιλος Καβάφης και η ποιητική της σεξουαλικότητας (*San k' emena kamomenoi: O omofylofilos Kavafis kai i piitiki tis sexoualikotitas*; *Created Like Me: Gay Cavafy and Sexual Poetics*), published only in 2014, is "the first book-length study of Cavafy through the lens of queer theory in Greece" (Boletsi, Review 202). Cavafy's work provides instructors with ample ways to introduce students to canonical texts and arguments under the umbrella of queer theory and to more recent turns toward temporality. Queer theory also provides a kaleidoscope for students to view Cavafy's poetry from a number of "slight" angles (Forster, "Poetry" 91), to generate fresh interpretations, and to develop a queer lexicon for describing how it feels to read Cavafy today.

NOTES

1. Sedgwick herself maintained a keen interest in Cavafy: see, for example, *Weather* 42–69. She also made a unique artist's book, in which she pasted numerous poems by Cavafy onto Edward Bulwer-Lytton's homophobic novel *The Last Days of Pompeii*. For discussion, see Edwards 307–400.

2. I assign Papanikolaou, "Days," as an optional reading that situates Cavafy more explicitly within contemporary sexological discourses.

3. As Kayalis shows, Cavafy's most probable source here was J. P. Mahaffy's *Empire of the Ptolemies*, whose antiquarian pose Cavafy parodies; Kayalis, "Cavafy's Historical Poetics."

4. See, for instance, Edelman; Halberstam, *In a Queer Time*; Freccero; Love; and Freeman.

5. For further context about Cavafy's bibliographic materiality, instructors might consider Stroebel, who articulates how Cavafy indefinitely deferred a complete, totalizing edition of his poetry; rather, the poems were cobbled together "like Frankenstein's monster" (292): heterogenous and typographically fluid.

Bringing Cavafy the Egyptiote into the Classroom

Hala Halim

Like the speaker in his poem "Alexandrian Merchant," C. P. Cavafy could have said, "I arrived in April; / I am leaving in April" (*Complete Poems* [Dalven] 229). He was born in Alexandria on 29 April in 1863, and he died in his native city on the same day in 1933. Biographical notes on the covers of English-language Cavafy books by and large designate him as Greek-born in Alexandria. A far more relevant term, *Egyptiote*, is hardly ever used, despite the fact that it is allegedly Cavafy's coinage (Kolaitis 27).[1] What is even more significant, in my view, is that some poems and prose texts in his corpus lend the term aesthetic and affiliative substance beyond an ethnic label, in a manner long overlooked by critics. The disregard for Cavafy as an Egyptiote is a consequence of Eurocentric readings that ascribe the poet exclusively to European imaginaries, whether Western European or Greek. I do not deny the dialogue in Cavafy's corpus with these imaginaries, nor would I write off Orientalist strains in his texts; rather, by presenting Cavafy as an Egyptiote I aim to foreground a dimension of his complex positionality and amplify a strand in his corpus that relates subtly to Egypt. Considering Cavafy as an Egyptiote, even as it evidently fits a comparative literature course, would enable the instructor in a modern Greek literature classroom to put pressure on the notion of him as a canonical Greek poet and to guide students in parsing the ethical and aesthetic import of his diasporic subjectivity; the material, additionally, can be adapted to a Middle Eastern studies course. Because of space considerations, I focus mainly on two of the essential primary sources for presenting Cavafy as an Egyptiote in the classroom—a poem, "27 June 1906, 2 P.M.," and a prose text, "On the Intellectual Affinity of Egypt and the West"—but also refer to other relevant texts that can be recommended as further reading.

I would open the classroom session with an overview of the Greeks as constituting the largest foreign community in modern Egypt. The Kavála-born Albanian ruler Muḥammad ʿAlī, the so-called founder of modern Egypt, welcomed the input of Europeans, not least among them the Greeks, into his nation-state building project in the first half of the nineteenth century. Favorable conditions for this influx were provided by the system of capitulations that granted the members of several foreign countries extraterritorial rights, guaranteeing for foreign merchants—such as Cavafy's father, who traded in cotton and grain—freedom of trade, exemption from taxation, and trials in consular courts. This system would be annulled, four years after Cavafy's death, by the Montreux Convention in 1937. Before then, the crushing of the nationalist ʿUrabi uprising and the British bombardment of Alexandria in 1882 would inaugurate the British occupation. Egypt remained nominally part of the Ottoman Empire until the beginning of World War I, when it was declared a British protectorate. The British occupation, which made Egyptian cotton the prize commodity at the heart of the system, installed British administrators while further securing the Greek community and providing opportunities for its prosperity. Cavafy was thus employed as a clerk in the Irrigation Service of the Ministry of Public Works under British bosses. In 1922, the year when he retired, Egypt was granted nominal independence under pressure from the nationalist movement, although direct British intervention in the affairs of the country would continue until the 1950s. It is under the aegis of this quasi-colonial situation that a discourse of Alexandrian cosmopolitanism would identify Cavafy as its principal icon. One long-standing interpretation of Cavafy's texts presents him as *the* modern Alexandrian Greek whose poetry hearkens back to the Hellenistic period, a view that thus sanctions European ascendancy in the country. Passed over in silence are Cavafy's Egyptiote affinities with the county of his birth and the aesthetic resonances of things Egyptian in his corpus.[2]

Cavafy's prose text "On the Intellectual Affinity of Egypt and the West"— undated and unpublished during his lifetime—is most likely to have been written in 1928 (Halim, *Alexandrian Cosmopolitanism* 115). It is something of a position statement and a set of recommendations made in response to a literary collective started by Paul Vanderborght, the Belgian poet, editor, and founder of the journal *La lanterne sourde* (*The Dark Lantern*), who at the time was living in Cairo. First based in Brussels, the collective would broaden its scope of intercultural dialogue internationally. In Cairo, Vanderborght founded the Amitiés belgo-égyptiennes (Belgian-Egyptian Friendship), followed by the Lanterne sourde d'Égypte, in which context he corresponded with Cavafy. Vanderborght's side of the correspondence, in 1928 and 1929, is available online at the *Onassis Cavafy Archive* (Letter [4 Dec. 1928], Letter [12 Apr. 1929]), while a letter from Cavafy in reply to him is reproduced in Mélanie Alfano's *La lanterne sourde, 1921–1931*, an extract from which should provide useful contextualization if there are any francophone students in the classroom (118). Cavafy approaches the mission of La lanterne sourde by way of pitting against the pursuit of "intellectual affinities" "obstacles [that] present themselves once the cultures come into contact," and specifically the concern that "the Western" and "the Eastern world represented in this case by Egypt . . . differ greatly from one another." The program of La lanterne sourde, as he relays it, is "the development of relations between the writers of Egypt and those of Europe and America," involving "receptions" of visiting "foreign scholars" as well as "lectures (some in Arabic and some in French)" and studies "in European periodicals" of Modern Greek, Arabic, and other Middle Eastern literatures (*Selected Prose Works* 68). The collective's program suggests an international mode of circulation, largely in French (and also in Flemish), that, together with Cavafy's essay, would benefit from being read in relation to a world literature theoretical framework.

An apt framework here would be Pascale Casanova's thesis about "Paris [as] the capital of world literary space," a consecration bestowed by that capital being the subject of contest among peripheral literatures (124).

Having registered a degree of skepticism about the Lanterne sourde project vis-à-vis Egypt, Cavafy goes on to laud the initiative and outline something of an order of priorities. Although the Egyptiotes come last in that order, by the end of the essay he adumbrates through them a different intercultural literary space, a Greek-Egyptian one. Egyptian Arabic literature should be the collective's priority, yet it is important to "convey to the European nations whatever specific contribution Arab writers in Egypt have to offer to [Western European] trends." Far from casting Egyptian arabophone writers as peripheral or assimilated by European literary trends, the statement underscores their agency and contribution to intercultural dialogue, with the additional caveat that "translation [must be] done most carefully" (*Selected Prose Works* 68). Suggesting here a degree of knowledge about Egyptian arabophone writers, evidence of which is discussed elsewhere (Tsirkas, *Politikos Kavafis* 79; Halim, *Alexandrian Cosmopolitanism* 113–15), Cavafy touches on the output of the francophone writers who include, in addition to Egyptians, "Greeks, Syrians, and [people of] other ethnicities," whom he is keen to designate the offspring of Egypt. He then turns to "the intellectual contribution of the Greeks in Egypt"—here clearly hellenophone—and despite specifying that their linguistic outreach is limited, he outlines for them quasi-indigenous credentials. Being "reared in the Egyptian environment," Greek intellectuals "produce or will produce works that possess or will possess something of this environment." Likewise, the Greek language, long spoken in Alexandria, is not unfamiliar in the city. Cavafy then assigns the Egyptiote intellectuals a mediatory role: their familiarity "with the Egyptian way of life" renders them "a well-suited constituency" for intercultural "initiatives." Astonishingly, and taking as a pretext La lanterne sourde's mention of conducting a rigorous exploration of contemporary Greek literature, he recommends that the collective become an instrument for acquainting "the Arabic-speaking public via condensed articles, written in Arabic or French—preferably Arabic," with the "intellectual activities of the Greeks of Egypt." He thus goes beyond an elite, francophone, presumably world literature sphere to reangle the collective's desired "affinity" toward a hellenophone-arabophone continuum (*Selected Prose Works* 69). In an interview about "the philological production" of the "Egyptioton Ellinon," or the Egyptiotes, published in Alexandria in 1930, Cavafy not only reiterates the recommendation that local Greek intellectuals' output be transmitted to arabophone intellectuals through short articles but also proposes that Egyptiote intellectuals acquaint the Greek public with the outlines of Egyptian arabophone literature. He also recommends a philological inquiry into the Egyptiotes' literary output that would bring out the imprint of the Egyptian environment, particularly Alexandria's Hellenism, and foreground its distinctive characteristics (Cavafy, *Peza* 155; see Halim, *Alexandrian Cosmopolitanism* 113–17).[3] Instructors can provide an example of what an inquiry into Egyptiote poetics and affinities might yield by reading with students Cavafy's poem "27 June 1906, 2 P.M."

I would frame "27 June 1906, 2 P.M." by emphasizing that it was written in 1908 in solidarity with Egyptians oppressed by the British occupation, and I would ask students to consider why Cavafy did not publish this poem and how that decision might have related to his positionality as an Egyptiote working in an office under British administration. The poem's historical context is an instance of horrendous British colonial injustice. On 13 June 1906, four British officers went hunting pigeons belonging to the inhabitants of Dinshiwai (or Dinshaway), a village in the Nile delta, without obtaining proper permission. Firing a shot, an officer inadvertently set fire to a threshing floor belonging to the local peasants, which resulted in a clash between the British and the villagers that turned violent. A peasant woman was wounded, and her fellow villagers attacked the British with sticks. An officer who had been hit on the head fled and later died of sunstroke, and a peasant who had been trying to help him was murdered (see al-Masadi 71–81; Esmeir 253). An abridged trial benefiting from a legal structure promoted by the British in the interests of the occupation established premeditation on the part of the peasants and pronounced sentences on 27 June. Four male villagers received execution sentences, two villagers were sentenced to life imprisonment with hard labor, several men were sentenced to hard labor of varying lengths, and several villagers were sentenced to be flogged. The executions and floggings took place, in full sight of the villagers, the following day at 2 p.m., roughly the same time of day when the incident had occurred.[4] The Dinshiwai incident escalated Egyptian resentment of the British occupation, was the subject of an anti-British campaign in European media by the nationalist leader Muṣṭafā Kāmil, and drew an international outcry. Supplementary material to be assigned to students could include an extract from George Bernard Shaw's "Preface for Politicians" in *John Bull's Other Island* (xlvi–lxii) and the British anti-imperialist Wilfrid Scawen Blunt's pamphlet *Atrocities of Justice under British Rule in Egypt*. Many Arabic literary texts about the incident were produced, including poems, folk ballads, and fiction (see Halim, *Alexandrian Cosmopolitanism* 102–04).

Students should be encouraged to consult Cavafy's handwritten draft of the poem available online in the *Onassis Cavafy Archive* (Cavafy, "Yussef Hussein Selim"). Even if the students do not know Greek, this activity would acquaint them with the practice of consulting manuscripts and might lead them to explore other archival material in that repository, to be drawn on in presentations and written assignments. Several translations of the poem may be provided as a reminder of its translated status and for the purposes of comparing versions, a practice that would reinforce close textual analysis; in a Greek-language classroom, the comparison would enable students to engage with the circulation of Cavafy's works in world literature. Readings could emphasize the empathic choice of diction and devices in relation to intertextuality with folklore, particularly Egyptian. But it would be instructive for students to dwell first on the title of the poem and for the teacher to introduce the notion of paratext. "More than a boundary or a sealed border, the paratext is, rather, a threshold . . . an 'undefined zone' between the inside and the outside," in Gérard Genette's words (1–2). Whereas the Cavafian poetic corpus contains quite a number of dates in titles, "27 June 1906, 2 P.M." stands out for including the hour, which is a "threshold" that cues us to the "outside" represented by "the extradiegetic 'empirical' temporality of medical and legal discourse, and the 'hard facts' of the newspaper report"; simultaneously, the hour cues us to the "inside" that is "the poem's contrastive diegetic modulation of the temporality of mourning and affective truth" (Halim, "C. P. Cavafy as an Egyptiote" 137). Students may be encouraged to browse contemporary newspapers, if accessible, but on the note of extradiegetic, legalistic temporality, one would cite Samera Esmeir's discussion, in *Juridical Humanity: A Colonial History*, of the Dinshiwai incident in relation to the British drive to establish "a special tribunal to try such offenses [of Egyptians against English soldiers], which was sanctioned by a khedival decree of 1895." During the legal proceedings following the incident, she continues, "[s]ummary trial and execution circumscribed the trial in time. The declared purposes of the summary nature of the trial were effectiveness and immediate deterrence" (254, 255).

Close reading of "27 June 1906, 2 P.M." may follow discussion of its title:

> When the Christians brought him to be hanged,
> the seventeen-year-old, the innocent boy,
> his mother, who was crawling and beating herself against the ground
> there near the gallows,
> under the harsh midday sun,
> now shrieked, and howled like a wolf, like a wild beast,
> and the next moment, exhausted, the martyr lamented,
> "You lived with me for only seventeen years, my child."
> And when they took him up the gallows ladder
> and passed the rope around and strangled him,
> the seventeen-year-old, the innocent boy,
> and he was pitifully dangling in the void
> with the spasms of black agony
> coursing through the well-formed adolescent body,
> the mother, the martyr, writhed on the ground
> and now she no longer lamented about the years;
> "For only seventeen days" was her lament,
> "For only seventeen days I took joy in you, my child."[5]

I would lead the discussion by focusing on three keywords, the first of which is Χριστιανοί ("Christiani"; "Christians"; Cavafy, *Krymmena piimata* 91). Pointing out that in the draft of the poem available online this word is Άγγλοι ("Angli"; "English"; Cavafy, "Yussef Hussein Selim"), the question may be posed to students whether the usage of "Christians" is Orientalizing in its attribution of a static, monolithic gaze to the villagers. I would then adduce two readings that have argued that the poem's intertext is likely to have been colloquial Egyptian folk texts, specifically مواويل (*mawawil*; "ballads") about the incident (Tsirkas, *Politikos Kavafis* 78–79; Halim, *Alexandrian Cosmopolitanism* 102). Next, in an opportunity for students to do comparative work, Cavafy's poem may be put into conversation with an English translation by Pierre Cachia, accompanied by a transliteration from Arabic of a ballad that uses النصارى "al-nasara" ("Nazarenes" or "Christians"; 250, 252) to describe the British (250–53); a virtually identical folk ballad that does likewise has been translated into Greek and quoted by Stratis Tsirkas, who disputes any fanaticism in the usage (*Politikos Kavafis* 78–79, 82).[6] Cavafy's word choice has also been interpreted as ironical commentary on the "un-Christian" behavior of the British (Tsirkas, *Politikos Kavafis* 83), whose actions fly in the face of Christian mercy and forgiveness (see al-Naqqash 265; Halim, *Alexandrian Cosmopolitanism*, 102). Cavafy's diction can be read as a riposte to the charge of Egyptian fanaticism leveled by the British and wielded to mitigate the international backlash (see Blunt 55; al-Sayyid, *Egypt* 174; Fahmy 179–80, 181–83).

Finally, the empathy asserted in "27 June 1906, 2 P.M." by a poet who, born into a Christian family, uses "Christians" in an ironic mode is reminiscent of a move Cavafy makes in his 1917 poem "For Ammonis, Who Died at 29, in 610." This poem is set in Alexandria in the last years of Byzantine rule and roughly three decades before the Arab conquest. The poet Ammonis, whose name marks him as a Copt, has died, and an epitaph for him has been solicited from Raphael, an Egyptian Hellenophone. As a group of young men plead with Raphael to infuse the epitaph with homoerotic allusions to the dead poet's beauty, the poem layers the personal mourning with hints, such as in the titular date, of an acute cultural and linguistic anxiety at a time of massive historical transformation. The speakers, almost a millennium after Alexander the Great's conquest of Egypt, do not know Greek; they might then fit a definition of *barbarian*, that Greek term for the other. Cavafy the Egyptiote affiliates himself with the so-called barbarians when he has the young men describe his language twice as ξένη γλώσσα ("a foreign tongue"; *Ta piimata* 83): "Our sorrow and love pass into a foreign tongue / Pour your Egyptian feelings into a foreign speech" (*Before Time* 64). I argue that the poems "27 June" and "For Ammonis" "are made into vehicles for specifically indigenous Egyptian (the *fellahin*, in this case predominantly Muslim, and the Copts, respectively) mourning" (Halim, *Alexandrian Cosmopolitanism* 103–04).

The next keyword in Cavafy's poem "27 June 1906, 2 P.M." is μάρτυσσα ("martyssa"; "the martyr"; *Krymmena piimata* 91), which provides another springboard for a discussion of different translations. Memas Kolaitis opts for "martyress" (Cavafy, *Greek Poems* 2: 70). Is the choice of the obsolete "martyress" justified and adequate, given that the original term is "uncommon" in Greek, according to Stathis Gourgouris (personal communication)? I would point out that most other translations opt for "martyr," and I ask students what strategies are used to feminize the word while withholding the unfamiliar feminine form. The second instance of the word, in verse 15, reads, ἡ μάνα ἡ μάρτυσσα (literally, "the mother the martyr"; Cavafy, *Krymmena piimata* 91). Daniel Mendelsohn opts for "his mother, martyr" (Cavafy, *Collected Poems* [Mendelsohn] 318), while both Theoharis Constantine Theoharis and Rae Dalven hyphenate the two words, and Theoharis additionally replicates "mother-martyr" in verse 7, where "mother" is not used in the original (Cavafy, *Before Time* 258; Cavafy, *Complete Poems* [Dalven] 267). The following questions may be posed: With what cultural allusions might the feminine form be charged? If "martyress" comes from a Christian register, how do we square Cavafy's use of this word with the rebuking use of "Christians"?

The word "martyress" interweaves Greek and Egyptian frames of reference. Critics have noted that the lamenting mother in this poem belongs to the "*mater dolorosa*" leitmotif in Cavafy's poetic corpus and cited the poem "Aristoboulos" (Liddell, *Cavafy* 92). I find a more representative poem to be "Supplication," in which the unknowing mother of a dead sailor prays for his safe return while the Virgin Mary's icon listens sorrowfully (Cavafy, *Complete Poems* [Dalven] 5).[7] But I would elaborate the Egyptian frame of reference by suggesting that "martyress" in "27 June 1906, 2 P.M." invokes the عديد *'adid* ("dirge" or "lament") genre, specifically the trope of the lamenting kinswomen of Dinshiwai, which appeared in different discourses at the time. In the local European-language press, fragments of the women's dirges were quoted, for example in the Greek-owned newspaper *Le phare d'Alexandrie* (*The Alexandria Lighthouse*; Tsirkas, *Politikos Kavafis* 76). Indeed, the women's keening was cited in the outcry in Britain against the sentences, so much so that on July 5, 1906, a local mouthpiece of the British administration in Egypt, *The Egyptian Gazette*, "strongly deprecate[d] the remarks . . . by certain irresponsible individuals in the House of Commons" concerning "the wailing of the women at the time of the execution," which is "the custom . . . in all cases of death, and had no other significance at Denishwai" ("Denishwai M.P.'s Sentimentalism"). In depicting the mother as a martyr, the poem ripostes to the silencing in colonial discourse of the voice of the subaltern. Cavafy would seem to have attended to the women's depiction in the press: the simile he uses for the mother's howling—σά λύκος, σά θηρίο ("like a wolf, like a wild beast"; *Krymmena piimata* 91)—appears to echo the coverage in the *Journal du Caire* of the executions in the Dinshiwai incident, which, as translated by Blunt, ends as follows: "Only the women, like hunted wolves, howl with rage and anguish" (62).

The third keyword, "seventeen," condenses multiple significations. One extant draft of the poem "27 June" carries as one of its titles "Yussef Hussein Selim," the name of the youngest man who was hanged in the incident, whom one historian states was in his early twenties (al-Masadi 91). The poem's commuting of his age to seventeen years collocates with the multivalent use of "innocent" in addition to a further solidaristic layer of the condensation of time, most visible in the mother's dirge, in which years are commuted to days. In his discussion of this poem, Tsirkas notes an affinity between Greek and Egyptian folkloric verse and persuasively relates the condensation of the grieving mother's "subjective time" to the workings of time in a folk song chanted by Upper Egyptian agricultural laborers to accompany strenuous work (*Politikos Kavafis* 86; see also 78, 87–89). In a seminar on Cavafy in which I elaborated on the intertextual resonances of Greek and Egyptian folklore in this poem (Halim, "C. P. Cavafy the Egyptiote"), I drew out examples of his engagement with Greek folklore—particularly the lament genre in his prose (the narrative "A Night Out in Kalinderi"; *Selected Prose Works* 68–69) and poetry ("It Was Taken"; *Collected Poems* [Mendelsohn] 335)[8]—and framed it in relation to Margaret Alexiou's monograph *The Ritual Lament in Greek Tradition*. In class, I would adduce Alexiou's discussion of the "antithetical style [that] remains a dynamic feature of the [Greek] folk lament," a "common technique of the modern" genre being "emphasis by contrast" (159), and I point out that the condensation has resonances in Egyptian *'adid* (see al-Asyuti 209; Halim, "C. P. Cavafy as an Egyptiote" 139).

Finally, the spelling of "seventeen" in the poem's original Greek, in the three instances in the mother's dirge, is unconventional—δεκαφτά (*dekafta*)—as distinct from the standard spelling in the two instances in the narrator's voice—δεκαεφτά (*dekaefta*; Cavafy, *Krymmena piimata* 91), as Dimitris Papanikolaou has noted (see Halim, "C. P. Cavafy" 148). To my mind, the elision recalls the Egyptian colloquial سبعتاشر (*saba'tashar*; "seventeen"), as distinct from the term in classical Arabic, سبعة عشر (*sab'at 'ashr*). Here I would cite for students Cavafy's 1892 poem "Sham el-Nessim," in which the poet transliterates the Arabic word مغني (*mughannī*; "singer") into Greek, μογάννι (*mughanni*), and adapts the Arabic name for Egypt, مصر (*Misr*), as Μισίρι (*Misiri*; *Apokirygmena piimata* 24), a Greek version of the name apparently used by an older generation of Egyptiotes.[9] The poem is about the country's spring festival and thematically and structurally appeals to local popular song. All of this suggests that Cavafy may have had some degree of proficiency in Egyptian colloquial Arabic. I would posit that the Greek Egyptian resonance in the elision in the word "seventeen" places a marker on the broader intercultural folkloric reverberations in this poem written in anticolonial solidarity (see Halim, "C. P. Cavafy as an Egyptiote," esp. 153). As such, it is a further instantiation of an Egyptiote-Egyptian continuum in Cavafy's corpus.

Depending on the class time allocated to the discussion of Cavafy as an Egyptiote, relevant supplementary material may be drawn on. In teaching this poem, I have screened a clip of dirges recited by female mourners in 'Atiyyat al-Abnudi's 1988 documentary about Upper Egypt, إيقاع الحياة (*Iqa' al-haya*; *The Rhythm of Life*; 46:34–51:27), to help students visualize a performance of *'adid*.[10] One literary text instructors may bring in for comparison is Mahmud Tahir Haqqi's novel عذراء دنشوای *'Adhra' Dinshiwai* (available in English translation as *The Maiden of Dinshway*), particularly the closing pages, which depict—in Egyptian colloquial Arabic in the original—the oldest of the Dinshiwai men to be hanged going up to the gallows and the dirges of his wife and daughter. The Egyptiote's anticolonial empathy with Egyptian affect would manifest in

Cavafy's keen interest in another cause célèbre connected to the Dinshiwai incident, namely the 1910 attempt by the pharmacist Ibrahim al-Wardani to assassinate the Anglophile Butrus Pasha Ghali in 1910. One of the reasons al-Wardani gave in court for wanting to kill Ghali was Ghali's role as chief justice in the Dinshiwai trial (al-Sayyid, *Egypt* 173). In a move that recalls his empathy with Egyptians' mourning over the incident, Cavafy kept several issues of the Alexandria-based *La réforme* newspaper's coverage of the trial, sentence, and execution of al-Wardani ("Newspaper") and wrote a note registering manifestations of Egyptians' mourning on this occasion (Liddell, *Cavafy* 92), all of which can be consulted in his archive.[11]

As the class discussion draws to a conclusion, I would clinch the argument about Cavafy as an Egyptiote by noting how, in contrast to the general anglophone critical disregard for "27 June 1906, 2 P.M.," the poem garnered endorsements in its Egyptian reception (Halim, *Alexandrian Cosmopolitanism* 104–09). The critic Raja' al-Naqqash, for example, who identifies contemporary Egyptian events as one of the sources, if a limited one, of Cavafy's poetry, designates "27 June 1906, 2 P.M." as one of the "Egyptian poems" in his corpus. Extolling it as "a beautiful, moving human tableau of great concision" (264, 267), he compares it to شنق زهران ("Shanq Zahran"; "The Hanging of Zahran"), a celebrated poem about Dinshiwai by the distinguished Egyptian poet Salah 'Abd al-Sabur (*Al-A'mal al-Shi'riyya al-Kamila* 195–98), who himself translated Cavafy and cited him in prose writings. Although the publication history of Cavafy's poem makes somewhat unconvincing al-Naqqash's argument about the intertextuality in 'Abd al-Sabur's poem—written in the mid-1950s—with "27 June 1906, 2 P.M.," the Egyptian critic's essay is an echo of the Greek Egyptian comparative work that Cavafy, in the late 1920s, was beginning to adumbrate. 'Abd al-Sabur's poem is available in English translation and might be circulated for comparison ("Hanging"). Refuting an assumption in anglophone criticism that Cavafy was uninterested in post-Arab-conquest Alexandria, Ahmad Mursi (or Ahmed Morsi)—himself an Alexandrian poet and artist who translated and made etchings inspired by Cavafy poems—cites "27 June 1906, 2 P.M.," among other poems, to demonstrate that the Egyptiote "shared the emotions and passions" of Egyptians ("Iskandariyyat Kavafi" 65). The appreciation by al-Naqqash and Mursi responds, decades later, to Cavafy's call for a mediatory role by Egyptiote intellectuals vis-à-vis their Egyptian counterparts and for interpretations that elicit the imprint of "the Egyptian environment" on Egyptiote intellectual output (*Selected Prose Works* 69).

NOTES

1. Of interest is the bilingual Greek-Arabic newspaper Αἰγυπτιώτης Ἕλλην / اليوناني المتمصر (*Egyptiotes Ellin / Al-Yunani al-Mutamassir*; *Egyptianized Greek*), published in Alexandria starting in 1932 and available at the Egyptian National Library (Dar al-Kutub) and the Hellenic Literary and Historical Archive. For a monograph on the newspaper, see

al-Imam. For a discussion of this newspaper's discourse on the Egyptiotes in relation to Cavafy's own discourse, see Halim, "C. P. Cavafy as an Egyptiote." Unless otherwise indicated, all translations from Arabic are mine. This essay abridges and revises points made in Halim, *Alexandrian Cosmopolitanism*, esp. 56–119, and "C. P. Cavafy as an Egyptiote." It also draws on a seminar I taught at the International Cavafy Summer School in Athens in July 2019; see Halim, "C. P. Cavafy the Egyptiote."

2. On Alexandria's economy in the nineteenth century, see Reimer. For short English-language references on the city's Greek community, see Gorman; Kitroeff, "Alexandria"; Trimi and Yannakakis. For a source in Arabic, see 'Ashmawi. For the outlines of Cavafy's biography, see Liddell, *Cavafy*.

3. My reading of this passage in Cavafy, *Peza*, depends on a translation provided by Eleni Tssagouri.

4. It is open to conjecture why the title of Cavafy's poem uses June 27, the day when the sentences were passed, instead of June 28, when they were carried out. On the 2 p.m. timing, see al-Masadi 77, 91, 171. Al-Masadi would be useful to assign in a Middle Eastern studies course. For relevant English-language scholarship, see al-Sayyid, *Egypt*; Fahmy.

5. I thank Demetres P. Tryphonopoulos for translating the poem for this essay.

6. I thank Michalis Chryssanthopoulos and Khalid Ra'uf for translating extracts from Tsirkas's book.

7. Tsirkas likewise adduces the imagery in the poem "Supplication" to explicate Cavafy's use of "martyress" in "27 June"; *Politikos Kavafis* 89–90.

8. For the narrative and the poem in Greek, see, respectively, Cavafy, *Ta peza* 308–09, and *Krymmena piimata* 108.

9. I am indebted to Persa Koumoutsi, the Egyptiote translator of Arabic literature into Greek, for the observation about this Egyptiote usage in a personal communication.

10. For a screening of the relevant clip, see Halim, "C. P. Cavafy the Egyptiote."

11. On Cavafy's response to the Wardani case, see Halim, *Alexandrian Cosmopolitanism* 100–03, and "C. P. Cavafy as an Egyptiote."

Cavafy and History:
An Interdisciplinary Approach

Kelly Polychroniou and Loren J. Samons

C. P. Cavafy famously called himself a ποιητής ιστορικός ("poet-historian"), and his work invites approaches from various angles, including the linguistic, philosophical, erotic, biographical, and historical.[1] Yet the historical approach has rarely been attempted in anglophone treatments of the poet, among which Glen Bowersock's studies of the poet form a notable exception ("Julian Poems," "Cavafy and Apollonios").[2] The fact remains that the poet's insistence on his work's historical aspect, as well as the preponderance of historical material in his work, invites this approach, even as one recognizes that attempting to categorize Cavafy's poems as merely historical or erotic can be misleading.[3]

In developing Cavafy and History, a new advanced undergraduate course at Boston University, we sought to combine historical, literary, and linguistic approaches to achieve a better understanding both of Cavafy's treatment of particular historical periods and of the poet's literary techniques. The course utilized an interdisciplinary method combining historical and source criticism with close reading and instruction for students in employing these tools themselves. In addition, rather than treating these poems primarily or exclusively as examples of Cavafy's poetic development, we approached poems about specific persons, events, or periods as discreet groups—even if the poems had been composed at different times—in order to discover if Cavafy displayed consistent attitudes toward particular historical subjects and to identify the ways he conveyed these attitudes poetically.

Students could register for the class through either classics or Modern Greek studies and thus satisfy requirements for, say, a minor in Modern Greek or a major in classical civilization. All enrolled students were required to complete the same set of assignments, the only difference being that advanced students of Modern Greek completed their written assignments in Greek while other students completed theirs in English. The class attracted a large audience for a Modern Greek course, and eighteen students ultimately enrolled. The students represented diverse backgrounds and interests and included native Greek speakers, Greek Americans with varying language skills, and non-Greeks—some of whom were studying Modern Greek, classics, or ancient Greek.

We intended to make the course truly interdisciplinary, although Loren Samons had primary responsibility for the historical material, and Kelly Polychroniou for the linguistic and poetic material. Development of the course began with a reading of Cavafy's corpus and the separation of the historical poems into groups based on the period and subject addressed. Although this grouping reflected a somewhat arbitrary distinction—some of the poems with historical settings probably do not reflect actual historical figures or events—the exercise produced a relatively clear set of temporal clusters. Cavafy did not approach history as a buffet, picking items here and there on which to compose poems. Rather, he fixed on a relatively small number of periods and subjects and then tended to write groups of poems devoted to these somewhat restricted areas (e.g., the emperor Julian, Julius Caesar, Ptolemaic Egypt). Cavafy returned repeatedly to subjects and periods after years of writing on other topics. Uncovering the possible reasons for Cavafy's focus on particular subjects provided another motivation for us to approach his historical poems in this fashion.

We identified and examined the following historical clusters in Cavafy's published poetry:[4] mythology and the Trojan War,[5] the Persian Wars, the Ptolemies and Seleucids in the third to second century BCE, the age of Caesar, Apollonius of Tyana, Julian, late antiquity, and Byzantium in the twelfth and fourteenth centuries. Another type of Cavafy poem treats real or fictional graves and epitaphs, which are often tied to a historical moment or environment. Other miniclusters could also be identified—the two poems on Nero, for example—or the categories arranged somewhat differently, especially if the unpublished and unfinished poems are included. Perhaps most striking in this list is the absence of such topics and figures as Periclean Athens, the Peloponnesian War, and Philip and Alexander—subjects that have typically formed the heart of any Greek history course. Cavafy's predilection for the more obscure or neglected subjects would be reaffirmed repeatedly over the term.

Course Structure

The course moved chronologically in terms of subjects addressed rather than the poet's biography. We nonetheless began with a week on Cavafy's background and life, including a guest lecture by Erik Goldstein (Boston University) on the poet's geopolitical environment. Particularly valuable here was the lecture's emphasis on Britain's impact on the Alexandria of Cavafy's youth and on the epochal events in the Greek world in the early 1920s. Cavafy's poetry—including the historical poems—can at times seem isolated from the larger political and historical environment in which it was composed. Goldstein alerted the class to the possibility that this apparent isolation might be an illusion. The geopolitical events involving Greece and the Greeks (including the diaspora) during Cavafy's life were of such a magnitude that it is extremely unlikely that Cavafy was unaffected by them, even if the chief effect was to cause him to return repeatedly to the past and to the question "What does it mean to be Greek?"

In our week on Cavafy's background and biography, we did examine some of the early, nonhistorical poetry, especially the poems that seemed to relate in some ways to the writer's early experiences (e.g., "Voices" [*Collected Poems* (Sachperoglou) 3], "Candles" [3, 5], "Walls" [13]). Although Cavafy continued to write a kind of personal poetry later in his career, these early poems do suggest a different and arguably more introspective approach to his compositions than much of the historical (and perhaps even the erotic) poetry he developed over the following three decades. Our introductory classes also included sessions in which each faculty member selected a poem and demonstrated for the students the kind of analysis we expected them to perform. We had determined to make student presentations an important part of the course, but since some of the students had never analyzed poetry formally, we also provided them with a set of terms and ideas used in poetic and literary analysis and discussed their definitions and applications.

Following the introductory meetings, the course took on its regular format. Each week the students were asked to read a set of poems on a particular topic or period as well as background material, including selections from Cavafy's sources or scholarly analysis. On Mondays, Samons presented a historical lecture designed to familiarize students with the period addressed by that week's poems and the poet's sources. On Wednesdays, Polychroniou analyzed one or more of the assigned poems for that week in terms of poetic structure, vocabulary, punctuation, meanings, and so on. In both sessions, students were encouraged to participate by asking questions or raising issues not addressed in the presentation. Friday classes consisted of student presentations (or, occasionally, presentations by outside speakers). The presentations included discussions of the historical sources and background of the chosen poem, poetic technique, vocabulary, punctuation, meanings, and the poem's potential relation to other Cavafy poems.

Beyond their presentations and occasional quizzes, students were responsible for writing one analytic piece on a poem not covered in class as well as a major research paper treating the poem addressed in their presentation. Every student was also required to bring to each class a written response to one of the poems assigned; these responses were collected by the instructors, read, marked, and returned to students in the subsequent class. Asking students to prepare responses meant that each student came to class with something to say, a procedure helpful in stimulating discussion and especially in drawing out students who might not otherwise feel comfortable speaking in class.

In terms of basic resources, our students were assigned Edmund Keeley's *Cavafy's Alexandria*, Richard Clogg's *Concise History of Greece*, and R. Malcolm Errington's *History of the Hellenistic World*. Students were frequently directed to online resources, especially the *Onassis Cavafy Archive*. We also provided them with online access to certain ancient and Byzantine texts and translations, as well as to some modern works like those of Edward Gibbon and Shakespeare. Another useful resource for the instructors was J. Phillipson's edition *Historical Poems* (Cavafy, *Historical Poems*). A self-published work by a lifelong student of Cavafy's work, it contains short essays on the historical background of virtually all the historical poems. Extremely useful in familiarizing readers with the historical environment of Cavafy's poems, Phillipson's book focuses on the historical events themselves rather than Cavafy's selection and use of sources. Not having been peer-reviewed, the work contains several errors as well as Phillipson's occasional (and apparently intentional) insertion of inaccurate or misleading information as a kind of inside joke. Therefore, although it is impressive as a testimony to a dedicated reader's love for Cavafy, Phillipson's work must be treated with caution.

The Cavafy text we used in class was Evangelos Sachperoglou's edition in the Oxford World Classics series, primarily because it includes facing Greek and English texts as well as useful notes and indices and a valuable introduction by Peter Mackridge (Mackridge, Introduction). Students were also encouraged to consult other translations to see the different ways competent translators might treat the same passage.

Julius Caesar and Caesarion

For our week on Julius Caesar and Caesarion, students were assigned "Theodotus" (*Collected Poems* [Sachperoglou] 35, 37), "The Ides of March" (33), "Caesarion" (85, 87), and "Sculptor of Tyana" (59, 61). For background and source material, we assigned Plutarch's *Life of Caesar*, Shakespeare's *Julius Caesar*, and a portion of Keeley's *Cavafy's Alexandria* (75–102). We focused on the two Julius Caesar poems, as Cavafy's interest in Caesarion seems as much aesthetic as historical, given the passage in "Caesarion" in which the poet describes how he Σ' ἔπλασα ("made") Caesarion beautiful (*Collected Poems* [Sachperoglou] 84, 85), alluding to his own role in creating a reality (at times) unbound by historical facts or sources. Since we were interested in the way Cavafy used his sources, the Caesar poems, and especially "The Ides of March," provided useful examples that the students could readily grasp. Cavafy's primary sources for this poem are arguably Plutarch's life of Caesar and Shakespeare's play. In this poem, Cavafy draws on Shakespeare's treatment of Caesar's death scene as well as on Shakespeare's sources (or the sources of Shakespeare's sources)—Suetonius's and, especially, Plutarch's biographies of the Roman leader.

Beyond the focus on the warning note that Caesar refuses to read—in Shakespeare because he refuses to give the appearance of valuing his own safety or interests above those of the public good—perhaps the most striking factor in Cavafy's treatment of Caesar's demise in "The Ides of March" is the almost total lack of sympathy shown for the Roman leader. While Cavafy seems to place the blame for Caesar's demise squarely on Caesar's shoulders as a function of the man's arrogance and feeling of superiority, the poet's sources (both ancient and modern) exhibit a marked sympathy for the ruler. This appears perhaps most strikingly in the phrase Suetonius claims Caesar uttered when he saw that even Brutus, the son of an old friend and someone he had pardoned and advanced, now sought to execute him, καὶ σὺ τέκνον ("Even you, child?" [63n3]), which becomes Shakespeare's more well-known "Et tu, Bruté? Then fall Caesar!" (3.1.77).

Cavafy goes out of his way here to contrast his poem with Shakespeare's work. Just before Caesar is struck down and utters those last words—showing that he recognizes his own doom once someone as dear to him as Brutus strikes him—Shakespeare suggests that Brutus has knelt before Caesar pretending that he seeks the dictator's indulgence. The conspirators have chosen to act as if they are supplicating Caesar to forgive a Roman who is out of favor, in order to approach closely and even to touch the dictator. Brutus's act of kneeling is thus a double treachery—he pretends to recognize and supplicate Caesar's authority even as he has joined in the conspiracy to kill him. Before he is struck down, Shakespeare's Caesar comments on Brutus's appeal: "Doth not Brutus bootless kneel?" (3.1.83). Cavafy seems to reference this line directly when the speaker in "The Ides of March" warns Caesar not to "fail to brush / aside all those who salute or bow" (*Collected Poems* [Sachperoglou] 33). This phrase, χαιρετοῦν καὶ προσκυνοῦν (32), brings the reader directly into the scene as recreated by Shakespeare, where Caesar is ringed by those pretending to beseech his mercy while intending to murder him. It is better by far, the speaker of Cavafy's poem tells us, to read that warning message as soon as you receive it and to trust no one—not even a kneeling Brutus. Cavafy here illustrates that he can employ historical or literary sources to portray the same subject as they do in a different light. He thus asks readers to reconsider their view not only of history but also of the sources themselves.

Julian

Cavafy's interest in Julian is deep and well known. We spent two weeks on the Julian poems and other poems concerning late antiquity that we believed were relevant to Cavafy's treatment of the famous apostate emperor and the relationships between pagans and Christians in the fourth century AD (e.g., "Myres: Alexandria 340 A.D." [*Collected Poems* [Sachperoglou] 187, 189, 191], "A Great Procession of Priests and Laymen" [163], "Ionic" [71]). We also asked students to read one of the unpublished poems, "Julian at the Mysteries" (*Collected Poems* [Mendelsohn] 290–91). For background and source material, we assigned Julian's own *Misopogon* (*Beard-Hater*) and the emperor's rescript on Christian teachers as well as Ammianus Marcellinus's and Edward Gibbon's treatments of the emperor. Gibbon's almost encomiastic treatment of Julian formed a particularly relevant study, since Cavafy's use of Gibbon is well known, and we can be certain the poet read the historian's presentation carefully.[6] Indeed, Gibbon's account of the tumultuous fourth century AD, arguably, presents readers with two virtually heroic figures: Julian, the apostate emperor who attacked Christianity with energy and cunning, and Athanasius, the sometime archbishop of Alexandria who vigorously defended the concept of the trinity, openly challenged imperial authority, and spent much of his career in flight or hiding. That Gibbon's choice to highlight the careers of these two figures influenced Cavafy is suggested by the poet's composition of an unfinished poem called "Athanasius" (*Unfinished Poems* 9), which depicts part of the archbishop's adventures at the moment of Julian's death.[7]

As an obvious admirer of antiquity who evinces some sympathy for the lost pagan gods ("Ionic" [*Collected Poems* (Sachperoglou) 71], "If Dead Indeed" [119, 121]) as well as someone with perhaps ambivalent feelings about the Orthodox Church, attitudes that may have derived in part from his homosexuality, Cavafy seems a likely admirer of the apostate Julian.[8] Students who do not have strong sympathies for the ancient Christians and are drawn to figures exhibiting independence from, and criticism of, religious orthodoxies and dogma might also see Julian as an admirable and tragic if not heroic figure. Yet contrary to expectations derived from Cavafy's biography and their own prejudices, contemporary readers of Cavafy's Julian poems do not find the poet evincing much admiration for the pagan emperor. The Julian poems consistently portray an imperial figure out of step both with his Christian critics and with the ancestral religion he claims to defend but that he arguably does not understand. Julian's enemies—the ostensibly Christian Antiochenes—have more in common with pagan voluptuaries than does the putatively pagan emperor. Julian's puritanical form of paganism, with its rejection of the pleasures of the flesh and insistence on the purity of a kind of pagan clergy, flew in the face of the traditional religious practices and social conventions of Greco-Roman society.

The irony of a puritanical pagan emperor opposing and opposed by thoroughly worldly Christians provided Cavafy with his richest vein of historical material, to which he returned repeatedly and with profit.[9] Perhaps his favorite source material appears in Julian's *Misopogon*,[10] which must form one of the most misguided attempts at improving public relations in the ancient or modern world. In this tone-deaf essay, which manages to offend everyone while reconciling no one, the emperor sought to defend himself against his Christian or Antiochene critics by ostensibly attacking them. In fact, the transparent attempt to portray his critics as officious buffoons backfired badly. The emperor's work surely did little to assuage the Antiochenes' feelings of revulsion at the emperor's paganism—or at his offending beard. Perhaps this affectation of Greekness by individuals like Julian—Hellenes who were Romans by birth (if not so much by education)—provides one explanation for Cavafy's fascination with the emperor. The issues of what makes a person Greek or constitutes Greekness feature repeatedly in the poet's work, and in Julian Cavafy found a subject that allowed him to approach this issue obliquely even as he luxuriated in the ironies of Julian's ascetic paganism, which contrasted with the Christianity of Julian's secularized foes. In other poems, such as "Julian in Nicomedia," Cavafy attacks the issue directly, associating Julian with the attempt to gain τῶν Ἑλλήνων τὰ ἰδεώδη ("Greek ideas"; *Collected Poems* [Sachperoglou] 144, 145). In "Julian, Noticing Negligence," one feels the bitter sarcasm in the description of the emperor's friends (and Julian himself) that ends the poem: Ἕλληνες ἦσαν ἐπὶ τέλους. Μηδὲν ἄγαν, Αὔγουστε ("They were Greeks, after all! Nothing in excess, Augustus"; 142, 143).[11]

Spartans and Greekness

Occasionally during the course, a common theme would emerge that spanned Cavafy's treatment of different historical periods or individuals. Perhaps the most interesting to us was the appearance of a paradigm of Greekness that some of Cavafy's poems attribute to Sparta and Spartans. The poem "Thermopylae" introduces this concept early in the canon (*Collected Poems* [Sachperoglou] 11), but it reappears repeatedly over Cavafy's career, perhaps most programmatically with "In the Year 200 B.C." (205). The speaker in this poem is a Greek pondering Alexander's famous dedication of Persian spoils as taken by the Macedonian king "and the Greeks except the Lacedaemonians" (205). The speaker goes on to ponder the awe-inspiring, new Greek world created by Alexander and his Hellenistic successors without the help of the Spartans. The speaker takes pride in being a member of this group—it is "we" Greeks who achieved all this:

> We: the Alexandrians, the Antiochians,
> the Seleucians, and the numerous
> other Hellenes of Egypt and Syria,
> and those in Media and those in Persia, and so many others. (205)

The speaker sums up by praising the common Greek speech now spread all the way to Bactria and India, ending thus: "Do we need to talk about Lacedaemonians now!" (205).

Yes, all this was achieved without those celebrated Spartans. Yet the reader knows what the bombastic speaker—who seems to overcompensate for his diasporic status[12]—does not know: the year 200 BCE sits at the border between a powerful Hellenistic world and one more or less completely dominated by Rome. Little more than a decade later, the Romans would defeat the powerful armies of Macedon (under Philip V) and Asia (under Antiochos III), and the age of Greek superpowers would be over. The decadent Seleucid and Ptolemaic monarchies left standing would swiftly become little more than supplicants before Roman might (as depicted in "The Displeasure of the Seleucid," "Of Demetrius Soter (162–150 B.C.)," and "Envoys from Alexandria" [*Collected Poems* (Sachperoglou) 47, 49; 117, 119; 81, 83]) until they too were swept away and their former empires became provincial Roman domains. The poem thus calls upon the reader's (superior) knowledge of events and, we would argue, knowledge of Cavafy's other poetry.

In particular, Cavafy implicitly contrasts the decadence of the Roman-era Seleucids and Ptolemies with the Spartan Cleomenes and his mother, Cratisicleia, who represent two of the most sympathetic and admirable figures in the poet's oeuvre. The relationship of son to mother was undoubtedly important to Cavafy (Liddell, *Cavafy* 95–102), but biography alone cannot explain the poet's tender regard for these figures in the trials they faced late in the third century BCE (see "In Sparta" and "Come, O King of the Lacedaemonians"

[*Collected Poems* (Sachperoglou) 175, 177; 195, 197). These figures suggest that whatever made Sparta admirable had not disappeared with the collapse of the southern Greeks before the Macedonians.[13] As at the Battle of Thermopylae, the Spartans exhibited in this later period something to which other Greeks can and do aspire—at least a part of which is the dedication to duty even in the face of certain defeat.[14] Yet Cavafy's admiration may have been as much linguistic as cultural and historical: perhaps no poet ever deserved the appellation "laconic" more than Cavafy.[15]

Over the course of the semester and taking the historical poems as a group, we found that Cavafy at times plays with the idea of Greekness, beginning with the Spartans as an ideal and extending outward through Greek, Macedonian, and Italiote identities to the diaspora and then to the non-Greek inheritors, usurpers, or impersonators of Hellenism ("Philhellene" [*Collected Poems* (Sachperoglou) 55]). In Cavafy's fixation on the question of what it means to be Greek, the Spartans arguably play a—if not the—central role.

Outcomes and Takeaways

Student reactions to this course were extremely positive. They enthusiastically participated in a contest at the end of the semester we called the Mimesis Challenge: each student composed a poem in imitation of Cavafy, and the class judged the (anonymous) results in terms of their potential for passing as poems by Cavafy. The experiment produced some remarkable student compositions on historical subjects ranging from Darius III of Persia to the Latin sack of Constantinople. One student went on to write his senior honors thesis on Cavafy's portrayal of Sparta and Spartans. We found the course to be one of the most enjoyable we had ever taught. Much of this reaction, of course, stems from the poet and the poems: Cavafy's work combines intellectual complexity with immediacy and accessibility in a way matched by few poets (or historians) in any language or period. Yet this course also benefited from the mix of students and faculty members involved. Historical interests met the literary and linguistic on equal terms. Some students excelled in their knowledge of Greek language, others in modern poetry, and still others in classical or modern history. These different interests and specialties allowed the students and instructors to inform, critique, and challenge one another in each class. Cavafy's historical poems perhaps offer as perfect a field of study as any for this kind of multidisciplinary approach.

Cavafy's preference for the backwaters of Hellenic history is well known. Yet Sparta and Laconism form an important theme for this poet obsessed with the issue of Greekness. His Spartans are arguably the most Hellenic of Hellenes, a stance that even the classical Athenians would have understood and (in many cases) endorsed. By treating the question of what it means to be Greek as central to his project, while approaching the issue from the historical and geographic periphery of Hellas, Cavafy challenged his fellow Hellenes to wrestle with their complex identity. Ironically enough, to paraphrase Philostratus (one of Cavafy's sources), the question of Greekness turns out to be a question about humanity itself: for the wise man, everywhere is Greece. Cavafy's poems describing historical individuals set in particular places and times continue to speak eloquently to the human condition.

NOTES

1. On the term ποιητής ιστορικός, which can mean "historical poet" just as easily as it means "poet-historian," see Ricks, "Cavafy."
2. See also Lee. Bowersock's "The Julian Poems" provides an illustrative treatment of Cavafy's use of historical sources over time and the poet's development of a particular historical point of view.
3. Misleading but perhaps not pointless. Mendelsohn argues that such a distinction is a "serious mistake," since time itself ultimately forms the subject of both the historical and erotic poems (Cavafy, *Complete Poems* [Mendelsohn] xxxvi). Nevertheless, the poet's different approaches to this larger theme surely justify an analytic distinction.
4. With a few exceptions, some noted later in the essay, we restricted the course to the so-called canon of 154 authorized poems.
5. On Cavafy's treatment of mythological and historical subjects in the same fashion, see Barnstone, "Real and Imaginary History"; Ricks, "Cavafy."
6. On Cavafy's reading and extensive annotations of Gibbon's work, see Haas, "Cavafy's Reading Notes," especially 44–54, covering Cavafy's notes on Gibbon's treatment of Julian and related subjects, and G. Savidis, *Mikra Kavafika A* 91–99. On Cavafy's quotation of Gibbon's dismissive view of the citizens of Antioch, see Lee 246.
7. On this poem, see Bowersock, "Julian Poems" and "Cavafy and Apollonios" 183. G. Savidis doubts that Cavafy could have been influenced by Gibbon in his decision to write about Julian; *Mikra Kavafika A* 96. Bowersock discusses the note Cavafy appended to his unfinished poem on Athanasius, to the effect that he could not locate the original (ancient) source of the story it describes and that he had decided not to publish the poem unless he could find the source; "Julian Poems."
8. See, for example, Lee; Bowersock, "Julian Poems." Bowersock maintains that since Cavafy saw himself as a Christian, his distaste for Julian stemmed, at least in part, from the emperor's intolerance of Christianity; "Cavafy" 189.
9. This irony plays out repeatedly in the Julian poems and renders insufficient any explanation of Cavafy as being motivated primarily by dislike of Julian, his hypocritical critics, or both (as Keeley came to see in "Cavafy's Voice" [164], after the initial publication of *Cavafy's Alexandria*). The Julian poems' subject matter (e.g., Christianity, paganism, philosophy, sensualism, and hypocrisy), personalities, and even locations (especially Antioch) provided an irresistible combination for Cavafy. On these poems and Cavafy's irony in general, see Keeley, *Cavafy's Alexandria*, 153–77, especially his critique of Beaton, "C. P. Cavafy." Beaton treats Cavafy's irony as pervasive and the poet's stances as relativistic, but Cavafy's implicit criticism of Julian and his critics stems partly from a recognition of the emptiness of hypocrisy and a firm belief in the beauty of both Christianity and pagan sensualism. Cavafy's almost pervasive irony does not always imply the absence of a conclusion.

10. Bowersock warns against assuming a single source for Cavafy's poems and notes that even when inspired by a secondary source, Cavafy insisted on reconciling his poetry with the original, ancient source on which his modern source had depended; "Julian Poems" 94–98.

11. Bowersock emphasizes Cavafy's apparent desire to reconcile his homosexuality with his Christianity as the primary reason for his revulsion at the intolerant and antisensualist emperor: "In the Julian poems he struggled for historical accuracy because it was clearly imperative for him to know that there really had been a world that could accommodate a sensualist, both Christian and Greek"; "Julian Poems" 103–04. Yet the appropriation of Greekness by those, like Julian, who either rejected or did not understand Hellenic tradition seems to have been an equal stimulant for the poet.

12. Phillipson notes that some commentators have taken the speaker's claims here without irony or even as expressions of Cavafy's own pride of Hellenism; Cavafy, *Historical Poems* 140. See, for instance, Sphaellou 40–45; Korsos 75–77. Yet Peridis recognizes that Cavafy distances himself somewhat from the speaker in the poem; 198–99. Cf. G. Savidis, *Mikra kavafika A* 344–46.

13. To recognize Cavafy's admiration is not to imply that no irony is possible in these poems. Beaton rightly stresses that Cavafy's irony applies even (or perhaps especially) to his treatments of Hellenism itself; "C. P. Cavafy" 521–28.

14. Tzouvelis emphasizes the importance of what he calls "the cycle of duty" in Cavafy's work; 31–36.

15. Mendelsohn maintains that this aspect of Cavafy's poetry is often overemphasized, since the term *laconic* "fails to convey the frequent strangeness of the diction" in the poems; Cavafy, *Complete Poems* (Mendelsohn) xlv. Yet from the standpoint of the classical Greeks, this Spartan strangeness was part of Laconic speech; see, for example, Thuc. 4.40.

Cavafy in Comparison: The Politics of Time

Natalie Melas

Michel Foucault formulates three questions as "the new questioning of modernity": "What is my present? What is the meaning of this present? And what am I doing when I speak of this present?" ("Art" 141). These questions guide my teaching of Cavafy's poems in the context of a comparative literature graduate seminar, Modern Poetry in and out of World Systems. The aim of the comparative framework this course develops is to situate a set of poets on a conceptual and historical world map of modern poetics. In so doing, the seminar attempts to decenter the premises of comparative accounts of influence that construe modern poetics or poetic modernity as moving unidirectionally from the European centers of imperial power, or of the world republic of letters (see Casanova), to peripheral locations where it is received and reproduced derivatively. The ground of comparison for Cavafy here is therefore philosophical and historical, and the intellectual aim of the seminar is to articulate the modern poetics at stake in Cavafy's poetry. The politics of time underlies various discourses of modernity and empire with which he grappled directly or indirectly as the queer modern Greek Alexandrian poet he became over the course of his writing life. The comparative approach to Cavafy here is thus mediated by the intersection of modern poetic form and theoretical questions relating to historical temporality and temporalization.

While the seminar includes some direct comparisons between poems and poets, the aim of comparison is mainly to constellate a set of poets and writers—chiefly Miraji (active from the 1920s to 1949) in India under the British Empire, Aimé and Suzanne Césaire in the French colony of Martinique (with a focus on 1939–56), and Cavafy in Alexandria, Egypt, under the British mandate (with a focus on 1897–33)—who occupied comparable sites in the modern imperial world system and responded explicitly from their peripheral positions to the modern poetics emerging from Paris, such as those of Baudelaire and subsequent movements and avant-gardes. These writers received and repurposed modern poetics in ways that mobilized through poetic form and lyric subjectivity their positions with respect to the uneven temporal and racial-cultural dispensations created by European empires. The pedagogical point is therefore *not* to compare the poets directly or to juxtapose one poem with another, but rather to situate their modern poetics comparatively on the world map of empire. The operative question about the three poets is, How did they become modern poets in the sites they inhabited and in the languages they possessed? How did Cavafy become, and what does it mean for him to become, a modern Alexandrian Greek poet? In Cavafy's case, the politics of time plays a particularly important part in this process.

What is the politics of time? The most immediate source of the phrase and the concept for this seminar derives from Peter Osborne's *The Politics of Time: Modernity and Avant-Garde*. Osborne's approach brings to debates about periodization a philosophical reflection on time that seeks to examine the conceptual logic at work in what are generally deemed to be chronologically distinct periods and forms. Osborne draws attention to what he usefully names the mechanics of temporalization, that is, how any given form or experience is constituted as temporal. For Osborne, the notion of the politics of time inheres in approaches to practice: "Associated with such temporalizations are both historical epistemologies (defining the temporal norms and limits of knowledge) and particular orientations towards practice, particular *politics of time*" (ix). This seminar approaches Cavafy's poetry theoretically—that is, *à thèse*. The working hypothesis posits Cavafy's poetry as, in Osborne's careful phrasing, an orientation "towards practice" that intimately engages historical epistemologies as well as social norms through the lens of aesthetics. Politics in this approach inheres in forms of temporalization rather than primarily in the poetry's content or in the advocacy of certain topical positions.

Two dimensions of Cavafy's poetic temporalization are taken up in the two seminar sessions devoted to Cavafy. The first, under the rubric Politics of Time 1: Decadence, Aesthetic and Historical: "Those People," takes up Cavafy's complex engagement in his poetry with history and historiography, with a particular focus on decadence. The second, under the rubric Politics of Time 2: Queer Temporality and Desire's Future Pasts, takes up the temporalization and historicity of what recent theorists call queer temporality, a countervailing temporality to that of reproductive futurity, emerging from the context, rhetoric, experience, and relationality entailed in homosexual desire.

Decadence as a literary movement and orientation, variously articulated in French and English literary circles in the second half of the nineteenth century, was, as Peter Jeffreys has demonstrated, the primary literary influence for Cavafy's early poetry and for his idea of poetic vocation. In keeping with the comparative approach outlined above, the seminar session Politics of Time 1 attempts to articulate the literary movement through historical accounts and ideas about decadence since these are particularly relevant to imperial valuations of the long, continuous history of Greek language and culture after classical antiquity, that period associated in the modern northern European historical imagination with various forms of decadence and decline. Edward Gibbon, in his magisterial enlightenment history, *The Decline and Fall of the Roman Empire, 1776–1789*, consigns the entire empire of the East to perpetual decline in a resounding phrase: "from the reign of Arcadius to the taking of Constantinople by the Turks, [it] subsisted one thousand and fifty-eight years in a state of *premature and perpetual decay*" (578; emphasis added). The stasis of this "premature and perpetual decay" was not fully remedied, in Gibbon's view, until the reassertion of reason and progress in the European enlightenment of his eighteenth-century present. Gibbon's may be a classic work of enlightenment historiography, but the idea of world-historical progress and the philosophy and politics of time his writing elaborates are the bedrock of European modernity.

In this world-historical view of modernity, the notions of a modern Greece and a modern Greek poetry are oxymorons. The enlightened rationalism imputed to Greek antiquity is the font of that Western civilization whose telos and true heir is northern European modernity. The inhabitants of territorial Greece and Modern Greek speakers more broadly are thus in the category of "Ottoman Orientals." The seminar readings for this session are premised on the thesis that Cavafy, in crafting his poetics as reflected mainly in the published canon of his works, marshals literary decadentism, against the philosophy of history undergirding accounts of historical decadence and the world-historical narrative that consigned the Greek culture of his time to a temporally stalled quasi-Oriental periphery. But in a converse or dialectical move, the seminar posits, Cavafy also marshals the actual long history of eastern Hellenism and a certain philosophy of history against European literary decadentism as a sheer aesthetic style and attitude. I use the term "decadentism" here to distinguish the decadence deliberately articulated by modern literary movements from the decadence described or diagnosed in historical discourses. The seminar approaches this complex dynamic starting from Cavafy's reading of Gibbon's magnum opus and the careful reading notes in which he recorded this encounter (see the appendix for a list of readings).

This first seminar session begins with one of the most important of Cavafy's reading notes on Gibbon, where the poet mentions Paul Verlaine's 1883 poem "Langueur" ("Languor"; *Jadis* 104), which, as it happens, was adopted as a manifesto of sorts for a short-lived avant-garde movement in Paris that called itself "décadisme" ("decadism"; Calinescu 171). Scholars have identified the literary and historical intertexts contained in this particular reading note of Cavafy's as a possible origin or source for the poems "Waiting for the Barbarians" and "Ionic." The conjunction in the note of a poetic expression of decadentism with an historical account of decadence in Gibbon's text quite marvelously stages for the students the complex and layered temporalization to be read in what is perhaps Cavafy's most widely known poem (though not one that students had read prior to the seminar), "Waiting for the Barbarians" (*Collected Poems* [Keeley and Sherrard, 1992] 18–19 and *Complete Poems* [Mendelsohn] 192–93), when it is considered in relation to Verlaine's "Langueur" through the prism of Gibbon's enlightenment history of decadence. This intersection of history and poetry, of historicism and aestheticism, opens a number of clear-cut paths for discussing Cavafy's poetry as a poetic orientation "towards [the] practice" of temporalization. We then extend these considerations to other poems that stage a discrepant encounter between poetry and history, poetics and periodization, starting with "For Ammonis, Who Died Aged 29, in 610" (Cavafy, *Collected Poems* [Keeley and Sherrard, 1992] 71) and "For Ammon, Who Died Aged 29, in 610" (*Complete Poems* [Mendelsohn] 71) and followed by whatever poems the students in the seminar are moved to suggest for discussion from among those listed in the syllabus.

This approach addresses two major challenges to the teaching of Cavafy in a graduate seminar in comparative literature in an American university: first, the fact that students are generally unfamiliar with Cavafy's poetry and with the literary and historical context of the eastern and southern Mediterranean, and second, the deceptive simplicity of the poetry itself, especially in translation. Of the nine graduate students in the seminar I taught in fall 2020, all of whom had scholarly commitments to modern lyric poetry in a number of languages (British and American English, French, German, Spanish, Hispanic Caribbean, ancient Greek, and Arabic), six had never heard Cavafy's name before, two had heard of him through someone they know, and one, a gay man, had discovered his poetry through his interest in the poetry of homoeroticism. From my experience teaching Cavafy in four different comparative literature graduate seminars over the years, this degree and kind of previous knowledge is typical. The aim of the readings for the first seminar session is to provide just enough context through primary texts (and a brief introductory lecture) to convey the stakes of Cavafy's engagement with literary and historical decadence for his poetics and particularly for the complex temporalization they instantiate. The layered intertexts also open a perspective for students on the many reverberations underlying the poetry's apparently simple diction. In that vein, I also follow David Damrosch's invaluable example of foregrounding the reading of translations in the context of world literature pedagogy (22–24), so that for every poem we read two translations, Keeley and Sherrard's as well as Daniel Mendelsohn's. In addition, I point students to Stathis Gourgouris's essay "Cavafy's Debt" for a fine-grained exploration of the poetics of translation that includes the poet James Merrill's unequaled translations of a few of Cavafy's poems.

The aim of the second seminar session on Cavafy, The Politics of Time 2, is to follow through on the complex layering of historicism and aestheticism explored in the previous session but with an emphasis on queer temporality. The session relies on a theoretical or critical frame that brings together two primary texts, Osborne's *The Politics of Time* and Lee Edelman's polemical articulation in *No Future* of queer temporality as set against heteronormative reproductive futurity (Edelman 1–21), along with a few other texts in the background (Foucault, "Art" 141). This theoretical nexus is complemented by Dimitris Papanikolaou's pioneering and rigorously contextualized approach to Cavafy's poetry in relation to homosexuality's discursive formations in the late nineteenth and early twentieth centuries ("Days"; see the appendix for a list of readings).

While ostensibly manageable for a week's reading, the readings for this seminar session may appear daunting in their multiplicity. I assign more reading than can be discussed in the span of two hours, and I pile on additional texts in the recommended reading section. Seminar time is further constrained by occasional ten-minute student presentations on secondary materials, for which students also formulate discussion questions. I always start the seminar with a twenty-minute lecture, giving an account of the day's readings, and often send students a message a few days prior to the seminar session suggesting orientations for their reading. But the underlying principle is that students will continue to engage with the material over the course of their studies in ways that are not foreseeable in my own planning for the seminar. The excess and experimental eclecticism of the materials are thus meant to authorize, inspire, or goad students into taking any aspect of the seminar's readings and intellectual premises into their own hands and for their own purposes. My professorial hope is that Cavafy's poetry will thus find new and unexpected reverberations in future comparative scholarship.

For the seminar session on queer temporality in fall 2020, two students presented, one on Osborne, the other on Edelman. I also sent a message before the seminar suggesting that students read the poems in clusters. The first cluster is "Hidden Things" and "Hidden" (Cavafy, *Collected Poems* [Keeley and Sherrard, 1992] 195 and *Complete Poems* [Mendelsohn] 319), "Comes to Rest" and "To Stay" (97; 88), "In the Tavernas" and "In the Taverns" (141; 134), and "The Next Table" (95; 82). The second cluster is "Days of 1908" (177; 173), "Days of 1909, '10, and '11" (161; 156), "Days of 1896" (146; 139), "Tomb of Iasis" and "Tomb of Iases" (76; 67), "In the Month of Athyr" and "In the Month of Hathor" (77; 70), and "Kleitos' Illness" and "Cleitus' Illness" (138; 131). I asked them to ponder the following question: What thoughts or questions do these clusters of poems prompt for you about the relation between desire and time, desire and belonging to a time? We begin this seminar's discussion with a close, translational consideration of the unpublished poem translated as "Hidden Things" and "Hidden," anchoring our analysis in Papanikolaou's comment on the poem in the context of "homobiographics," where Papanikolaou argues that the poem and the note that echoes it "show a homosexual man who decides to use strategically the discourses that have codified homosexuality, turning them into a point from which to speak, a constitutive mark of the self, an assertion and further reshaping of subjectivity and, even, minoritarian community" ("Days" 269). The poem "Hidden" asserts the hidden nature of the poet's speech about who he was and how he lived his life, and it ends with an analogical projection into the future: "Later, in a more perfect society / someone else made just like me / is certain to appear and act freely" (Cavafy, *Collected Poems* [Keeley and Sherrard] 195).

From here the discussion moves to the poetic juxtaposition of desire in antiquity and in modernity, what one might tentatively call the historical temporalization of homosexual desire in Cavafy's poetry, with particular attention to "Days of 1909, '10, and '11," whose last stanza draws a direct comparison between beautiful, desired, and desiring young men in modern and ancient Alexandria in its life account of a modern blacksmith's apprentice. Following on that temporal comparison, we discuss the poems "In the Tavernas" and "In the Taverns" and "The Next Table," noting the qualities of seriality and exchangeability or transferability across time and epochs these settings of desire foreground. After the student presentations on Osborne and especially on Edelman, the discussion turns to how these theoretical elaborations frame or direct our analysis of Cavafy's poems and how the poems echo or contest some of the positions elaborated in the theoretical works. The questions relating to how Cavafy's poetry posits the meaning of the present and what it is doing, or *poiein* ("making"), when it speaks of its present or actuality, recall the guiding questions from Foucault and come into sharper focus here. The discussion is particularly pointed and lively around Edelman's polemical antifuturity, to which Cavafy's "Hidden" is already a kind of retort, and this opens onto a more fine-grained appraisal of the form and disposition toward futurity in the homoerotic poems of Cavafy. From here we begin, really just as a preliminary adumbration, a discussion of what difference the explicit poetic articulation of Cavafy's Alexandrian location makes for the temporalization his poetics undertake as a multifaceted project across the canon of his published work. Part of taking account of Cavafy's location entails acknowledging the dimensions of that geopolitical space that are nearly absent from his poetry, namely modern Egypt under the control of the British Empire. I point students to the groundbreaking analysis in Hala Halim's *Alexandrian Cosmopolitanism: An Archive*, where, in the chapter on Cavafy, Halim undertakes a thorough and penetrating appraisal of Cavafy's relation to modern Egypt partly through the lens of the complex interplay in his poetry between Greeks and barbarians.

It's fashionable in neoliberal approaches to pedagogy to spell out and measure learning outcomes, but such tidy commensuration is not possible in the context of the graduate seminar on the Humboldtian model, which designates this particular format as a space in which knowledge is not transferred unidirectionally from the one who knows to those who do not yet know but rather is generated collectively in the process of discussion among a disparate community of knowers. From a certain angle, the best measure of the outcome of such a learning environment may be how much the professor learns, how much in the discussion surprises her and prods in new directions her own thinking about the poet and about teaching his poetry in a given time and place. The greatest challenges of teaching Cavafy *à thèse* within the theoretical frame of the politics of time has to do with moving from the microregister of discussing the implications of word choice in translating a poem, repetition in the poem, or its line breaks to the macroregister of the world-historical dimensions of decadence and theories of the politics of time. There is a gap in the modality of expression between history, theory, and poetry. And there never seems to be enough time to get to the bottom of it. But both ends of the spectrum are necessary. Without a close reading of a poem or two, the poetry as such does not come to life as an object of thought, and without a consideration of larger questions, the poetry is cut off from the frames of analysis that give it a context and open up its potential worldly relations. This is particularly important in the case of a major modern poet like Cavafy who remains outside the mainstream of known poets in the American academy.

The lively new debates around the question of world literature overwhelmingly focus on the novel as a form that can be theorized and historicized on a world scale (see Moretti; Schwarz). The category of world poetry, conversely, has drawn little theoretical or historical attention and has tended to be treated on an anthological register concerned primarily with the tricky determination of who might be selected as the greatest or most characteristic poets from all the regions, nations, or languages of the world. Cavafy's poetry offers a particularly telling resistance to this anthological mode because it is so unique and because it resists from many angles attempts to view it as characteristic or representative of a nation or a bounded territorial ethnos. Reading the poetry as a dynamic intervention in the politics of time that informs his position as a modern Greek Alexandrian poet offers another framework for inquiring into the worldliness of Cavafy's poetry. The comparative constellation of my seminar, which sets Cavafy among other modern poets engaging a structurally similar situation in their poetry, goes some way toward approaching world poetry as a category from the perspective of a materialist analysis of form, rather than of ethnically or historically referential content amenable to anthologization. Cavafy's early symbolist and decadentist poems intersect powerfully with Miraji's eclectic allusions to and translations of Baudelaire in a modern Urdu literary context (Patel 157–63), even as the neoprimitivist, antiracist dimension of Aimé Césaire's great poem of negritude articulates precisely the inverse of the static Orientalist decadence in the discursive map of empire to which Cavafy's poetry responds. Through the innovative intersection of poetic form and content and the elaboration of a modern lyric voice crafted by nonnormative, often explicitly racialized persons situated discrepantly in nonmodern places, the works studied in the seminar can productively be read as addressing the present of modernity as a dynamic and fractured contemporaneity in which poetics constitute an intervention into the politics of time.

I have found that Cavafy's poetry is invariably a revelation to graduate students in comparative literature seminars, most of whom work within the confines of northern European languages. It not only introduces them to a unique and innovative modern poet with important connections to familiar figures from the French and English tradition of modern poetics but also perhaps more cogently expands their understanding of the historical and theoretical dynamics of approaching modern poetics transnationally and comparatively as a worldly force.

Natalie Melas   71

APPENDIX: THE POLITICS OF TIME SEMINAR READINGS

The following readings are for the sessions Politics of Time 1: Decadence, Aesthetic and Historical: "Those People" and Politics of Time 2: Queer Temporality and Desire's Future Pasts.

Politics of Time 1: Required Readings

Verlaine, "Langueur" (*Jadis* 104), with Cavafy, "Waiting for the Barbarians" (*Collected Poems* [Keeley and Sherrard, 1992] 18–19 and *Complete Poems* [Mendelsohn] 192–93) and "For Ammonis, Who Died Aged 29, in 610" and "For Ammones, Who Died Aged 29, in 610" (71; 71).

Haas, "Cavafy's Reading Notes" (25–26, 56–62), with Cavafy's "The God Abandons Antony" (*Collected Poems* [Keeley and Sherrard, 1992] 33 and *Complete Poems* [Mendelsohn] 10), "Ionic" (34; 44), "Alexandrian Kings" (41; 26), "Kaisarion" (82; 61), and "A Prince from Western Libya" (157; 150).

Politics of Time 1: Recommended Readings

Poggioli; Jeffreys, "Translating Baudelaire" (*Reframing Decadence* 26–56); Halim, "Of Greeks" (*Alexandrian Cosmopolitanism* 57–119).

Politics of Time 2: Required Readings

In Cavafy, *Collected Poems* (Keeley and Sherrard, 1992): "Hidden Things" (195), "Days of 1908" (177), "Comes to Rest" (97), "Days of 1901" (150), "Days of 1896" (146), "Kleitos' Illness" (138), "Tomb of Iasis" (76), "The Next Table" (95), "Ithaka" (36), "In the Month of Athyr" (77), "In the Tavernas" (141), "He Had Come There to Read" (129).

In Cavafy, *Complete Poems* (Mendelsohn): "Hidden" (319), "Days of 1908" (173), "To Stay" (88), "Days of 1901" (143), "Days of 1896" (139), "Cleitus' Illness" (131), "Tomb of Iases" (67), "The Next Table" (82), "Ithaca" (13), "In the Month of Hathor" (70), "In the Taverns" (134), "He Came to Read" (121).

Edelman 1–21; Foucault, "Art"; Osborne 1–29; Eliot, *What* 29–32; Papanikolaou, "Days."

Politics of Time 2: Recommended Readings

Halberstam, "Queer Temporality"; Said, "Glimpses"; Papanikolaou, "'Words.'"

Why Cavafy? Why Postcolonial? Teaching the Postcolonial Cavafy

Martin McKinsey

Cavafy enters the range of postcolonial criticism by virtue of living most of his life within a diaspora community in a key territory of the British Empire. For my purposes, his particular subject position within that empire is less relevant than the responsiveness of his verse—above all, the poems on historical or pseudohistorical themes—to the questions that postcolonial criticism, for several decades now, has been asking of literature from the so-called Third World. My case for Cavafy's postcoloniality here is based on materials presented in an early article entitled "Cavafy on Shakespeare: Two Essays and a Poem" (McKinsey, "Cavafy") and in my comparative study *Hellenism and the Postcolonial Imagination: Yeats, Cavafy, Walcott* (McKinsey, *Hellenism*), as well as my experiences of bringing Cavafy into the English literature classroom.

When I think of teaching the postcolonial Cavafy in the twenty-first-century classroom, two questions come to mind: first, Why Cavafy? and second, Why postcolonial? The first question might arise in connection with a course offered under the postcolonial rubric in an English literature department such as mine. Why does the work of an Alexandrian Greek deserve a place on a syllabus replete with writers from South Asia, sub-Saharan Africa, and the Caribbean? What makes him postcolonial? The short answer might run as follows: first, Cavafy spent his adult life within the bounds of the British Empire (as a lifelong resident of Egypt, which in 1882 was occupied by the British); second, from an early age, he revealed in his writings a deep involvement with and conflicted indebtedness to British literature and culture; third, he used the colonial language, English, for his earliest poetry and prose and for personal notes throughout his life; fourth, he was employed for thirty years in the British colonial administration in Alexandria, where he answered to English superiors; and fifth, he wrote poems about empires, diasporas, and hybridization.

Yet despite this profile, I see three potential hurdles to Cavafy's inclusion in a course on postcolonial literature in English: his European ethnicity, his language, and his choice of genre. The first objection is akin to those raised after Edward Said, in "Yeats and Decolonization," proposed that the work of W. B. Yeats and, by implication, modern Irish literature as a whole can be understood as postcolonial. For both instances, the objection can be countered with evidence of the historical racialization of Greek and Irish identities in the heyday of European colonialism. That Cavafy was Levantine as well as Greek compounds the categorical ambiguity of his position—though to dwell too long on questions of ethnic origin is to slip into essentialist ways of thinking that have been a prime target of deconstructive postcolonial critique.

As for the second hurdle—that his poems were not written in English and therefore are not assimilable to the body of works normally found on the syllabi of English literature courses—this objection reflects the disciplinary constraints of the traditional English department, with its historic Anglocentrism, its corresponding bias against translation, and its unilinear, nation-based model of literary history.[1] On the other hand, the recent push by many colleges and universities to internationalize their curricula provides an opportunity to diversify literature offerings by the inclusion of writers like Cavafy who write in a language other than English. As for the third obstacle, it is a fact that postcolonial theory and criticism, like most poststructuralist discourses, have grounded themselves in the study of prose fiction and other narrative modes, often at poetry's expense. Here one can only hope that a number of prominent works on postcolonialism and poetry, from Jahan Ramazani's groundbreaking *The Hybrid Muse* to Robert Stilling's *Beginning at the End*, have opened up postcolonial literature courses to poetry.

The second question I pose above about teaching the postcolonial Cavafy—Why postcolonial?—would pertain to a course on modern Greek literature, with readings either in English translation or in the original, offered within the framework of a Modern Greek program. If the course were an introductory survey, I would need to point out Cavafy's distinctiveness as an Egyptian Greek before asking, Why postcolonial? In a course devoted exclusively to Cavafy, however, or to Cavafy and one or two other Greek authors, where the instructor is able to introduce a range of critical perspectives on Cavafy's work, then the postcolonial aspect ought to be included. Such an approach has the advantage of rooting Cavafy's work in time (the age of empire) and place (viceregal Egypt). Until recently, Cavafy's poetry has been read primarily within the larger framework of European modernism, an approach that privileges qualities like allusiveness, irony, and the rejection of received notions of aesthetic value. Postcolonial criticism complicates this profile and helps us appreciate the peculiarities of Cavafy's situation as a semi-European living in the semiperiphery, at the doorstep of Africa and the Middle East, but with one ear turned on Western Europe. Such criticism foregrounds his status as the product of diaspora and as a member of an ethnic and religious minority in a land that was overwhelmingly Arab and Muslim but that was under the political and military control of the British. It emphasizes the intersectionality of his identity as Hellenic, Αἰγυπτιώτης (*Aigyptiotis*; "Egyptiote," or "Greek Egyptian"), European, and queer. In practice, it allows us to bring his work into dialogue with the work of writers from other colonized or formerly colonized parts of the world who, like Cavafy, write about empires, hybridity, and diasporas.[2]

How, then, does one go about teaching Cavafy postcolonially? In practical terms, a postcolonial approach to his work might begin by highlighting two key rhetorical strategies that underlie many of his poems: counterdiscursivity and displacement.

Counterdiscursivity

Postcolonial literature has been conceptualized as a counterdiscourse to the discourse of post-Enlightenment Europe and its enshrinement of a particular set of cultural and racial values. Counterdiscursivity is the essence of the Rushdian meme "Writing Back to the Center."[3] Counterdiscursivity as a totalizing theory has several acknowledged drawbacks, but the term does serve to describe the productive combination of resistance and dialogism characteristic of a sizeable body of postcolonial literature. In its most recognizable form, it involves rewriting a Western canonical work from the point of view of that book's other, a category of writing Helen Tiffin has called "canonical counter-discourse" (22). Thus, we have Charlotte Brontë's monstrous Bertha Mason rewritten as the unhappy Antoinette Mason in Jean Rhys's *Wide Sargasso Sea*, and Shakespeare's Caliban newly empowered in Aimé Césaire's *Une tempête*. It was with such examples in mind, when writing "Cavafy on Shakespeare," that I approached Cavafy's 1899 poem "King Claudius" (*Collected Poems* [Keeley and Sherrard, 2009] 338–43). In that essay I propose that in rewriting the plot of Shakespeare's *Hamlet*, Cavafy was performing a discursive inversion of the Elizabethan play, in which the story as we know it is turned on its head. As the essay summarizes, in the context of growing Egyptian dissatisfaction with British rule at the turn of the century,[4]

> [i]n Cavafy's version, [Shakespeare's villain] Claudius is portrayed as a mild, peace-loving ruler, a friend of the people, in contrast . . . to his hawkish predecessor, Hamlet's father. . . . Claudius, in fact, is the model of a benign monarch, egalitarian in sympathies ("he treated everyone with respect, / both great and small"), with parliamentary leanings (he "always / . . . sought advice / from seasoned, serious counselors"). . . . In the context of Cavafy's poem, Shakespeare's *Hamlet* is . . . the official story of those who came out on top.   (McKinsey, "Cavafy" 7)

We can think of the poem as a subaltern history of the events in Denmark, one whose contrary account gives the lie to the storyline of the most famous play by England's most celebrated poet.

Six months after composing "King Claudius," Cavafy wrote "When the Watchman Saw the Light" (*Collected Poems* [Keeley and Sherrard, 2009] 345), an equally skeptical take on master narratives. Here Cavafy's intertext is not Elizabethan but a work from the classical archive: Aeschylus's *Agamemnon*, the opening play in the *Oresteia* trilogy—itself a key document in the genealogy of the European Enlightenment. Cavafy's poem uses the Watchman's familiar prologue as the basis for a deflationary meditation on the nature of dynastic power and the discourse that underpins it. Cavafy doesn't revise the play's storyline so much as tell it from a different perspective, one in which a representative speaker—or perhaps speakers, something of an alternative chorus—gives little weight to the dynastic power struggles at the trilogy's heart. The voices in both poems are those of the disenfranchised who feel remote from the levers of power but who, in compensation, are granted a dry clarity, both perceptual and intellectual, and an ingrained skepticism of the discursive machinery of power.

Displacement

As Cavafy matured as a poet, historical intertexts, especially those treating the hellenized Middle East in the age of Roman ascendency, came to replace literary ones as his sources of creative inspiration. Cavafy's fascination with Greek history was real, but it would be a mistake to confine his poems on historical subjects to the past. Joseph Brodsky describes Cavafy's technique in these poems in terms of a metaphor's division into "tenor" and "vehicle": "What Cavafy did, almost from the very beginning of his career as a poet, was to jump straight to the second part [of the metaphor]: for the rest of [his] career he developed and elaborated upon its implicit notions without bothering to return to the first part, assumed as self-evident. The 'vehicle' was Alexandria; the 'tenor' was life" (56). Life, however, is a large concept, one that can be broken down in an infinite number of ways. Somewhere between life writ large and the infinitesimal is life as it was lived in colonial Egypt and the Levant. Political realities, as they cascade down through the social, cultural, and economic lives of diverse communities and individuals, lie at the heart of a postcolonial analysis of Cavafy's work. In practice, this means reflecting on how the situation in a poem, the attitude of its speaker, or the behavior of its subject resonate within the established paradigms of postcolonial literature and within the Egyptian context in which it was written, and on what this resonance, in turn, tells us about the views or intention of the poet who wrote it: a native of Egypt, a Greek by descent and language, and a colonial subject who, upon achieving adulthood, forfeited his British citizenship.

The first book to do justice to this dimension of Cavafy's verse was Ο Καβάφης και η εποχή του (*O Kavafis kai i epochi tou; Cavafy and His Times*), by the Greek Egyptian author Stratis Tsirkas. For Tsirkas, Cavafy was principally a symbolist poet whose symbolism—in earlier poems like "Walls" (*Collected Poems* [Keeley and Sherrard, 2009] 3), "The City" (51), "Windows" (25), "Trojans" (39), and "Thermopylae" (27)—encrypted potentially objectionable commentaries on Egyptian and more specifically Alexandrian affairs under the British. At the same time, Tsirkas characterized Cavafy's later turn to ancient history as evidence of a loss of nerve: the poet's engagement with the political impasse of his time giving way to an arcane antiquarianism (444). It was only twenty years later, in his second book on Cavafy, Ο πολιτικός Καβάφης (*O politikos Kavafis; The Political Cavafy*), that Tsirkas credited some of these later poems with a political conscience. In a section entitled "Pax Romana id est Pax Britannica" ("The Roman Peace Is the British Peace"), he writes convincingly of the parallels between the puppet masters of ancient Rome—as encountered in poems like "The Displeasure of Selefkidis" (*Collected Poems* [Keeley and Sherrard, 2009] 121), "Envoys from Alexandria" (165), and "Of Dimitrios

Sotir (162–150 B.C.)" (191)—and the British power brokers of the Middle East in the time of Evelyn Baring, the Earl of Cromer. Yet Tsirkas's reading of Cavafy's historical metaphor as the superimposition of ancient Roman imperialism onto the modern British equivalent does not exhaust its metonymic possibilities. The poetry's representation of the processes of hellenization in the realm of culture, for instance, invites comparison with the cultural effects inseparable from the colonial project, whether that means anglicization in the context of Britain's English-speaking colonies or its less parochial cognate, westernization, a process well underway in Egypt before the arrival of the British.

Referring to Tsirkas's work, a Greek critic once remarked that to speak of a political Cavafy was to not talk about the homosexual Cavafy. And to the extent that Tsirkas's book was an attempt to rescue the poet from the ranks of the decadent bourgeoisie to which Marxist purists had consigned him, this may indeed have been the case. Yet there is no inherent reason why the two sides of Cavafy should be kept apart. It is a truism that trying to categorize Cavafy's poems as either historical or erotic is futile since the erotic element, specifically the homoerotic element, so thoroughly permeates the historical element. One could make a similar argument regarding the political and the erotic in his poetry. Both queer and diasporic writing constitute minority discourses, and it is not feasible to attribute Cavafy's handling of power and powerlessness, insiders and outsiders, and those working the gap between to a single source. The elusive border these elements share awaits further exploration.

Practicum

The previous section makes the case for the validity of a postcolonial reading of Cavafy and its suitability for college teaching and offers two schemata that might serve to structure such an approach. How one introduces this reading of the poet to college students will vary depending on the nature of the class. In an undergraduate course on postcolonial literature, students are likely never to have heard of Cavafy. For another group, the name may be familiar, but as a poet of Greece, not as a subject of the British Empire. The classes I teach belong to the first category, where even the notion of a Greek Egyptian is likely to be an alien concept.

As with much great poetry, meaning in a Cavafy poem comes in layers. The first layer of a historical Cavafy poem is the Hellenistic and Byzantine world in whose continuum it participates. It is best to assume that college students have little or no knowledge of either the poet or the historical milieu favored in his mature poems. Providing students with the tools and historical framework they will need if they are to understand Cavafy is a challenge shared by all who teach his historical poems. A postcolonial approach asks students, once they've grasped the multiple factors at play in such a poem, to then reread these dynamics in the light of its author's colonial background and in the context of a larger corpus of postcolonial writing, both imaginative and critical. I have taught Cavafy in graduate and undergraduate seminars and learned that when it comes to Cavafy and the postcolonial, context is everything. Mindful of likely lacunae in my students' knowledge of modern history—and given that postcolonial studies' main focus continues to be on the anglophone and francophone literatures of Africa, South Asia, and the Caribbean—I have found that a good place to start is with a map showing Britain's considerable presence in the Middle East before and immediately after the First World War,[5] which corresponds roughly to the period of Cavafy's greatest productivity.

How much biographical background to supply depends on one's preferences and time constraints, but a sketch of the role England played in Cavafy's life should include his childhood years in Liverpool and London, the loss of his family's home in Egypt after the 1882 British bombardment of Alexandria, and his employment as a correspondence clerk in the British colonial administration, a position he held for thirty years. Today's students may also need refreshing when it comes to the history of the Ottoman Empire, especially in its nineteenth- and early-twentieth-century role as "the sick man of Europe." Beyond such details, I let our discussion of the poems be shaped by parallel and ancillary readings from the syllabus.

I have taught Cavafy's work in graduate courses with titles like Writing as Translation and Traveling Poetries, which, while not exclusively postcolonial in focus, overlapped with the field in terms of readings and aims.[6] Writing as Translation combined translation theory with an exploration of modes of writing that resist the monolingual, first-language model that has shaped the study of literature in this country. The reading list included works by Samuel Beckett (*Molloy*) and Brian Friel (*Translations*) and poetry by Paul Celan, Nuala Ní Dhomhnaill, M. NourbeSe Philip, and Derek Walcott (*Selected Poems*). Cavafy came in the unit Writing Diaspora, as did excerpts from memoirs by Eva Hoffman and Meena Alexander. Conversations in this instance were guided by Gilles Deleuze and Félix Guattari's concept of "Minor Literature," as laid out in their book on Kafka (*Kafka*). Judging by students' online discussion, this pairing worked well, though one student wondered whether a particularizing approach wasn't preferable to the conceptual or political one proposed by Deleuze and Guattari. The student was not sure writers can escape their "foundational political milieu."

Another student, however, found the concept of minor literature effective both as a critical fulcrum for individual poems and as a way of framing Cavafy's linguistic attitudes. This student pointed out that Raphael (in "For Ammonis, Who Died at 29, in 610"; *Collected Poems* [Keeley and Sherrard, 2009] 133) must express his own life in the majority language, thereby reducing the "territoriality of the dominant language." A third student deployed George Steiner's notion of the "extraterritorial" to similar ends, noting how Steiner quotes from Theodor Adorno on the poetry of Heinrich Heine: "Only he who is not truly at home inside a language uses it as an instrument" (5). This student's association of Adorno's remark about Heine with Cavafy strikes me as particularly insightful, an argument for the use of comparative methodologies in treating Cavafy's mature work.

78   POSTCOLONIAL CAVAFY

Two years later, my graduate seminar Traveling Poetry positioned itself at the intersection between poetry and globalization, with the *de*-location of culture as its underlying theme. At stake were the organicist assumptions, dating to the Romantic era, of the indissoluble bond between poet, place, and language—long the a priori of nation-based models for literary development and courses of study. Key terms in this class were *exile, expatriation, migration,* and *diaspora,* along with related concepts like hybridity, authenticity, errancy, and the rhizome. The reading list, bookended by T. S. Eliot's *The Waste Land* and Walcott's *Omeros,* included works by expatriate poets like W. H. Auden (*Collected Poems*), A. K. Ramanujan, and Paul Muldoon; poems of travel by Elizabeth Bishop and Allen Ginsberg; and poems of displacement by Cavafy and the contemporary Iraqi poet Saadi Youssef (*Nostalgia, Without*), the other non-anglophone poet on the syllabus. One theoretically sophisticated student essay from that semester applied Homi K. Bhabha's concept of a cultural "third space" to several of Cavafy's historical poems (54). However, the essayist translates Bhabha's spatial metaphor into temporal terms, locating the third space in the gap between the poem's historical time and the enunciatory present. For this student, a poem's tonal irony implies a critique that gestures to futurity by opening the door to alternative forms of action.

After a lengthy hiatus, Cavafy made a reappearance in my teaching when I agreed to take over a colleague's undergraduate course Postcolonial Fiction, with the understanding that our readings would not be limited to fiction. Two class sessions were devoted to Cavafy. Thinking a more guided approach was in order at the undergraduate level, I split the twenty-odd students into five groups and assigned each group a key term from postcolonial criticism and a corresponding set of Cavafy poems.

Key Term	**Poems**
Diaspora	"Poseidonians" (*Collected Poems* [Keeley and Sherrard, 2009] 357), "Exiles" (371), "Aimelianos Monae" (173), "Going Back Home from Greece" (369), "The City" (51)
Hybridity	"In a Town of Osroini" (129), "Alexandrian Kings" (77), "Aimilianos Monai, Alexandrian, A.D. 628–655" (173), "For Ammonis, Who Died at 29, in 610" (133)
Center/Margin	"Philhellene" (73), "Exiles" (371), "In a Town of Osroini" (129), "Going Back Home from Greece" (369), "That's the Man" (49)
Mimicry	"Alexander Jannaios and Alexandra" (311), "A Prince from Western Libya" (299), "For Ammonis, Who Died at 29, in 610" (133), "Philhellene" (73), "Going Back Home from Greece" (369)
Religion	"Priest at the Serapeion" (267), "Myris: Alexandria, A.D. 340" (307), "Of the Jews (A.D. 50)" (185), "Kleitos' Illness" (263), "A Great Procession of Priests and Laymen" (271)

Our first class was devoted to group work: each group used online resources to research the postcolonial dimensions of the key term and discussed its bearing on the poems. In the second class, group members took responsibility for individual poems, and during class time we cycled through all the groups as poems were discussed in terms of specific themes or in the context of previous readings. Students later posted their general reactions on our online discussion board. One characteristic of the postcolonial condition that students noticed in Cavafy's work was the persistent sense of intellectual and emotional dividedness. A student in the Religion group wrote, concerning the poem "Of the Jews (A.D. 50)," that the Jew portrayed in the poem is "caught between" Greek and Jewish culture, which is a "concept of identity seen through many other works covered in class." And a student from the Mimicry group commented that the colonized "mimic men" are "stuck in between" the cultures of colonizer and colonized. Another student, equally alert to the cultural dividedness of Cavafy's characters, invoked W. E. B. Du Bois's concept of double consciousness. A student in the Center/Margin group, writing of the poem "Philhellene," remarked that the small-time king from his capital on the eastern border of the Hellenistic empire, "wants [his] coin to be 'Greek enough'" while still representing his own culture. Another student from the Mimicry group, writing on "A Prince from Western Libya," incorporated a phrase from Bhabha in remarking that the result of mimicry is "never a reproduction but a 'blurred copy.'" From the Diaspora group came a comment that in "Poseidonians," a poem about a Greek colony on the Italian peninsula that has been "cast aside" by Hellenism because the colonists have forgotten their original language and customs, "Cavafy exhibits nativist views," which the student described as uncharacteristic in the light of the favor that Cavafy shows the hybrid in other poems. Students recognized Hellenism for the essentialist concept it can easily become—even, though rarely, at Cavafy's hands.

Not all students responded fully to the poems. One student wondered whether Cavafy's poems belonged in such a course, while another admitted that they would not have thought of Cavafy as postcolonial if encountering his work on their own, at least not in the sense that Chinua Achebe and Derek Walcott are postcolonial. And it's true, Cavafy is not postcolonial in the sense that these other writers are; such a Cavafy would be a historical anachronism, at least if the *post* in *postcolonial* retains any historico-temporal value. There are elements of resistance in his verse, seen especially in the counterdiscursive impulses discussed above, but Cavafy was a product of his origins in the comprador bourgeoisie—as an Anglo-Greek who retained the trace of an English accent when speaking his so-called native language—and he was a product of his age, which predated the great surge of anticolonial sentiment that crested in the decades following the Second World War. If Cavafy had a cause, that cause was not decolonization, which would imply political solidarity with the emergent Arab nationalism of his era, not merely the sympathy he expressed in a variety of contexts. His liberatory impulses, as his "Notes on Art and Morality" make clear, were focused elsewhere, toward the easing of miserable laws and prejudices regulating human sexuality (Cavafy, *Clearing* 66). Nevertheless, Cavafy lived his life in the Mediterranean lap of empire, and his reimagining of the ancient hellenized and romanized Middle East shaped itself around that nexus of opposing European, Egyptian, and Ottoman ambitions.

Edward Said has written, "One of the main strengths of postcolonial analysis is that it widens, instead of narrows, the interpretive perspective, which is another way of saying that it liberates instead of further constricting and colonizing the mind" ("Reflections" 179). One way of achieving this widening perspective in a course on modern Greek literature would be to bring Cavafy into dialogue with the work of writers from other parts of the postcolonial world—*Waiting for the Barbarians*, by J. M. Coetzee, being the salient example. Other pairings might include the Cavafy poem "Ionic" (*Collected Poems* [Keeley and Sherrard, 2009] 63) and Seamus Heaney's "On Toome Road" (*Opened Ground* 143); "Poseidonians" and Keki Daruwalla's "The Poseidonians" (*Collected Poems* 260–62), which begins, "All it takes to blight a language / is another sun"; or Derek Mahon's intriguingly oblique adaptions of several Cavafy poems (as found in Kruczkowska 133–96).

Cavafy's poems about remote places during remote periods of history still speak to us because they are transtemporal; their world translates easily into our own. But our world is a variable element. Increasingly, a part of that world is an awareness of the imbalances built by colonialism (imperialism in its older, statist form) and colonialist discourse into center/periphery relations. Cavafy writes about the political, cultural, and personal fallout of those power differentials, employing history as his medium, often with an irony that can make it difficult to determine his stance. The fact that we are now living in a period of historical flux only adds to the sense of recognition that instructors and students experience when reading his poems. There are other ways of reading Cavafy than postcolonially, and the present essay does not seek to limit the interpretive richness of Cavafy's Hellenistic world, a richness to which first-time readers should be allowed access. However, in a pedagogical setting it would be foolish to ignore the role colonial Egypt and the once-powerful British Empire played in the making of that vividly imagined world.

NOTES

1. Unfortunately, the language barrier is in danger of being institutionally reinforced by the recent trend of relabeling positions in "postcolonial literature" as positions in "world anglophone literature"; Srinivasan 309.

2. Such a dialogue was inaugurated by the South African writer J. M. Coetzee in his 1980 novel *Waiting for the Barbarians*.

3. This assertion that the English language needs to be decolonized is stated most directly in Salman Rushdie's "The Empire Writes Back with a Vengeance." For a discussion of the phrase and its meaning, see Srivastava.

4. See al-Sayyid, *History* 93–95; Kazamias 268–269.

5. Such a map might identify the region as the Arab world after the First World War; see Boustani and Fargues 15.

6. These two graduate courses go back over fifteen years, and were I to teach either of them today, I would want to accompany Cavafy's poems with a relevant work of queer theory, something along the lines of Benjamin Kahan's excellent "Conjectures on the Sexual World-System."

TRANSLATING, DISCOVERING, AND INTERPRETING CAVAFY

Cavafy Constructed: Archive, Editions, Translations

Karen Emmerich

Virtually all works of literature are brought to readers by complex processes of mediation; multiple nonauthorial actors are almost always involved in creating the editions (print and digital editions, as well as editions in translation) that represent those works to varied audiences. Particularly for canonized figures whose work often exists in multiple editions or versions even in a single language, these processes can involve disputes, competition, and discord—but even for less celebrated figures, editions and translations (among other "sponsored images" [Eaves 108] or forms of "rewriting" [Lefevere])[1] reflect distinct interpretations that shape readers' experiences of the works in question. With Cavafy's poetry, these processes are especially evident since Cavafy chose not to publish a single volume of poems during his lifetime, at least in the conventional sense, though he did make his poetry public, both in periodicals and in the extremely variable handmade collections he distributed through a network of friends and acquaintances. After his death, if the work was to be read beyond the relatively small circle of individuals with access to those roughly 2,200 unique collections, intermediaries were needed: editors first and foremost, who could give the poetry a shape stable enough to be reproduced in commercial editions, and eventually also translators, who would facilitate the poems' growth into other languages. The publication history of Cavafy's work has thus been marked by repeated attempts to give a solid shape to this amorphous, changeable body of work. In Gregory Jusdanis's words, the poet's refusal of fixity gave way after his death to the formation of a fixed oeuvre "by mechanisms beyond the poet's control"

(*Poetics* 60)—though, conversely, that fixity has also been destabilized by the sheer multiplicity of editorial versions, in Greek and other languages.

Neither of these facts—the stabilizing or destabilizing of Cavafy's work—is necessarily to be bemoaned. While we may prefer some versions of the work over others, mediation is an unavoidable reality of almost all literary production and circulation. As Jerome McGann has written, "[A]n author's work possesses autonomy only when it remains an unheard melody. As soon as it begins its passage to publication, it undergoes a series of interventions which some textual critics"—and certainly many scholars and readers—"see as a process of contamination, but which may equally well be seen as a process of training the poem for its appearances in the world" (51). For those who teach Cavafy's poetry, the posthumous shaping of the poet's work by editors and translators is what makes it possible for us to bring the poems into our classrooms in the first place. Moreover, treating that history of mediation as a subject for exploration can deepen and enrich our classroom discoveries, opening up fascinating questions about literary production, circulation, and reception and about the discursive formation of literary canons and canonized figures. Where does Cavafy's body of work begin and end, and who is involved in its construction? How have its contours been drawn not only by the poet but by editors, translators, scholars, teachers, and communities of readers—that is, by the countless rewriters of Cavafy who continue to produce images, representations, or versions of his work in the public sphere? If Cavafy's poetry is subject to endless reconfiguration and re-presentation by others, and if readers encounter it in a diverse array of forms—in Greek, English, Albanian, Portuguese, Thai, and so on, and in textbooks, stand-alone volumes, anthologies, newspapers, blogs, or even the recently released digital platform of the Cavafy Archive, which offers open-source images of over two thousand archival documents—what if anything ties these forms together? What ideologies or assumptions underly these various sponsored images of Cavafy and his work? What are the confluences between them, and where are the points of tension? This brief essay cannot answer these many questions, nor can it offer a comprehensive account of editions of Cavafy even just in Greek. It instead gestures to how paying attention to the many forces that have shaped the forms that represent the poet's words, in Greek and other languages, can deepen our understanding not only of the poetry but also of the uses to which it has been put. Bringing a discussion of some of these forms of mediation into the classroom thus allows us to treat not only the content of the poems themselves but also the historical, social, literary, and political contexts of Cavafy's reception—a reception that is also always an interpretive coconstruction.

In the flood of posthumous sponsored images of C. P. Cavafy, the work of one scholar, George P. Savidis, stands apart. Savidis was not the first to publish a commercial edition of Cavafy's work; the lavishly illustrated, large-format volume edited by Rika Sengopoulou and published in Alexandria in 1935 was the first to bring together the 154 poems that would become known as the Cavafy canon. Yet over the course of three decades, Savidis wrote dozens of biographical and critical texts and prepared numerous editions, not only of the poems Cavafy semiprivately distributed, but also of other poems, notes, and even diaries found among the poet's papers after his death, which Savidis obtained from Kyveli Sengopoulou (the second wife of Alekos Sengopoulos, Cavafy's heir) around 1968. Savidis's initial contact with Cavafy's papers had come several years earlier, when a "large suitcase full of manuscripts, photographs, and printed matter" was shown to the young scholar (*Archio* 29), who was subsequently entrusted with the task of cataloguing these materials. By the end of 1963, he had organized and photographed them and had also published several of what would become a lifetime's worth of texts about editions of Cavafy's work, including his two-volume edition of the canon, Ποιήματα, Α΄, 1896–1918 (*Piimata, A', 1896–1918; Poems 1, 1896–1918*) and Ποιήματα, Β΄, 1919–1933 (*Piimata, B', 1919–1933; Poems 2, 1919–1933*). Until his death in 1995, Savidis produced an ambitious string of editions that involved the piecemeal release of materials that, after 1968, he owned and to which he granted access only to a select few. Many of Cavafy's writings thus entered both the Greek and the world canon in forms that were shaped by Savidis's editorial hand. Even the now common (though certainly not uncontested) division of the poems into the "published" poems of the "canon" and into the "repudiated," "unpublished" (or "hidden"), and "unfinished" poems was reinforced by Savidis's critical works and by the forms of the editions he produced.

By far the most influential of Savidis's many editions is *Poems 1* and *Poems 2*, which present the 154 poems Sengopoulou had gathered in her edition, but in a very different format and arrangement. While Sengopoulou ordered the poems roughly chronologically by year of completion (already a thorny enterprise, given Cavafy's habit of lifelong revision), Savidis divided the poems into two volumes, on the basis of a bibliographic difference he observed in the hand-compiled groupings Cavafy had put into circulation. The first volume presents the poems from two θεματικές συλλογές (*thematikes sylloges*; "thematic collections"; Savidis's term, which has been widely adopted by subsequent scholarship) that were actively being shared at the time of the poet's death, poems from an earlier collection Cavafy had printed in 1904 but may not have circulated, and two poems that were not included in any of these collections but had already appeared in Sengopoulou's edition. The second volume presents the poems included in the "chronological" sheaves and packets of poems Cavafy created plus an additional poem, Εις τα περίχωρα της Αντιόχειας ["Is ta perichora tis Antiochias"; "On the Outskirts of Antioch"], that Cavafy never included in any of his collections but that Savidis judged to have been "ready, one might say, for the printer" at the time of Cavafy's death (Cavafy, *Piimata, B'* 154), implicitly differentiating it from the numerous "unpublished" as well as "unfinished" poems that were likewise left behind in the archive.

This popular edition of Cavafy's so-called published poems went through several bibliographic configurations: it initially appeared in two volumes in 1963, which were united under a single cover in 1984 and then revised back into two volumes in 1991, each time with slight changes to the texts and ordering of the poems; the title, too, changed slightly since Savidis revised the date on the first poem included from 1896 to 1897. Even with these variations, these plain, small-format books have shaped our understanding of Cavafy and his work more than any other books; they have gone through countless printings, can be found on bookshelves and in bookstores across Greece, and have formed the basis for countless translations as well as other Greek-language editions that replicate Savidis's edited texts, often without acknowledgment. Savidis's introduction, meanwhile, legitimizes the editor's choices by presenting the resulting edition as the fullest available embodiment of an editorial fixity toward which Cavafy was headed—that is, as a completion of the editorial work Cavafy was engaged in during the last two decades of his life: Savidis writes, Την λαϊκή έκδοση των ποιημάτων του, μπορούμε να πούμε ότι την είχε σχεδιάσει και πραγματοποιήσει, ως ένα σημείο, ο ίδιος ο ποιητής ("We can say that the popular edition of his poems was planned and carried out, to a point, by the poet himself"), a process cut short by Cavafy's death, of which Savidis writes rather lyrically in the introduction's opening paragraphs. Even the form of this edition, which brings the poet's last two "thematic collections" together under a single cover, is tentatively attributed to Cavafy: Αν είχε ζήσει περισσότερο ("Had he lived longer"), Savidis notes a few sentences later, δεν αποκλείεται να είχε ενοποιήσει τα δύο αυτά τεύχη ("it is not out of the question that he might have combined these two volumes"; Cavafy, *Piimata*, A' 15). Savidis's inclusion of "On the Outskirts of Antioch" is another instance in which an interpolation about what Cavafy might have done has come to be taken for granted, such that other editions, including those in translation, routinely include it as part of the established canon of "published" poems.

If Savidis's introductory note ventriloquizes Cavafy to substantiate the editor's choices, the 1963 edition ends with twenty-nine densely printed pages of notes that likewise attempt to guide a reader's encounter with the texts; in the 1991 reissue, the notes have mushroomed to an astonishing 106 pages.[2] While Savidis insists that εστάθηκα πολύ φειδωλός στην παράθεση ερμηνευτικών σχολίων από εργασίες τρίτων (συμπεριλαμβανομένων και των δικών μου) ("I have been very sparing in quoting interpretive comments from the writings of third parties (including my own)"); Cavafy, *Piimata*, A' 16), his commentary is in fact thoroughly interpretive in nature. For instance, he identifies many of the poems as either ιστορικογενή (meaning "based on historical events and figures"), ιστορικοφανή (meaning "building on historical context but featuring fictional persons"), or ψευδοϊστορικά (meaning "evoking a sense of historicity without an actual historical underpinning"). While he was not the first to introduce any of these terms (which are usually attributed to Michalis Pieris, I. M. Panagiotopoulos, and George Seferis, respectively), his categorization of particular poems according to this rubric has influenced the way subsequent scholars read and discuss them. In addition, Savidis offers interpretive glosses of certain phrases in about two-thirds of the poems and provides information about

Cavafy's life that implicitly encourages a biographical reading: the fairly generic κίτρινη όχθη (*kitrini ochti*; "yellow shore") in Θάλασσα του πρωϊού ("Thalassa tou proiou"; "Morning Sea") is identified as η παραλία της Αλεξάνδρειας ("the shore at Alexandria"; 148), while the notes to Καισαρίων ("Kaisarion") clarify that the lamp in line 24 is a *gas* lamp—a reading supported by the fact that [τ]ο διαμέρισμα του Καβάφη . . . δεν είχε ηλεκτρικό· φωτιζόταν είτε με κεριά είτε με λάμπες πετρελαίου ("Cavafy's apartment . . . had no electricity; it was lit either by candles or by gas lamps"; 156), an observation that implicitly conflates the poem's speaker with Cavafy himself. This same comment appears with reference to Απ' τες εννιά—("Since Nine O'Clock—"): the notes to that poem suggest, with regard to the phrase πένθη της οικογένειας ("family mourning"), that Ο Καβάφης είχε χάσει διαδοχικά τον πατέρα του (1870), τον αδελφό του Πέτρο (1891), την μητέρα του (1899), και τους αδελφούς του Γεώργιο (1900), Αριστείδη (1902) και Αλέξανδρο (1905) ("Cavafy had successively lost his father (1870), his brother Petros (1891), his mother (1899), and his brothers Georgios (1900), Aristeidis (1902) and Alexandros (1905)"; 153). Equally noteworthy are the glosses of individual words and phrases that abound in Savidis's notes, which often seem to correct Cavafy's Greek, as with τον επρότεινε = του επρότεινε ("he suggested to him"), changing the case of an article to accord with standard usage, or μνήμες = αναμνήσεις (Cavafy, *Piimata, B'* 116), shifting the meaning from memory as the capacity for remembering to memory as the product of that capacity. At other points, these intralingual translations are obviously designed to clarify meaning, as when κομάτι is equated with λιγάκι in one poem (117) but with ολίγον τι in another (119), offering differently shaded interpretations of the "a little" or "slightly" implied by the word. Taken together, these elements betray a strong desire on Savidis's part to shape the way in which readers encounter the work—a desire also manifested, as discussed above, in the organization of the edition at large.

A close look at the structure and paratext of Savidis's other editions of Cavafy's work—including most centrally the 1968 Ανέκδοτα Ποιήματα, 1882–1923 (*Anekdota piimata, 1882–1923*; *Unpublished Poems, 1882–1923*), the 1983 Αποκηρυγμένα Ποιήματα και Μεταφράσεις, 1886–1898 (*Apokirygmena piimata kai metafrasis, 1886–1898*; *Repudiated Poems and Translations, 1886–1898*), and the 1997 Κρυμμένα Ποιήματα, 1877–1923 (*Krymmena piimata, 1877–1923*; *Hidden Poems, 1877–1923*)—would elucidate other ways in which the interpretive labor of this one scholar has shaped readers' and other scholars' understanding of Cavafy's poetic output. Indeed, even the separation of the poems into the discrete categories of the "canon" of published poems and the "repudiated," "unpublished" or "hidden," and "unfinished" poems (first made available in the 1994 edition Ατελή Ποιήματα, 1918–1932 [*Ateli piimata, 1918–1932*; *Unfinished Poems, 1918–1932*], edited by Renata Lavagnini) continues to underlie many scholarly discussions and readerly experiences of the work, even as many individual poems assigned to these categories could easily find a home in a competing category. The lasting power of Savidis's system of categorization may largely be due to the fact that the Savidis family maintained control of Cavafy's archival materials until 2012, and scholars—much less general readers—therefore had little opportunity to check his work, particularly for poems that exist only in manuscript forms.

The field of Cavafy scholarship has been radically opened and expanded by the recent release of the digital platform of the Cavafy Archive, whose materials are now owned and maintained by the Alexander S. Onassis Foundation.[3] The digital platform attempts to create the environment of an online reading room, offering an image and a description of every item in the archive and organizing items into fonds, sub-fonds, series, files, and sub-files that categorize the materials according to both philological and bibliographic criteria. The sub-fonds dedicated to Cavafy's work, for instance, contains four series: Poems, Prose Works, Notes, and Translations and Works of Others on C. P. Cavafy. Poems, in turn, contains three files: Poems (manuscript), Poems (printed), and Lists. The file of printed poems is further subdivided into Pamphlets–Broadsheets, Issues, and Collections; the last of these contains twenty items, including multiple copies of C. P. Cavafy Poems (1907–1915) and C. P. Cavafy Poems (1908–1914), with extensive descriptions that help guide the scholar and reader toward points of bibliographic divergence. While references to each item's place in the G. P. Savidis Historical Catalogue have also been provided, the archive has been catalogued anew, and the user's experience is now shaped by entirely different modes of organization.

The Cavafy Archive's digital platform comprises yet another chapter in the necessarily interpretive history of Cavafy's reception: digital archives are not transparent windows onto some untouched reality but are themselves shaped according to certain assumptions both about the particular materials in question and about the needs of the scholars and readers the archives seek to serve. For instance, the Cavafy Archive clearly imagines a global readership for Cavafy but also a readership able to work in either Greek or English, the two interface languages for the archive's digital presence. While certainly still limited in its reach, this dual-language interface makes it newly possible for readers of Greek to compare the editorial choices of posthumous print editions of Cavafy to the collections the poet himself created and his habits of semiprivate publication, while also helping readers of English explore the archive's contents, access the manuscripts for particular poems, and understand why, for instance, there might be a remarkable bibliographic variance in editions of Cavafy in translation, as we can see from a sampling of titles and contents of volumes in English. Rae Dalven's *The Complete Poems of Cavafy* (Cavafy, *Complete Poems* [Dalven]) and Edmund Keeley and Philip Sherrard's *Selected Poems* arrange poems chronologically by year, and both contain some "unpublished" poems in addition to those of the "canon"; Dalven also includes a section of the so-called repudiated poems, which she simply calls "early" (xxii). Of the much more recent spate of translations, Aliki Barnstone's *The Collected Poems of C. P. Cavafy* includes all the published poems and twenty unpublished ones; rather than separating them out, she orders all 174 chronologically by year (Cavafy, *Collected Poems* [Barnstone]). John Chioles's *The Poems of the Canon* (Cavafy, *Poems* [Chioles]) and Stratis Haviaras's rather oddly titled *The Canon: The Original One Hundred and Fifty-Four Poems* (Cavafy, *Canon*) contain the same one hundred fifty-four poems as Savidis's edition but in different orders. Avi Sharon's *Selected Poems* offers these same 154 poems in yet another order, which he explains at length in his translator's note (Cavafy, *Selected Poems* [Sharon]). In his 2009 *One Hundred Sixty-Six Poems*—the 154 plus twelve additional "unpublished" poems—Alan Boegehold presents them all in one straight run and offers no explanation of his selection criteria (Cavafy, *One Hundred Sixty-Six Poems*). Daniel Mendelsohn's *Complete Poems* hews perhaps most closely to Savidis's categorization and organization, with sections for each of the "thematic" and "chronological" collections as well as the "repudiated" and "unpublished" poems; his notes exceed even Savidis's for length and detail (Cavafy, *Complete Poems* [Mendelsohn]).[4]

Anthony Hirst, who edited the Greek texts for the bilingual *Collected Poems*, with translations by Evangelos Sachperoglou (Cavafy *Collected Poems* [Sachperoglou]), has written extensively on Cavafy's methods of selective self-publication and Savidis's largely invisible role both in defining the contours of Cavafy's work and in shaping particular texts (e.g., Hirst, "Philosophical"). In an essay that predates this volume by many years, Sarah Ekdawi and Hirst propose that Savidis's categorization scheme be replaced by a far simpler one: the term *collected* should be used for poems the poet brought together in a quasi-publication during his life, and *uncollected* for all the others (79). Hirst and Sachperoglou's volume is the only one to follow this usage. The volume also includes Hirst's extensive explanation of the editorial strategy, which takes a bibliographic approach to Cavafy's handmade collections: it presents the poems included in two of Cavafy's collections, in the order he gave, while also indicating the order of two additional collections so as to account more fully for the multitude of forms in which the poet circulated a remarkably small number of poems. In a nod, perhaps, to the tyranny of readerly expectations, Hirst and Sachperolgou also include the poems Savidis (like Sengopoulou before him) added to flesh out the so-called canon, but in a separate section, distinct from those devoted to Cavafy's own groupings. Of course, Hirst's gesture to the bibliographic multiplicity of these forms inevitably remains just that, a gesture: given the 2,200 unique collections that Cavafy compiled over twenty years, a comprehensive reproduction of these forms seems beyond the reach, or even the goals, of a mass-produced edition.

One can see from this quick overview that descriptors like *complete*, *collected*, and *original* shed their usual meanings in this context. And if the structure and contents of these editions in translation vary so much, so of course do the lexical choices demonstrated by the translations themselves, which give shape to translators' particular interpretations of texts whose relative fixity or instability can also now be gauged by consulting the facsimiles of manuscripts and print versions in the digital archive. In my courses on Modern Greek and comparative literature, usually taken by undergraduate students with little or no knowledge of Greek, I routinely teach multiple translations of individual Cavafy poems side by side—my perennial favorite is Εν τω μηνί Αθύρ ("En to mini Athyr"; "In the Month of Athyr"), which lends itself to discussions of textual mediation, reading as interpretation, and the obstacles to understanding put in place by both linguistic and temporal distance. When I teach larger selections of Cavafy's work, rather than asking all students to read from a single edition in translation, I encourage them to purchase or borrow a translation of their choosing; the interpretive choices of a range of translators as well as the editorial configurations of the volumes themselves thus become fodder for rich classroom conversations, above and beyond the content of the poems. In other words, my courses routinely treat not only Cavafy's work but also the many ways in which it has been posthumously shaped or rewritten by others. We also now make extensive use of the Cavafy Archive's digital platform and analyze its mode of presentation and organization. In urging students to consider the role archivists, editors, and translators, among others, have played in shaping our conception of Cavafy and his work, we can also help them understand that they, too, are participating in this tradition of coconstructive reception: they, too, are necessarily confronting the limits of what can be considered Cavafy's work and redrawing its lines for themselves. Discussions of this sort almost always reach beyond Cavafy's work to address issues of representation and manipulation in other spheres as well. Indeed, given the confluence of identity issues that Cavafy represents—as a queer, migrant, diasporic, minority figure who was also part of a colonial enterprise and inhabited positions of both privilege and financial hardship over the course of his life—the example of Cavafy and the mediating forces that construct various versions of his work is a particularly powerful one, sensitizing students to the responsibility involved in creating and analyzing rewritings of all sorts. As André Lefevere avows, "Rewriting manipulates, and it is effective. All the more reason, then, to study it. . . . A study of rewriting will not tell students what to do; it might show them ways of not allowing other people to tell them what to do" (9). The example of Cavafy is a potent source for thinking on this front.

NOTES

All translations from Greek are my own.

1. Eaves identifies three categories of material objects that contribute most centrally to the process of canon formation, "the bibliography, the critical study, and the edition." Eaves gives editions pride of place, suggesting that in them, "sponsorship takes physical form"; 108. "Rewriting," meanwhile, is Lefevere's term for a range of practices including editing, translating, literary criticism, anthologization, book reviewing, and more.

2. As I learned from conversations with Edmund Keeley, many of the additional notes had been written for Keeley and Philip Sherrard's 1975 English edition, a fact that helps explain, for instance, the inclusion of a rhyme scheme for all rhyming poems, information

that may be of use to English-language readers but is arguably redundant for Greek-language ones; Cavafy, *Collected Poems* [Keeley and Sherrard, 1975].

3. For more on the Onassis Foundation Cavafy Archive, see the essays by Angeliki Mousiou and Takis Kayalis in this volume.

4. Mendelsohn was also the first to publish the unfinished poems in a companion volume; Cavafy, *Unfinished Poems*. Economou's *Unfinished and Uncollected* contains translations of these poems as well. Both rely on Lavagnini's 1995 genetic edition of the poems, which presents selected manuscripts as well as edited "last texts," which Lavagnini considers closest to what Cavafy had arrived at when he died; Cavafy, *Ateli piimata*. See Emmerich 131–60.

Which Cavafy?
Selecting the Right Translation

Sarah Ekdawi

Modern Greek studies programs in the United Kingdom are now largely mediated through classics and comparative literature departments. The only UK university that still offers a bachelor of arts program in Modern Greek is Oxford, where the syllabus focus is more broadly cultural than strictly literary. Modern Greek studies is offered at the master's level at Birmingham University and King's College London (formerly, these universities also offered BA programs in Modern Greek). Both Oxford and Cambridge offer a Modern Greek option to classics students; this option is popular and can be rewarding to teach since classics tends to attract extremely able students, original thinkers who are almost always willing to do extra background reading. The frame of reference they bring to the work of C. P. Cavafy is also valuable. Programs in Modern Greek for classicists focus on literature and make use of translations, essays, and commentaries. Oxford has recently introduced a new master's degree in comparative literature and critical translation. This reflects a burgeoning interest in translation studies and also allows students another (interdisciplinary) pathway into Modern Greek literature.

Teaching Cavafy in contexts where students may be unable to read Greek raises questions about translations and how they are used. A translation can serve as a tool to help readers decipher a text in a partially known language or as a substitute if they have no knowledge of that language. The focus in translation studies is on the translation itself, including the translator's aims and how different translators often offer radically divergent solutions to the same problems. It is also worth noting that translations, in the form of assignments and examination papers requiring candidates to translate set passages, are used to evaluate the linguistic competence of students reading for degrees in ancient and modern languages.

The plethora of available translations of Cavafy's poetry is a unique case in world literature, both in terms of sheer quantity and in view of the fact that many of the published translators are native speakers of Greek but not of English. Three factors inform my choice of translation for my students: their academic needs, my understanding of translation theory, and the views of Cavafy himself on translation, insofar as these can be inferred. My students need to be able to read Cavafy's Greek but cannot do so without assistance. They therefore need a translation that they can relate almost word-for-word to the Greek texts. Translation theory comes into play when we evaluate together, in a preliminary class, the range of options on offer, as I discuss in the last section of this essay. I turn now to Cavafy's own understanding of translation.

How Cavafy Understood Translation

Cavafy had near-native competence in English and high-level competence in French. He spoke Italian, and there is some anecdotal evidence that he could communicate in Arabic at a basic level. He lived in multilingual times in a multilingual community in a multilingual city where foreign-language knowledge was not viewed as a rare, abstruse, or hard-won skill but was the norm. Cavafy had been partly educated in England in the 1870s. At that time, the school curriculum was firmly rooted in the classics; students had to "read," that is translate from Greek and Latin. Similarly, today's classics students are used to translating texts from ancient Greek and Latin into English. Translations from the classics at a BA level are basically exegetical, not literary; close textual (linguistic and literary) analysis is taught and practiced in these programs but translation theory is not addressed. This most probably mirrors the kind of instruction that Cavafy himself would have experienced in the classics during the English phase of his education.

Everything we know about Cavafy's attitude to translation, specifically the translation of his poetry into English, indicates that he made three basic assumptions: that a nonnative speaker of English could do it, that poetry is not lost in translation, and that the poet is the ultimate arbiter of translations of his work. We know that Cavafy wanted his poetry to reach the English-speaking world. In fact, one of his earliest publications, from 1897, was in the form of a parallel Greek-English text, Τείχη ("Tichi"; "My Walls"; Savidis, *I Kavafikes ekdosis* 30), and he collaborated with at least two translators (both of them Greek) over an extended, overlapping period: circa 1896–1921 and circa 1915–33. He also cooperated with E. M. Forster's attempts to have translations of his poems published in literary magazines. In or around 1916, Cavafy himself had initiated Forster into his poetry by translating orally for him Απολείπειν ο θεός Αντώνιον ("The God Abandons Antony") as they both pored over the Greek text (Harvey 40). This initiation was facilitated by the fact that Forster had learned ancient Greek at school.

"The first English translation of Cavafy was made by Cavafy." So begins Forster's account of the translation history of Cavafy's poetry, referring to Forster's own encounter with the poet (qtd. in Harvey 40)—and like so much in Forster's presentation of the poet, this account stands at a slight angle to the truth. For the first translations of Cavafy were made by Cavafy's brother, John (see Cavafy, *Sixty-Three Poems*). This fact was carefully concealed from Forster by the poet, almost certainly because he had realized years earlier that John's translations were inadequate but was too loyal to say so. The Onassis Foundation Cavafy Archive holds several translating notebooks that bear witness to the long-term collaborative efforts of John and Cavafy. Cavafy may well have objected to John's translations on the grounds that they were too artistic or poetic; as a lesser Victorian poet with decidedly offbeat literary English, John's attempts to replicate effects such as rhyme had some rather unhappy results.

Cavafy's second and preferred translator was George Valassopoulo. In letters to Forster, Cavafy describes Valassopoulo as his "ideal translator" (Jeffreys, *Forster-Cavafy Letters* 62), refers to revising the translations himself with Valassopoulo (89), and states that "Valassopoulo's translations are so faithful that they facilitate a great deal the forming of an accurate idea of the work" (44). Valassopoulo's English is somewhat stilted and sometimes reads strangely; he makes no attempt to poeticize his translations. These qualities and Cavafy's characterization suggest that Cavafy took a pragmatic view of translation as a transfer of content rather than of form. He makes no mention of attempting to preserve the acoustic texture of his poems. This cannot mean that Cavafy did not care about the formal features of his own writing. He wanted to be read in English by a wider audience, but he also wanted to be read in Greek by the smaller group of Greek speakers. Readers like Forster, with his knowledge of ancient Greek, could be initiated into the Greek text by a translator like the author.

In a poem that refers directly to an act of translation, Γιὰ τὸν Ἀμμόνη ποὺ πέθανε, 29 ἐτῶν, στὰ 610 ("Gia ton Ammoni pou pethane, 29 eton, sta 610"; "For Ammones Who Died Aged 29 in 610"; Cavafy, *Collected Poems* [Sachperoglou] 94, 95), grief and a sense of lost (human) beauty have to be conveyed in a foreign language, of which the proposed writer has great mastery but is not a native speaker. The "Egyptian feeling" of a group of Coptic speakers must be "poured," or translated, into Greek. This staging of a small group of speakers of a minority (in this case, dying) language who need to communicate in the current language of power, Greek, is instructive for the present discussion. Nor is it accidental that the "translation" to be produced by the Coptic poet Raphael is an epitaph for another Coptic poet, Ammones. Cavafy, prescient in so many ways, must have been alert to the growing dominance of English in the wider world. Only a poet can do what Raphael is required to do, so it is small wonder that Cavafy's instructions to his own translators, John Cavafy and George Valassopoulo, were altogether more prosaic, focusing on semantics rather than the "elegant and musical" use of language (95).

In working toward the specified (examined) syllabus objectives, I encourage students to consider Cavafy's attitude toward the translation of his work and to think about translation issues more generally. We discuss the fact that there is an extraordinarily large array of Cavafy translations to select from and that a surprising number of his translators are Greek native speakers. In addition to essays, students are required to write commentaries in which details of form are identified and discussed in relation to content. I therefore aim to give students a basic tool kit for close readings, providing them with a grounding in Modern Greek prosody. The use of meter and rhyme in modern Greek poetry has no real equivalent in ancient Greek prosody, and it is interesting for students to explore this contrast. By learning to make objective observations about Cavafy's use of language, including syntax and poetic devices, students can begin to appreciate how style informs content—a transferable skill in literary analysis. For example, the use of rich rhyme in all but the closing couplet of Τοῦ Μαγαζιοῦ ("Tou magaziou"; "Of the Shop"; *Collected Poems* [Sachperoglou] 66, 67) points up the contrast between the jeweler's masterpieces and the more ordinary items offered for sale, and the fifteen-syllable lines in the noncanonical Πάρθεν ("Parthen"; "Taken"; *K. P. Kavafis: Ta piimata* 552; *Complete Poems* [Dalven] 281) situates the poem, possibly ironically, within the tradition of the folk songs to which it alludes.

Leading Students to the Greek Text

Since classics students often find Cavafy's language difficult because of their limited knowledge of Modern Greek, I have devised techniques for increasing their confidence in dealing with the unfamiliar (e.g, by focusing on textual repetitions). I recently asked a group of Cambridge students to use colored marker pens to highlight all the repetitions in the poem Επέστρεφε ("Epestrefe"; "Come Back"; Cavafy, *Collected Poems* [Sachperoglou] 73, 74), with unexpected results: the key line stood out in black and white since it contained no repetitions. The density of repetition in this one short poem is striking, adding to its musicality and incantatory effect. This can be a fruitful approach to Cavafy's highly crafted poems and also serves to destabilize the idea of Cavafy's translatability. Students could be asked to suggest ways in which the repeated vowel sounds in the poem (notably the short *e*) could be replicated in English; they could also explore the sound texture of Evangelos Sachperoglou's translation by reading it aloud and consider the possibility of reproducing the sounds of one language in another. For radically different approaches to the question of reproducing the spirit or the letter of poetic texts, I refer students to two excellent discussions: Willis Barnstone's *The Poetics of Translation*, and Matthew Reynolds's *The Poetry of Translation*. Barnstone argues that the translator should attempt to give the reader an impression of the linguistic texture of a poem, even at the expense of literal meaning, while Reynolds advocates more "respectful behavior" toward the source text (72).

In her recent, groundbreaking study of literary translation, *Literary Translation and the Making of Originals*, Karen Emmerich alerts us to the dangers of referring to so-called original or source texts. This warning is particularly pertinent in the case of Cavafy, whose poems went through multiple revisions and were sometimes altered by hand in one printing but not in another. Behind the Cavafy canon lie the unelucidated decisions of editors, most notably George Savidis, who selected and repunctuated apparently final versions of the poems collected by Cavafy himself for publication. The unfinished and unpublished poems obviously present an even greater degree of textual instability, but these are outside the scope of the syllabus. At the undergraduate level, I teach one class called How Cavafy Made a Poem because I think it is important that students acquire some knowledge of the poet's complex self-publishing practices, including postpublication revisions. Interested students may look at digitized manuscripts of the unfinished poems and even create their own final versions. They can do this by visiting the newly digitized Cavafy archive on the Onassis Foundation Cavafy Archive website, and ideally, I would devote one session to introducing and exploring this complex and exciting new tool (e.g., see "God").

For pedagogical purposes, it seems sensible to choose translations of Cavafy's poems that mirror as closely as possible his Greek; a comparison of all the different translations available and the aims and achievements of the translators is a task for translation studies rather than for (Greek) literary studies. This being said, I teach at least one class session on comparing several versions of a well-known poem, just to give students an idea of the complexities inherent in translating poetry in general and Cavafy's poetry in particular. For the reasons outlined, I use and recommend the Oxford World Classics edition of Cavafy's collected poems (the canon), translated by Evangelos Sachperoglou with parallel Greek text (Cavafy, *Collected Poems* [Sachperoglou]). The translations sound quite odd, and even at times dissonant, as English text, but this is because they are very close to the originals in word order as well as meaning. My students take Modern Greek language lessons and can also, to a certain extent, utilize their knowledge of ancient Greek to decipher the text with the aid of the translation. Sachperoglou's versions help them to access the linguistic structure of the poetry. In this way, the students follow Cavafy's own approach to unlocking his poetry in English. I also recommend that students have access to the more readable translations of Daniel Mendelsohn, both because these are more literary and because of the excellent introduction and notes provided (Cavafy, *Complete Poems* [Mendelsohn]). There is some useful information in the "Language and Style" section of Peter Mackridge's introduction to Sachperoglou's translations (Mackridge, Introduction xxix–xxxii), and Anthony Hirst's useful note on the Greek text in the same volume is essential reading (Hirst, Note).

An introductory session might consist of comparing translations of a single poem, initially without recourse to the Greek. This would work in a comparative literature as well as a classics context. The aim of this session is to provoke discussion and reflection on the possibilities and limitations of translating poetry.

Lesson on Translation

A poem I have found fruitful for this kind of comparative translation session is "The God Abandons Antony." This poem typifies some of the difficulties inherent in translating Cavafy (discussed below); its English versions illustrate a vast range of approaches, from John Cavafy's Victorian poesy and Valassopoulo's close renderings to Lawrence Durrell's ham-fisted attempt to rewrite it as an English poem and Leonard Cohen's radical appropriation and reworking of it as a love song. The poem also raises issues of allusion, appropriation, continuity (from ancient to Modern Greek), colonialism, and gender politics. Finally, it exemplifies Cavafy's influence on twentieth- and twenty-first-century literature, from Durrell's *Alexandria Quartet* onward. At least sixteen translations of "The God Abandons Antony" are readily available in print, online, or both. All but two are by men; seven of the translators whose versions are cited in note 1 are Greeks.

When I teach translation techniques that are not part of the program in Modern Greek for classicists, I ask students to begin by identifying the translation problems of the set passage. So, their assignments begin with notes on these issues, and then they present their translation with its proposed solutions for discussion. I have identified what I call "seven headaches for the translator" in this particular poem, and there are no doubt more. I list these items and then comment briefly on each: the use of ancient Greek for the title; the poem's stated and unstated literary sources and cultural agenda; lexical and morphological equivalence in the title; the word σάν (or σά); the poem's flexible Greek syntax; stylistic and affective issues (or pragmatics) in the poem's sound texture; and grammatical gender and gender politics.

Use of Ancient Greek for the Title

Some ancient Greek is comprehensible to Modern Greek speakers; there is no direct English equivalent to this phenomenon. The poem's title is a partial quotation from Plutarch, which creates two problems: it is in ancient Greek, the sole parent language of Modern Greek (Anglo-Saxon wouldn't work as a replacement in an English rendering), and it doesn't have a finite verb. The closest equivalent to the ancient Greek infinitive ἀπολείπειν (*apolipin*; "to leave") in this context of reported speech would probably be the gerund form, and some translators have adopted this solution. Although technically this version has an incomplete or hanging verb form in English, "The God Abandoning [or Deserting or Forsaking] Antony" does not sound incomplete to an English speaker since this form is often used in the titles of paintings (such as *St. George Slaying the Dragon*): it describes an action that is happening and therefore fails to convey the incompleteness (dependency on a missing finite verb) of the Greek infinitive.

Literary Sources and Cultural Agenda

Although Cavafy's title quotes Plutarch (in ancient Greek, underlining linguistic and, by implication, cultural continuity), Shakespeare is almost certainly the real source. This assertion of a Greek source and downplaying of an English one reflects Cavafy's wider poetic practice, with its unacknowledged debts to Oscar Wilde and Robert Browning among others. This point can lead into a broader discussion of cultural appropriation and postcolonialism. Cavafy offers a rare example of a writer in a so-called minor language borrowing from the literature of a colonial power without acknowledgment. I have argued elsewhere that Cavafy had other reasons for omitting any overt reference to Wilde; in Ἐν πόλει τῆς Ὀσροηνῆς ("En poli tis Osroinis"; "A Town in Osroene") he again replaces an English source reference, Wilde's "Charmides," this time with the almost tautological phrase "Plato's Charmides" (Ekdawi, "Erotic Poems" 43).

Lexical and Morphological Equivalence in the Title

The poem's title has been translated as "The God Abandons [or 'Abandoning,' 'Forsakes,' 'Forsaking,' or 'Leaves'] Antony." The connotations of all these words are different. For example, *forsake* is archaic and exists in the marriage service vow—"forsaking all others"; it also appears in the adjectival *godforsaken* and Christ's words from the cross, "My God, my God, why hast thou forsaken me?" *Leave* is altogether more prosaic—as in "He left his wife behind" or "The train leaves at 9:15." Although *desert* has not been used by any of the translators, it is worth considering that this is the usual English rendering in Homeric instances where gods abandon mortals they had formerly supported. The connotations of *abandon* are not exactly the same as for *desert*; *abandon* gives a latent sense of leaving something half done, but "The God Abandons Antony" at least scans and has the advantage of sounding like the title of a poem.

Σάν or Σά

There are six instances of σάν, or its variant σά, in the poem; they constitute an essential part of the poem's semantic, syntactical, and acoustic structure and provide its opening word. This short, simple word has an exact English equivalent, *as*, but cannot always be rendered by *as*, which can also mean *because* in English, depending on the context. The translation therefore loses the connection between <u>σάν</u> έξαφνα ("As suddenly") and <u>Σάν</u> έτοιμος . . . <u>σά</u> θαρραλέος ("As if prepared . . . as if brave"; *Collected Poems* [Sachperoglou] 34; my trans.), which in the Greek emphasizes, through repetition and sound patterning, the contrast between suddenly being caught off guard and pretending to be prepared and brave. However, the repetition of this word (six times in a nineteen-line poem) is an essential structuring device. The English translator has no real option but to render it differently in the opening line and later lines. The English word *as* can be used in a temporal sense ("As I was sitting on my chair"), but in second-person structures it tends to be replaced by *while* ("while you were sleeping") to avoid ambiguity (compare "as you say" or "as you're tired"). In this circumstance, all the translators have opted for *when* except John Cavafy, who bizarrely uses *if*. All the other instances in the Greek poem invoke the comparative sense of σάν. The translators variously use *as*, *like*, *as if*, or *as though*, necessarily losing the connection between <u>σάν</u> έξαφνα ("When suddenly") and <u>σάν</u> έτοιμος άπό καιρό, <u>σά</u> θαρραλέος ("As one long since prepared, as one courageous"; Cavafy, *Collected Poems* [Sachperoglou] 34, 35).

Flexible Greek Syntax

Greek syntax permits object-verb-subject constructions as well as subject-verb-object ones, but in modern English, the first structure is unnatural and can be quite confusing. In the poem's title, "The God" and "Antony" are juxtaposed after the verb that relates them to each other (literally, "Abandons the God Antony") rather than separated by the verb, as they are in English. In Sachperoglou's English version, lines referring to the addressee's frustrated life plans have objects that end up sounding like the subject, such that the plans themselves are apparently "needlessly lament[ing]" (Cavafy, *Collected Poems* [Sachperoglou] 35). Students may be encouraged to think of other creative solutions to this syntactical conundrum.

Sound Texture

Cavafy's use of language involves alliteration and assonance, as in the following terms in the poem's first two lines:

ὥρα (*ora*; "hour")	ἀόρατος (*aoratos*; "invisible")
ἀκουσθεῖ (*akousthi*; "is heard")	θίασος (*thiasos*; "procession")
ἔξαφνα (*exafna*; "suddenly")	νὰ περνᾶ (*na perna*; "passing")

These effects have largely been replaced with plain, prosaic language in the poem's translations. In general, Cavafy's translators have downplayed or ignored the subtle acoustic texture of his poetry, and most of them have decided against prioritizing sound texture in this poem. This is an accepted position among translators of poetry, because sound effects can never be precisely reproduced. The English-speaking reader, however, deserves to be told (even in a footnote) that here, as elsewhere, Cavafy's use of language involves alliteration and assonance. Students can fruitfully discuss how these effects contribute to meaning. By using such a dense acoustic texture in the poem, Cavafy subtly underlines the beauty of the procession, its musical accompaniment, and the city that Antony is losing. These features are also relevant to the closing discussion of Leonard Cohen's setting of the poem to music.

Grammatical Gender and Gender Politics

It is notable that Cavafy completely erases Cleopatra from his account but uses feminine nouns Ἀλεξάνδρεια (*Alexandria*; "Alexandria") and πόλι (*poli*; "city") coupled with verbs of loss and leaving. This simply cannot be done in English. Suppressing Cleopatra is thus related to another translator's headache: the feminine gender of the city, Alexandria. In Shakespeare's play (Cavafy's suppressed source), Antony frequently addresses Cleopatra as "Egypt." Antony is not just losing Alexandria or Egypt; he is losing the woman he loves. But Cleopatra's absence from the poem is not absolute; she is implicit in the city (as its genius), and the happy accident of a feminine noun coupled with verbs for departure and loss hints at this implication in a way that translators cannot reproduce in English without sounding forced and artificial. In English, ships are sometimes referred to as *she*, but cities are not. Mendelsohn uses "the Alexandria, *whom* you are losing" (Cavafy, *Collected Poems* [Mendelsohn] 10; emphasis added), which just sounds odd. Thus, Cavafy's subtle displacement of Cleopatra becomes more absolute in English. Students can be encouraged to compare this displacement with the gender-ambiguous subjects of Cavafy's early erotic poems. The English-language translator must choose *he* or *she*, whereas in Greek, the ungendered third-person subject is contained in the verb.

Safe, Free, and Radical Translations

Rather than attempt a line-by-line comparison of the many available versions of "The God Abandons Antony," I ask students to read a selection of translations and to choose two or three to compare.[1] I introduce Leonard Cohen's song adaptation toward the end of the session. Another approach (possibly as a follow-up session) would be to do a creative translation workshop, in which students work from the Sachperoglou version to produce a poem of their own.

Cohen's song "Alexandra Leaving," which is based on the Mavrogordato translation, is a radical appropriation of "The God Abandons Antony." Cohen rewrites the poem as a love song addressed to a woman called Alexandra, who replaces the city of Alexandria in this evocation of loss. The song refers to "the god of love"; its refrain concludes with the phrases "Alexandra leaving" and "Alexandra lost." Cohen's rewrite is subversive in many ways. He removes this poem from the historical category of Cavafy's work and places it in the erotic category. He makes it heterosexual like its unacknowledged source: Shakespeare's *Antony and Cleopatra*. He characterizes the god as "the god of love," that is, Eros, rather than Dionysus, and he makes explicit—some might say illogical—use of Christian imagery: "crucifix uncrossed." All these changes are worth discussing in the context of the overall impact of the song and the fact that most listeners will be unaware of its source.

Cavafy's appeal is universal, crossing geographic, linguistic, cultural, and gender boundaries. As he himself foresaw, he was, and is, "un poète des générations futures" ("a poet of the future"; *Anekdota peza keimena* 82; my trans.). Cavafy was also aware of the aphorisms of Wilde: "there is only one thing in the world worse than being talked about, and that is not being talked about" (Wilde, *Oscar Wilde* 50). He might well have appreciated all these different translations, versions, and appropriations of his poetry and (beyond the scope of the present essay) all the imitations and even parodies inspired by it. Thus, Forster's assessment of Cavafy's readership aspirations seems wide of the mark: "To be understood in Alexandria and tolerated in Athens was the extent of his ambition" (qtd. in Harvey 40).

My classes, lectures, and workshops on Cavafy aim to give students a broad understanding of both the difficulties and the creative possibilities of literary translation as well as some insight into the linguistic structure and acoustic texture of the poems themselves. By selecting the most literal translation as a basis for instruction in programs in Modern Greek for classicists, I facilitate the reading of the Greek texts in a way comparable to Cavafy's own initiation of Forster into his work. Through comparison of a wide range of different approaches, both theoretical and practical, I allow students to explore many different versions of Cavafy's work in the hope that they will develop their critical skills, understand that different translations do not cancel each other out but rather complement and augment each other, and gain confidence in expressing and supporting their own insights into the extraordinary contribution of the Alexandrian poet to world literature.

NOTE

1. Cavafy, *Sixty-Three Poems* 31; Jeffreys, *Forster-Cavafy Letters* 168; Cavafy, *Poems* [Mavrogordato] 26; Cavafy, *Complete Poems* [Dalven] 30; Cavafy, *Collected Poems* [Keeley and Sherrard, 1992] 60–61; Cavafy, *Before* 8; Cavafy, *Collected Poems* [Barnstone] 45; Cavafy, *Selected Poems* [Sharon] 30; Cavafy, *Complete Poems* [Mendelsohn] 10; Cavafy, *Greek Poems* 1: 20; Cavafy, *Canon* [2nd ed.] 84–85; Cavafy, *Poems* [Chioles] 12–13; Cavafy, *One Hundred Sixty-Six Poems* 65; Cavafy, *Collected Poems* [Sachperoglou] 35; Cavafy, *Selected Poems* [Connolly] 23; Cavafy, *Complete Plus* 65; Durrell, *Justine* 25.

The Poetics of Liminality:
Anti-Economy and Cultural Politics in Cavafy

Panagiotis Roilos

In general, cultural politics concerns a two-way process: it refers, on the one hand, to the impact of political ideologies and practices on the production, circulation, and consumption of cultural products and, on the other hand, to the intricate ways in which the latter respond to, and even shape, aspects of the former. As I often stress in the classroom, cultural politics and Cavafy can be explored from many different but, as a rule, complementary perspectives. For instance, teaching Cavafy may involve the following questions: How is his work received by agents of politically determined or at least politically informed ideological discourses and activities (nationalism, postcolonialism, gender and queer studies, etc.)? How and to what extent may particular poems by Cavafy reflect specific political and social concerns in his contemporary Alexandria or in wider Greek contexts? Or in what ways did the themes of his mature work (produced and published from the late 1890s onward but especially after 1911) as well as his discursive choices undermine dominant socioaesthetic premises?[1]

My emphasis in this essay is on this last aspect of the complex topic of Cavafy and cultural politics. Cavafy's work is the main focus or an important comparative constituent in a number of graduate and undergraduate courses that I offer in the Departments of Classics and Comparative Literature at Harvard University. In addition to seminars devoted specifically to his poetry or to Greek modernism, Cavafy looms large in different courses of mine that cover a broad spectrum of topics and research areas; these range from gender and queer studies to the reception of Greek antiquity in nineteenth- and twentieth-century European and American literature and thought, and extend to irony, allegory, and "ritual poetics" (Yatromanolakis and Roilos). When I teach Cavafy, I ask students to consider mainly the ways in which his often subversive cultural politics redefined established approaches to the historical past, hegemonic ethical principles, and dominant economic concepts, practices, and priorities. Cavafy's approach to these three thematic orders (history, ethics, economy) was formulated, I argue, in terms of a distinctive liminality that promoted synthesis and inclusiveness rather than taxonomic or hierarchical polarization. The most important instructional aim of this methodological and interpretive focus is to familiarize students with interdisciplinary approaches to literature as a sociocultural phenomenon that, going beyond formalistic analyses, situates it within broader synchronic discursive contexts.

Against Grand Narratives

Cavafy, who famously declared that, if he were not a poet, he would have most happily been a historian, demonstrates an astute historical, economic, political, and, of course, aesthetic sensitivity throughout his published and unpublished work, especially from the middle of what I have called his allegorical period, in the 1890s, onward (Roilos, *C. P. Cavafy* 15–44). Concerning Greek history, he subscribed to the tripartite periodization scheme advocated by the patriarch of nineteenth-century Greek historiography, Konstantinos Paparrigopoulos, whose work he was deeply familiar with and greatly admired: antiquity, Middle Ages (Byzantium), and modern history. However, in contrast to cultural and ideological paradigms dominating his contemporary Greek and broader European intellectual production, Cavafy was particularly attracted not so much to the achievements of the famous classical past as to transitional periods of ancient and medieval Greek history: the era following Alexander the Great's expeditions to the East and the establishment of the Hellenistic kingdoms, late antiquity, and Byzantium.

Not unlike betwixt-and-between phases in the life of an individual or a community, such periods frequently bear the symptoms of an ambivalent liminality that is determined to a great extent by critical (potentially both destructive and creative), risky, and reinvigorating tensions between different conceptual, ideological, and broader sociocultural categories (e.g., familiar/unfamiliar, foreign/domestic, us/others, and past/present). Liminal eras in history, at least as perceived and approached by Cavafy, are to some degree marked by open-endedness, inclusiveness (syncretism), and fluidity. Although Cavafy wrote many decades before postmodernity, his interpretation of history and especially of the premises and practices of historiography is comparable to postmodern approaches to history—for example, those put forward by Hayden White.[2] A number of Cavafy's so-called historical poems focus on obscure, forgotten, or marginal episodes and figures of history, with a view to rehabilitating their multifarious significance, highlighting their relevance for broader socioaesthetic issues, and exposing the subjectivity inherent in hegemonic constructions or reconstructions of the historical past. Cavafy often illustrates how alleged documents are the products of fabrication, and thus have the status of monuments, or of apparent artifacts whose authority derives from the manipulation of specific discursive and ideological hierarchies.

When I discuss this pivotal dimension of Cavafy's poetry in class, I invite students to explore the ways in which the constructed nature of historical sources or narratives and the broader structures of political or discursive authority that determine historical developments are foregrounded in texts such as Πρέσβεις απ' την Αλεξάνδρεια ("Envoys from Alexandria"; *K. P. Kavafis: Ta piimata* 286)[3] and the unfinished poem Ζηνοβία ("Zenobia"; *Ateli piimata* 277–78, 280). The first of these poems describes the distress of the priests of Apollo in Delphi who have received expensive gifts from two rival members of the Ptolemaic dynasty, Ptolemaios VI Philometor and his brother Ptolemaios VIII Euergetes. The priests panic since they do not know which of their two benefactors they should promote through their oracular authority. Truth, even in its most sanctioned representations such as sacred endorsements or instructions, is exposed here as the product of intricate political and economic transactions. In "Zenobia," the homonymous queen of Palmyra orders two σοφιστάς ("sophists" or "scholars") to fabricate her genealogy and write a history that would prove her descent from the Greek kings of Egypt (*Ateli piimata* 278).

A characteristically Cavafian mode of engaging with history is the interrogation of dominant "grand narratives" by supplementing them with neglected snapshots or figures of the historical past. This is eloquently illustrated, for instance, in Καισαρίων ("Kaisarion") and Οροφέρνης ("Orophernes"; *K. P. Kavafis: Ta piimata* 280–81, 256–58). As is clearly stated in these poems, existent historical accounts do not provide many details about the lives and deeds of the two heroes (Kaisarion and Orophernes), and the narrators take it upon themselves to remedy this omission by providing their own versions. The result is a corrective and highly aestheticized retelling of history that highlights the subversive potential of minor versus grand narratives.

In "Kaisarion," the narrator admits that he creates an imaginary portrait of the homonymous son of Cleopatra, who was the tragic victim of political machinations. In fact, the poem extols poetry's creative intervention into dominant representations of history and poetry's power to foreground suppressed or undervalued aspects of the past. "Orophernes" exemplifies the liminality of Cavafy's discourse in all three thematic domains that I mention above: the homonymous hero, king of Cappadocia, was a minor figure of Hellenistic history, το τέλος του ("whose end"), the speaker stresses, η ιστορία ... δεν καταδέχθηκε ("history did not deign") to record (*K. P. Kavafis: Ta piimata* 258). Based on the pictorial and epigraphic evidence of a coin, Cavafy creates his own poetic story of that marginal figure that pertains to his overall socioaesthetic project. In an ironic twist of discursive expectations, the poem exalts those aspects of Orophernes's life that put into question the very socioeconomic principles on which the manufacture and function of monetary tokens like the coin are based. When he became a king, Orophernes, who in his early youth had abandoned himself to ελληνικά ("Hellenic") forms of sensual pleasure (256), indulged in what Aristotle would call χρηματιστική τέχνη ("the accumulation of wealth for its own sake"). According to the ancient philosopher, χρηματιστική is sustained by a desire with no τέλος ("end" or "purpose") and is thus determined by unrestrained υπερβολή ("excess"; Aristotle, *Politics* 1257a–1258a). By stalling circulation and economic exchanges, χρηματιστική ("the compelling storing of money") goes against the most fundamental condition of οικονομική ("economics"), that is, the free flow of monetary units. Furthermore, Orophernes's penchant for unreserved hedonism, which the poem glorifies, constitutes a marked form of excess, which resulted in the king's eventual self-expenditure. I have noticed that "Orophernes," although not as famous as other poems by Cavafy (e.g., Ιθάκη ["Ithaca"; *K. P. Kavafis: Ta piimata* 229–30], Η πόλις ["The City"; 216–17], or Απολείπειν ο θεός Αντώνιον ["The God Abandons Antony"; 225–26]), is especially appealing to students, thanks not only to its discursive complexity but also to its use of material intertextual sources: like other numismatic poems of Cavafy's (e.g., Φιλέλλην ["Philhellene"; 223–33]), "Orophernes" draws its inspiration from ancient coinage. I thus have the opportunity to invite students to compare images on those coins with Cavafy's poetic rendition of them.

Toward an Anti-Economy of Jouissance

The aestheticization of Kaisarion and Orophernes by Cavafy should be viewed in connection with his overall subversion of hegemonic ethics, as this was powerfully manifested in his outspoken celebration of homoerotic desire mainly in his mature years. His redefinition of aspects of the aesthetics and ethics of so-called Hellenic love was based on a radical destabilization of moral, sociocultural, and even economic principles that had become dominant in late industrial European societies. In his rearticulation of Hellenic love, Cavafy engaged in a creative dialogue with major representatives of British aestheticism, most notably with Walter Pater and Oscar Wilde. Cavafy's celebration of homoerotic desire and poetic creativity were conceptualized and articulated in terms of what I call the anti-economy of jouissance, a kind of economy that prioritizes excess, consumption, and self-expenditure at the expense of the dominant economic principles of profit and utility. The anti-economy of jouissance refers to any kind of nonproductive or antiproductive consummation of economic-libidinal desires (see Roilos, *C. P. Cavafy* 199–200).

The son of an affluent businessman and the grandson, on his mother's side, of a wealthy Constantinopolitan diamond merchant, Cavafy manifested a keen interest in economy early in his early literary production. Since this is a neglected aspect of the development of Cavafy's poetics, I often ask students to read systematically his literary production in the 1890s and identify those texts that attest to the significance of economy for his poetry and thought. My discussion of the subject in class focuses mainly on the following texts. In "The Four Walls of My Bedroom," written in 1893 and published posthumously, the personified walls are portrayed as involved in relationships with humans that are more authentic than the interaction between objectified men, who fall prey to the hegemony of commodification. Cavafy presents gift offering as an economic process promoting ephemeral and counterfeit values and replicating trade transactions, thus predating by almost one century Jacques Derrida's similar critique of established views about gift giving. Another early, unpublished poem, "The Bank of the Future," calls into question the credibility of the banking system. Investment in future profit and the concept of interest are dismissed by the narrator of this text as utterly devious. In addition to the poetry, several other texts by Cavafy attest to his preoccupation with economic matters. Notable is his piece on the function of the stock market in Alexandria, where he worked as broker from the mid-1890s to 1912 (*Prose Works* 264–66). In another text, an essay on Lucian's Περὶ τῶν ἐπὶ μισθῷ συνόντων ("On Salaried Posts in Great Houses"), he discusses the socioeconomic status of Greek scholars in the houses of Roman patrons in late antiquity (98–104).

"Ithaca" is an iconic Cavafian poem that propagates a similar redefinition of economic priorities as that in "Orophernes." Every time I teach this text, I discuss mainly two aspects of its poetics and thematics: first, its use of allegory, a trope that characterized Cavafy's poetic production especially in the 1890s and that marks, to my mind, his poetry's transition from metaphoric and Romantic to more metonymical and "prosaic" discursive modes; and second, the poem's subtle subversion of sanctioned economic priorities and promulgation, instead, of major principles of dandyist cultural politics and economics. In a sense, in "Ithaca," Ulysses's journey is approached as a risky enterprise undertaken by a prototypical entrepreneur who, however, indulges in the collection and private enjoyment of luxurious tokens of an aesthetic capital devoid of any use value (σεντέφια και κοράλλια, κεχριμπάρια κι έβενους / και ηδονικά μυρωδικά κάθε λογής ["mother-of-pearl and corals, amber and ebony, / and hedonic perfumes of any kind"; *K. P. Kavafis: Ta piimata* 229–30]) rather than in the acquisition of products that enter the circle of financial transactions. Indicative of the economic parameters of Cavafy's reinterpretation of Ulysses's journey is a comment of the poet's on Dante's innovative retelling of the ancient myth: "simplicity and sincerity permeate the whole discourse [of Dante], and thanks to them, the *entrepreneurial sparkle* [ἐπιχειρηματικὴ φλόξ] of the hero glows even more vividly" (G. Savidis, *Mikra Kavafika B* 178; emphasis added).

In "Ithaca," archetypal desire is associated with opulent and infertile consumption and not with utilitarian production and circulation. Accumulating precious symbols of dandyist aestheticism promotes compelling repetition, which I prefer to define in terms of metonymy, that is, successive instantiations of the same desiring force. In this respect, "Ithaca," like many other poems by Cavafy that thematize desire and anti-economy, should be read, I argue, in conjunction with the depiction of the liminality of Eros, the embodiment of desire, in Plato's *Symposium*, which is formulated in memorable economic terms: being a δαίμων ("demon") and the son of Πόρος ("Resource") and Πενία ("Poverty"), Eros occupies a liminal position between humanity and divinity, mortality and immortality, affluence and deprivation. According to Socrates, who mediates between his initiator into matters of eros, the priestess Diotima, and his interlocutors, "on the same day Eros thrives and lives, when he has resources, and then he dies; but again, thanks to the nature of his father, he is revived, but any resources he may acquire flow away, so that he is never completely deprived or affluent" (Plato, *Platonis Opera* 203e). As is evinced in several of his writings, Cavafy was familiar with Plato, whose *Symposium* had become emblematic in the circles of British aestheticists and especially the proponents of the so-called Uranian love.[4]

Economy and Art

The anti-economic function of the fine goods touted in "Ithaca" is comparable to the withdrawal from the market of the exquisite creations of the paradigmatic Cavafian artist in Του μαγαζιού ("Of the Shop"; *K. P. Kavafis: Ta piimata* 243).

The goldsmith in the poem does not sell his most precious products but keeps them for his own enjoyment, thus exemplifying the aesthetic dogma of art for art's sake. In this case, economic profit is sacrificed to pure aesthetic pleasure. In contrast to this artist, the musician in the rejected poem Τιμόλαος ο Συρακούσιος ("Timolaos the Syracusian"; 414–15) and the sculptor in Η συνοδεία του Διονύσου ("Dionysus and His Crew"; 208) illustrate the alienating effect of market economy on artistic production. If enmeshed in economic transactions, artists tend to trade aesthetic authenticity for profit and to succumb to the expectations of their patrons, as Cavafy illustrates in these poems but also in an interesting comment on the relationship between writers and their intended or envisaged readers that I discuss below. Timolaos's priority is to satisfy the demands of his audiences. In the end, the commercialization of art is experienced by Cavafy's fictional musician as a source of utter alienation: Ἀλλὰ ἐν μέσῳ τῶν ἐπαίνων τῶν πολλῶν, / ἐν μέσῳ τῶν πολυταλάντων δώρων, / περίλυπος εἶν' ὁ καλός Τιμόλαος ("But amid the many praises, / amid the gifts that are worth many talents, / good Timolaos is very sad"; 415).

Despite the fact that the story of "Timolaos the Syracusian" is situated in antiquity, it should be read as a comment on the conditions of Cavafy's contemporary art market and his own concerns about authenticity in poetry. Charles Baudelaire, whose work was an important intertext for Cavafy's poetry, had memorably described poetry's commodification in terms of prostitution and explored the drama of modern poets who are forced to enter the arena of economic transactions. One year after the composition of "Timolaos the Syracusian," Cavafy, apparently inspired by Lucian's "On Salaried Posts in Great Houses," wrote Λαγίδου φιλοξενία ("Lagides's Hospitality"; *K. P. Kavafis: Ta piimata* 476), which also focuses on the economic terms that determine the circulation and consumption of intellectual products. In Η συνοδεία του Διονύσου ("Dionysus and His Crew"), the fictitious sculptor Damon creates, despite his artistic refinement, with a view to acquiring social prestige and wealth that would allow him to go into politics. The way in which the artist's political and economic aspirations are presented in the poem indicates that the narrator views them as potentially detrimental to Damon's artistic individuality and as responsible for Damon's entrapment in the alienating gregariousness of the ἀγορά ("agora").

It is important to keep in mind that this poem appeared in Παναθήναια (*Panathenaia*) in April 1907, some months after that Athenian journal published a study on the crisis of the book market in Greece. Cavafy had been invited to share his views on the subject with the readers of the journal. He wrote a short note in which he stressed the importance of the writer's independence from any utilitarian practices and economic transactions. Commodification of literature is bound to have a corrosive effect on its authenticity: "No matter how sincere and [how much of] an idealist an author is, there will be moments that (almost without wishing it, almost without realizing it), knowing how the public thinks and what it likes and what it buys, he will make some sacrifices; he will formulate this passage in a different way and he will omit that one" (Cavafy, *Peza* 193).

Cavafy never sent this note to *Panathenaia*; instead, he had "Dionysus and His Crew" published in the journal—perhaps as a characteristically Cavafian, ironic comment on the concept and function of the book market that *Panathenaia* had explored in previous issues.

No doubt, Cavafy's exposure of the restrictive impact of the art market on artistic individuality was in accord with the views of other European aestheticists, most notably Flaubert, Baudelaire, and Wilde. The last of these writers, throughout his work but most systematically in his essay "The Soul of Man under Socialism," advocated the independence of artistic talent and creativity from any sort of financial transactions and elevated individualism to a supreme moral, aesthetic, and political value. Cavafy was familiar with Wilde's text; it is reported that he had commented on its value with the following words: "a world founded on the ideas of this work would be beautiful" (qtd. in Catraro 42).

I should stress that, despite these affinities with other European proponents of pure aestheticism and absolute freedom from the restrictions of book market and economic exchanges, Cavafy was the only one who remained loyal to this principle: he never had a book published by a publishing house. He preferred to have his poems printed privately in broadsheets or little pamphlets, which he would stitch together into folders, and to maintain absolute control over their free distribution. In class, I often invite students to disentangle the complex ideological and discursive ramifications of this combination of pure aestheticism and attraction to apparently socialist values, which at first sight seems to constitute a conceptual and ideological paradox.

The Erotics of Self-Consumption

To help students appreciate this ostensible paradox more spherically, I offer them a general outline of major, more or less synchronic developments in economics. I place particular emphasis on the fact that by the time dandyist aesthetics and Cavafy's poetry reevaluated hegemonic principles of the market economy, the so-called marginalist economists in Europe, mainly in England and Austria, such as William Stanley Jevons and Carl Menger, had shifted the focus of economic theory from production to consumption and individual desire as the main factors and criteria for determining value in economy (see especially Jevons; Menger). Although no direct connection between these developments in art, literature, and economics can or should be established, their contemporaneity indicates a broader reassessment of traditional conceptualizations of value, subjectivity, individuality, and desire in these and related discursive fields (e.g., philosophy and science).

For Cavafy, poetry constitutes an exemplification of radical anti-economy since it often involves creation through self-expenditure and loss, or—in terms of ritual poetics[5]—through self-sacrifice. His understanding of poetic creativity as an instantiation of a broader economic-erotic liminality is eloquently expressed in a poem that bears the characteristically ritualistic title Πέρασμα ("Passage"), in which initiation into the world of poetry is indeed described as a rite of passage.

"Passage," which was written in 1914 and published in 1917, illustrates how a παιδί απλό ("simple youth") is admitted to the realm of poetry on condition that he offers his καινούριο και ζεστό ("fresh and warm") blood to the personified, all-consuming ηδονή ("hedonic pleasure")—a major principle of Cavafy's ideal Alexandrian way of life (*K. P. Kavafis: Ta piimata* 268).

This approach to art can be compared to the ideas about general economy that Georges Bataille would develop in the 1930s and most systematically in his *Accursed Share*, published in 1949. Expenditure and excessive consumption are major categories of Bataille's revolutionary economic theory. General economy's main focus is on the ways in which surplus energy is consumed. Sacrifice, including self-sacrifice, constitutes a major form of such consumption, one of the most paradigmatic exemplifications of which is poetry.

Self-expenditure as a necessary prerequisite for genuine artistic creation is an idea that can be traced back to Cavafy's allegorical period. In the prose poem "The Regiment of Hedonic Pleasure," the homonymous personified force is glorified by means of a paradoxical subversion of conceptual and economic norms. Fundamental notions and principles of financial affairs like supply and demand, labor and compensation, are superseded by excessive consumption and counterproduction. Although ηδονή ("hedonic pleasure") is described as the highest form of liberally granted life, its climax coincides with death, the ultimate "reward" for absolute devotion to art:

> Do not shut yourself in your house; do not deceive yourself with theories of justice, with ill-made society's superstitious ideas about rewarding. Do not say "my labor is priced at this amount and as much I must enjoy." Like life, which is a sort of inheritance and you did nothing to acquire it as a reward, Hedonic Pleasure, too, must be a kind of inheritance. . . . Service to pleasure is a continuous joy. It exhausts you but it exhausts you with marvelous intoxication. And when, in the end, you will fall in the street, even then your fortune is enviable. As the procession of your funeral will be passing, the Figures that your desires have created will spread lilies and white roses in your coffin, and adolescent Olympian gods will lift you on their shoulders and entomb you in the Cemetery of the Ideal where the mausoleums of poetry coruscate in their white color.
>
> (Roilos, *C. P. Cavafy* 236–38)

Self-expenditure and consuming indulgence in the anti-economy of jouissance determine not only an artist's genuineness but also the transformation of the self-sacrificed subject into the embodiment of what Cavafy considered to be pure aestheticism and ideal eroticism; individuals experience the apogee of jouissance at the moment they themselves become monuments, artworks of utmost desire.

This theme is explored mainly in poems published around the same time or after "Passage."[6]

In Cavafy's unfinished poems, for instance in Η είδησις της εφημερίδος ("The Report of the Newspaper"; K. P. Kavafis: Ta piimata 567–69), Έγκλημα ("Crime"; 606–07), and Συντροφιά από τέσσαρες ("Company of Four"; 617–18), self-expenditure manifests itself also in criminal acts. The aestheticization of outlaws in Cavafy's poetry is in accord with his repeated characterization of homoeroticism, his ideal form of love, as έκνομος ("illegal"). Already in his earlier unpublished poem Δυνάμωσις ("Invigoration"), unlawful behavior is hailed as a fundamental prerequisite of intellectual vivification:

> Όποιος το πνεύμα του ποθεί να δυναμώσει
> να βγει απ' το σέβας κι από την υποταγή.
> Από τους νόμους μερικούς θα τους φυλάξει,
> αλλά το περισσότερο θα παραβαίνει
> και νόμους κι έθιμα κι απ' την παραδεγμένη
> και την ανεπαρκούσα ευθύτητα θα βγει.   (K. P. Kavafis: Ta piimata 525)

> He who desires to invigorate his spirit
> should go beyond respect and obedience.
> Some of the laws he will keep,
> but he will mostly breach
> laws and customs, and go beyond accepted
> and insufficient straightness.

It is mainly because of its illegality that the commercialization of love is not dismissed but rather elevated into the status of idealized sensuality in Cavafy's mature poetry. This is the case as early as 1904 with the composition of Σταίς Σκάλαις ("On the Stairs"; K. P. Kavafis: Ta piimata 529), but especially after 1915—for instance, in Μιά νύχτα ("One Night"; 271), Κάτω απ' τὸ σπίτι ("Outside the House"; 292), the unpublished Κι ἀκούμπησα καὶ πλάγιασα στὲς κλίνες των ("And I Reclined and Lay on Their Beds"; 544), the unfinished Ἡ είδησις τῆς ἐφημερίδος ("The Report of the Newspaper"; 567–69), Κ' ἐπὶ πᾶσιν ὁ Κυναίγειρος ("In Any Case Kynaigeiros"; 577–78), Στὴν προκυμαία ("On the Dock"; 580), and the canonical Εὔνοια τοῦ Ἀλεξάνδρου Βάλα ("The Benevolence of Alexandros Ballas"; 313). In Μέσα στὰ καπηλειά ("In the Taverns"; 348), Σοφιστὴς ἀπερχόμενος ἐκ Συρίας ("Sophist Leaving Syria"; 351), Μέρες τὸ 1909, '10, καὶ '11 ("Days of 1909, '10, '11"; 379–80), Ὡραία λουλούδια κι ἄσπρα ὡς ταίριαζαν πολύ ("Beautiful White Flowers That Became Him Well"; 379–80), and the unfinished Τιγρανόκερτα ("Tigranokerta"; 610–11), Cavafian narrators refer directly or indirectly to spaces and forms of erotic commerce in antiquity and modernity. Despite its apparent conformity to established financial principles and practices, in Cavafy's socioaesthetic system, investment in erotic excess eventually and essentially goes against sanctioned economic hierarchies, to the extent that it constitutes a form of antiproductive, infertile, illegal, and instantaneous consumption and expenditure of surplus libidinal energy. Closely connected with this idiosyncratic poetic exploration of the commodification of eros is the reversed discursive innovation encountered in Cavafy's late work: the eroticization of aspects and places of economic transactions, especially in "He Was Asking about the Quality," the unpublished "Half an Hour," or the unfinished "Company of Four."

Cavafy's poetry, a particularly multilayered discursive phenomenon of early-twentieth-century European literature, lends itself to complex interdisciplinary approaches, both in scholarship and in educational praxis. Inviting students to explore Cavafy's work also in terms of its reaction to hegemonic economic hierarchies and practices exposes them to one of the most innovative manifestations in world literature of poetry's potential to redefine, subtly but forcefully, socioaesthetic and political priorities.

NOTES

1. These choices involve mainly the gradual development of a poetic discourse that was, at least according to the established criteria of poeticity of the time, closer to prose than to poetry and, as such, was an inherently liminal discourse. Socioaesthetics is a concept put forward in Yatromanolakis's studies in ancient Greek cultural history; see especially *Sappho*.

2. White has memorably exposed the discursivity of historiography and its close connections with literary practices (e.g., the narratological strategy of emplotment) and rhetorical tropes, irony being, to his mind, the dominant one in postmodernist historiography; see, for instance, *Tropics* and *Figural Realism*.

3. All translations are mine, unless otherwise noted.

4. Uranian love refers to homoerotic love between men. The term derives from Plato's distinction between common and Uranian Aphrodite in his *Symposium*; cf. Dowling.

5. The concept of ritual poetics is put forward in Yatromanolakis and Roilos.

6. These poems include Ἰγνατίου τάφος ("Tomb of Ignatios"; *K. P. Kavafis: Ta piimata* 277), Ἰασή τάφος ("Tomb of Iases"; 274), Ἰμένος ("Imenos"; 297), Μέσα στά καπηλειά ("In the Taverns"; 348), Ἕνας νέος, τῆς Τέχνης τοῦ Λόγου—στο 24ον ἔτος του ("A Young Poet in His Twenty-Fourth Year"; 361), Μέρες το 1909, '10, και '11 ("Days of 1909, '10, and '11"; 373), and Ὡραῖα λουλούδια κι ἄσπρα ὡς ταίριαζαν πολύ ("Beautiful White Flowers That Became Him Well"; 379–80).

INTERTEXTUAL APPROACHES

Cavafy's *Iliad* in the Classroom

Stamatia Dova

This essay discusses teaching methodologies on C. P. Cavafy's reception of the *Iliad* in the context of an undergraduate classics elective course entitled The World of Greek Heroes,[1] offered at Hellenic College, with a reading list including all of Homer.[2] Through close readings of four of Cavafy's Iliadic poems—Τὰ Ἄλογα τοῦ Ἀχιλλέως ("Ta Aloga tou Achilleos"; "The Horses of Achilles"; *Canon* [2nd ed.] 26–27; *Collected Poems* [Keeley and Sherrard, 1975] 6–7), Ἡ Κηδεία τοῦ Σαρπηδόνος ("I Kidia tou Sarpidonos"; "The Funeral of Sarpedon"; 30–33; 10–13), Ἀπιστία ("Apistia"; "Perfidy"; 48–49; 28–29), and Τρῶες ("Troes"; "Trojans"; 60–61; 38–39)[3]—the class examined the dynamics of poetic inspiration against the backdrop of the multiformity of Homeric tradition. The method of instruction consisted of lectures and audiovisual presentations followed by class discussions. All readings were in English, and course assignments included a class trip to the Boston Museum of Fine Arts and biweekly reflection papers amounting to a minimum of thirty pages for the entire semester.[4] Class discussions were informed by recent scholarship and enriched with viewings of ancient Greek art from the online collections of the Metropolitan Museum of Art, the British Museum, and the Louvre. As stated on the syllabus, the course's learning objectives included helping students acquire a comprehensive understanding of concepts of the Greek hero in the archaic and classical period; develop a deep appreciation for ancient Greek literature, mythology, and culture; and identify and analyze the classical roots of twenty-first-century European and North American civilization. The poems by Cavafy contributed to a profound internalization of Homeric poetry by inviting the class to discover the metapoetic essence of reception as well as its creative energy. Our methodology, based on reader-response theory and reception theory (Hardwick and Stray 1–5; Martindale and Thomas 1–13; Tompkins 1–24), revolved around the question, How do we relate to Cavafy's reading of the *Iliad*?

The first step in our reading of Cavafy's Iliadic poems was to analyze the literary statement the poet makes through his selective reception of the original passage. Our class's search for Cavafy's *Iliad* began by juxtaposing his reception poems with the text that inspired them. Though seemingly passage-specific, this parallel reading branched out to incorporate the entire *Iliad* and its tradition. Our working assumption was that Cavafy's selective focus both constitutes evidence of his authorial intention and illuminates his reasons for composing on Homer. Furthermore, we worked on the premise that Cavafy's way of internalizing Homer does not differ from our own view of Homeric poetry as a timeless contemplation of the forces that govern the human experience. For the purposes of our discussion, this view, far from discounting the *Iliad*'s function as oral poetry composed in archaic Greece and performed in a variety of contexts throughout antiquity, identifies the poem's diachronic ability to express the human psyche and its concerns about mortality. Central to these concerns is the anxiety over the power of death to undo personhood, an element that also forms the basis of Cavafy's intellectual kinship with the *Iliad*.

In our analysis of the *Iliad*, students were given the opportunity to employ Cavafy's poetry as a hermeneutic tool for examining Homeric poetry. To this end, "The Horses of Achilles" proved remarkably successful since it provides a comprehensive overview of the *Iliad*'s discourse on mortality. In fact, the Iliadic scene that inspired Cavafy's poem (17.426–56) encapsulates a multiplicity of tensions between mortality and immortality by engaging the categories of god, human, and animal. Achilles's immortal horses, Xanthos and Balios, begin to weep at the news of Patroklos's death. Born to Zephyr (the west wind) by Podarge, one of the Harpies (16.149–50), these extraordinary animals connect Achilles to the etiology of the Trojan War, where the young hero will meet his fate: they were given by the gods as a wedding gift to his father, Peleus, at the very occasion where Aphrodite promised to give Paris the most beautiful woman for a wife, thus bringing forth his abduction of Helen and the Achaean expedition against Troy. The son of a goddess and a mortal hero, Achilles embodies the inherent contrast between immortal and mortal (Dova, *Poetics* 75–82). As my student Carolyn Catherine Holder writes, "[t]his marriage tied together strands of mortality and immortality which were never meant to do anything more than briefly cross, and the resulting knot created a problem in the fundamental order of the universe by subverting the hierarchy of place and station." In the *Iliad*, Achilles's mortality generates the poem's anxiety over heroic choice: set on pursuing κλέος (*kleos*; "glory"; *Homeri Ilias* 16.438), Achilles goes to Troy knowing that he will never be granted a νόστος (*nostos*; "homecoming"; 433). This foreknowledge of death informs the hero's actions both on the battlefield, where he unquestionably excels above all the Achaeans and Trojans, and in the assembly, where he is insulted by Agamemnon's threat to deprive him of his war prize (Dova, *Greek Heroes* 102–04; Burgess, *Death* 43–55). The threat carried out, Achilles withdraws from battle, also keeping Patroklos and the Myrmidons away from the battlefield. It is only following Patroklos's intense pleas that Achilles allows him to assist the exhausted Achaeans. Wearing Achilles's armor, Patroklos dies at the hands of Hektor, shot by Euphorbus's arrow and stricken by Apollo, Troy's patron god and Achilles's god-antagonist; his death, carried out in three acts, bears the symbolism of a sacrifice demanded by divinity and offered by mortals. The pattern of dual causality leading to Patroklos's death is to be replicated in Achilles's own death, which will result from an arrow shot by Paris and guided by Apollo. Not only does Patroklos's death constitute a rehearsal of Achilles's untimely demise, but it also initiates the chain of events that will bring it forth; as made clear by his mother, Achilles must die if he kills Hektor to avenge Patroklos's death (*Il.* 18.98–100).

A moment pregnant with tragedy, the realization that Patroklos has been killed is masterfully highlighted in the *Iliad* through the grief experienced by Achilles's horses. At this point in the *Iliad*, Achilles does not know yet of his friend's death. Despite his efforts, Automedon—Achilles's and, in this context, Patroklos's skilled chariot driver[5]—is unable to control the horses because they refuse to move, lowering their heads, stomping, and shedding hot tears (Schein, *Homeric Epic* 11–26). In a magnificent simile, the Homeric text likens them to σῆμα γυναικός τε καὶ ἀνέρος ἐκτάδιον τ' ἀνέστη / καὶ τεθνηῶτος ("a grave stele, a monument marking the burial site of a man or woman who has died"; *Homeri Ilias* 17.434–35).[6] Though summarized in ἡνιόχοιο πόθῳ ("lament for their charioteer"; 439), their emotions encompass anguish, despair, and longing for a lost loved one. As I argue elsewhere, Achilles's death is the result of πόθος (*póthos*; "longing") for dead Patroklos (Dova, *Greek Heroes* 45, 66n177, 159). Yet the horses of Achilles, unable to die, can only experience shock and despondency at the irreversibility of death. Their pain raises Zeus's pity, and the god hurries to admit his error in having gifted them, creatures ageless and immortal, to a mortal; he also vows to instill in them strength so that they don't fall into Hektor's hands. Indeed, right after Zeus's soliloquy, Automedon's chariot speeds through the melee and eventually reaches the Achaean camp, Patroklos's body is rescued, and his death eventually avenged.

None of these arguably lesser victories enters "The Horses of Achilles." On the contrary, Cavafy maintains a sharp focus on human mortality and its devastating effect on personhood by describing Patroklos as

ἄψυχο—ἀφανισμένο—
μιὰ σάρκα τώρα ποταπὴ—τὸ πνεῦμα του χαμένο—
ἀνυπεράσπιστο—χωρὶς πνοὴ—
εἰς τὸ μεγάλο Τίποτε ἐπιστραμμένο ἀπ' τὴν ζωή. (*Canon* [2nd ed.] 26)

lifeless, annihilated,
now merely contemptible flesh—his spirit gone,
defenseless, without breath,
sent back from life to the great Nothingness.

While in the *Iliad* the horses κλαῖον ("weep"; *Homeri Ilias* 17.427) at the news of Patroklos's death, in Cavafy they begin to cry as soon as they see him killed: τὸν Πάτροκλο σὰν εἴδαν σκοτωμένο ("when they saw Patroklos killed"), ἄρχισαν τ' ἄλογα νὰ κλαῖνε τοῦ Ἀχιλλέως ("the horses of Achilles began to weep"; *Canon* [2nd ed.] 26). As it begins to explore aspects of human mortality, Cavafy's poem incorporates a compressed encomium for the fallen warrior, ποὺ ἦταν τόσο ἀνδρεῖος, καὶ δυνατός, καὶ νέος ("who was so brave, and strong, and young"). The poem also contrasts Zeus's misguided regret for his role in exposing the horses to πρόσκαιρες συμφορές ("ephemeral misfortunes") with the true reason for their tears: Ὅμως τὰ δάκρυά των / γιὰ τοῦ θανάτου τὴν παντοτεινὴ / τὴν συμφορὰν ἐχύνανε τὰ δυὸ τὰ ζῶα τὰ εὐγενῆ ("Nevertheless, the two noble animals kept shedding their tears for the eternal calamity of death"; 26).

Students responded enthusiastically to Cavafy's perspicacious characterization of Zeus, identifying the antithesis between "the attitude of the horses, who mourn the *eternal* disaster of mortality, with the attitude of Zeus, who, looking down at the whole tragic scene, mourns the *ephemeral* disaster of mortality," as Holder puts it. It can be said that the difference in perspective between Zeus and the horses of Achilles explains why the two animals display such strong emotions on account of Patroklos's death, as if they were previously unacquainted with mortality. Yet, in addition to having witnessed countless warriors die in battle, Xanthos and Balios have also lost their mortal yokemate Pedassos (*Il.* 16.466–76), a fine stallion killed by Sarpedon's errant spear aimed at Patroklos. As Holder notes, "[t]he horses seem both shocked and somewhat disgusted by the death of their mortal companion, as if they want to get away and move on without dealing with the implications of mortality presented in the situation. Automedon in the heat of the battle immediately steps in and cuts the dead horse free, in a sense complying with the wish of the immortal horses to move on."

In Cavafy, the horses are overwhelmed with indignation and sorrow over Patroklos's death: ἡ φύσις των ἡ ἀθάνατη ἀγανακτοῦσε / γιὰ τοῦ θανάτου αὐτὸ τὸ ἔργον ποὺ θωροῦσε ("their immortal nature was resentful / at this deed of death it witnessed"; *Canon* [2nd ed.] 26), to which it remains intrinsically alien. By highlighting the contrast between the horses of Achilles as entities that belong jointly to the categories *animal* and *immortal* and Patroklos, who embodies the combination of *human* and *mortal*, Cavafy makes the most of a unique opportunity provided by the *Iliad*: to bemoan the human and its insignificance by showing representatives of the categories *god* and *animal* lamenting human powerlessness before fate. Now bitterly regretted by Zeus, the horses's conveyance— ἐκεῖ χάμου / στὴν ἄθλια ἀνθρωπότητα ποῦναι τὸ παίγνιον τῆς μοίρας ("down there, / to wretched humanity, destiny's plaything")—has come to underscore the incompatibility between mortal and immortal that also overshadows the union between Peleus and Thetis. As my student Anastasis Phyrillas writes, "Zeus regrets giving the horses as gifts because now he sees them experience death without dying, and he can relate to the type of pain that is."

In the *Iliad*, the horses of Achilles and the death of Sarpedon "build the understanding of immortality experiencing mortality," as Phyrillas puts it. Zeus is tempted to violate the universal order of things and save Sarpedon (*Il.* 16.433–38); reminded by Hera, however, that not even he can defy fate, he becomes resigned to it, with sole consolation that Sarpedon's body will be rescued from the battlefield by Apollo, taken to his native Lycia by the twin gods Death and Sleep, and given a splendid funeral. In "The Funeral of Sarpedon" Cavafy explores the compensatory potential of the funeral honors offered to Sarpedon. It can be said that "The Horses of Achilles" and "The Funeral of Sarpedon" reflect a dialogue within the tradition of the *Iliad*, an antiphonal exchange that also guides Cavafy's reception. As Dimitrios N. Maronitis has observed in Κ.Π. Καβάφης: Μελετήματα (*K. P. Kavafis: Meletimata*; *C. P. Cavafy: Studies*; 107), in this poem Cavafy displays unusual compliance with his Iliadic model. The impossibility of physical immortality for the hero is somewhat remedied by the rituals marking his passing. While "The Horses of Achilles" voices the grief caused by the death of the hero-warrior, "The Funeral of Sarpedon" is primarily preoccupied with the cultural mechanisms that will ensure the preservation of his memory. As a result, the premise for the latter poem is Zeus's acceptance of the necessity for the death of his son, which Cavafy, in accordance with his Iliadic model (*Il.* 16.441–42), articulates as ὁ Νόμος ("the Law"; *Canon* [2nd ed.] 30). At Zeus's command, Apollo cares for the hero's lifeless body, and that care functions as an act of restoration: treated with ambrosia and dressed in Olympian robes, the dead warrior is likened to a young king who is resting after his victory at a famous race (Jeffreys, *Reframing Decadence* 79; Maronitis 119–22; Paschalis 166; Ricks, *Shade* 107–10). Won μ' ἅρμα ὁλόχρυσο καὶ ταχυτάτους ἵππους ("with a golden chariot and the fastest horses"; *Canon* [2nd ed.] 30), this victory constitutes the gateway to the hero's cultural immortality by connecting his posthumous radiance with a fictitious yet appropriately imagined triumph. Cavafy's powerful grasp of the Homeric simile in its narrative and aesthetic functions is made evident here, as the idealized image of the handsome youth oscillates between death and sleep. Like Homer's dead Hektor (*Il.* 24.757), whose youthful body is returned to Troy looking fresh and unsullied thanks to divine protection (Monsacré 75; Segal 70), Cavafy's dead Sarpedon is translated into a state that respects his heroic perfection.

Such gentleness remains outside the scope of Patroklos's treatment in "The Horses of Achilles." His lifeless body is referred to only in negative terms, and we are given to understand that no funerary rite can effect healing. Situated outside the social domain of death rituals, the horses connect directly to Zeus, who feels their sorrow and appreciates their difficulty in coming to terms with it. As internal and external audiences of the *Iliad* may infer, the horses' grief is also anticipatory since Patroklos's death is to be followed by that of Achilles. The similarities between book 16, line 776, and book 18, line 26, in the *Iliad* provide further evidence of this connection. As my student Andreana Klein points out, "In the *Iliad*, Homer goes so far as to describe Achilles' grief for Patroklos as if he has already died himself." Indeed, in book 19, lines 408–17, the horses share with Achilles their foreknowledge of his upcoming death and wish to be exonerated of any responsibility for it. This passage served as the inspiration for Henri Regnault's 1868 painting *Automedon with the Horses of Achilles*, which the class saw during a field trip to the Boston Museum of Fine Arts. Like Cavafy's poem, this monumental painting encapsulates the pathos of the helpless animals as they refuse to submit to Automedon, their chariot driver, out of fear that they might bring Achilles, their chariot fighter, to his death.[7] Unlike Achilles, however, who remains disarmingly aware of the cost for *kleos* throughout the *Iliad* (19.421–22), Patroklos, deceived by Apollo, labors under the misapprehension that the gods may allow him to take Troy. This illusion proves catastrophic for the young Achaean, who, like Sarpedon before him and Hektor after him, entertains the false hope that he will survive the crucial encounter with an awe-inspiring enemy. By the time the hero and his near and dear are disabused of this unrealistic expectation, it is too late. Fate has taken its course, no matter how unpredicted the outcome.

Cavafy incorporates this element of disbelief into "Perfidy." As indicated by its epigraph, the poem joins the diachronic list of Homeric audiences trying to make sense of Achilles's death. Inspired by Plato's discussion of a passage from Aeschylus's no-longer-extant tragedy Ὅπλων κρίσις ἢ Αἴας (*Oplon krisis i Aias; The Judgement of the Arms of Achilles* or *Aias*; Radt fr. 350), Cavafy incorporates into his poem the *Republic*'s multilayered response to the rivalry between Achilles and Apollo.[8] As Ruth Scodel has shown (56–57), the title of Cavafy's poem demonstrates that the poet had made the connection between the Aeschylean fragment and book 24, line 63, of the *Iliad*, where Hera addresses Apollo with the adjective ἄπιστος ("apistos"; "untrustworthy"). In response to Apollo's condemnation of Achilles's desecration of Hektor's body, Hera objects to the suggestion that Achilles, the son of a divine mother, and Hektor, a mere mortal, should be considered equals. To prove her point, she reminds Apollo that Thetis is her protégée, concluding, πάντες δ' ἀντιάασθε θεοὶ γάμου· ἐν δὲ σὺ τοῖσι / δαίνυ' ἔχων φόρμιγγα κακῶν ἕταρ', αἰὲν ἄπιστε ("and you yourself sung at her wedding, companion of evil, always untrustworthy"; *Homeri Ilias* 24.63–64).[9]

Concerned with the moral education of the guardians of the ideal republic, Socrates and Adeimantos condemn Aeschylus's portrayal of Apollo as unreliable and perfidious (Plato, *Republic* 383a7–c5). Their censoring of the Aeschylean passage makes a powerful statement on truth and poetry, to which Cavafy responds with his poem (Zamarou 77). As Jonathan Burgess notes, this version of Achilles's death is not attested anywhere else ("Untrustworthy Apollo" 22). Inevitably, our discussion in class had to explore why Cavafy singles it out. In

"Perfidy," he provides his audience with a thought-provoking commentary on Homer that originates outside of Homer. Does Cavafy think of Aeschylus's fragment as the metatext to a lost epic tradition or as tragedy's adaptation of an epic theme? Similarly, are we to identify in the profound tension he creates between Thetis's trust and Apollo's deceit an authorial intention to negotiate the polarities between Achilles's excellence and untimely death? Our conclusion was that Cavafy employs the discrepancy between Apollo's words and deeds to illustrate the self-contradictory nature of human fate. Thetis's assumption that Achilles's beauty, admired by all Thessaly, is somehow connected to Apollo's prophecy is meant to lead Thetis astray, even though initially Apollo's words seemed to her a kind of ἐγγύησις γιὰ τὸ παιδὶ της ("guarantee for her child's future safety"; Cavafy, *Canon* [2nd ed.] 48).

By deviating from the Iliadic tradition of Thetis's foreknowledge of Achilles's impending death, "Perfidy" casts Thetis as the emblematic mater dolorosa, stressing her anger, devastation, and disbelief in the face of tragedy. Her divine status notwithstanding, Thetis protests the unfairness of her son's fate as would the mother of any fallen soldier (Zamarou 85–88). Furthermore, by discrediting a prophecy issued by the god of divination himself (spontaneously and not in response to inquiry), the tradition echoed in Aeschylus's play presents Apollo's words in a different light. While it is only fitting that Apollo would forecast health and longevity for the offspring of the newlyweds at whose wedding feast he sang, as patron god of Troy he retains the right to kill the city's greatest enemy. Thus, we wondered whether Cavafy is contextualizing Apollo's role in a similar way, reading his contradictory behavior toward Achilles as evidence for humanity's vulnerability. Students saw in Apollo's conduct a twofold potential: to exemplify the treachery of the gods, in accordance with the *Republic*, and to seal Achilles's cultural immortality by bringing forth his untimely but glorious death. From this point of view, "the prophecy did come true in some way," as my student Elias Pappas puts it, underlining the analogy between a long life and the immortality obtained by heroic death.[10] Nevertheless, while the Iliadic hero strives incessantly for "unwilting glory" (Nagy 184), "Perfidy" seems to deprive the handsome warrior of this much-coveted prize. Cavafy's selective focus is on the sudden reversal of fortune that spares no one, not even the son of a goddess. The poet's brilliant connection between the two passages featuring Apollo's untrustworthiness exposes the perfidy of the god by unmasking the fallacious confidence his prophecy inspires in the young hero's mother.

The same notion of pernicious optimism is inextricably interwoven with Hektor's profile in Cavafy's "The Trojans." The poem begins with a simile that drastically reduces the conceptual distance between the poet and his audience, on the one hand, and the residents of ancient Troy as featured in Homer's *Iliad*, on the other: Εἶν' ἡ προσπάθειές μας, τῶν συφοριασμένων· / εἶν' ἡ προσπάθειές μας σὰν τῶν Τρώων ("Our efforts are those of men akin to calamity, / our efforts are like those of the Trojans"; Cavafy, *Canon* [2nd ed.] 60).[11] Cavafy's depiction of the Trojans as a people prone to catastrophe rests on the *Iliad*'s characterization of Hektor shortly before his fatal encounter with Achilles. Interestingly, Cavafy enjoins the burden of mortality exclusively on the Trojan prince, casting his opponent as the agent of fate, a fate Hektor's parents discern and mourn all too quickly on the walls of Troy. Hektor's death, however, is yet another rehearsal of Achilles's own demise, a new stage in the *Iliad*'s prodromal discourse on the death of the archetypal hero-warrior. Placed beyond the *Iliad*'s narrative domain, Achilles's death becomes the culmination of a series of heroic deaths. Our methodology of juxtaposing Cavafy's reception poem and its locus of inspiration worked well in this case, too, helping us fully unravel the analogy between "we" and "the Trojans" in the poem. The fall of Troy, foreshadowed by the death of Hektor, which Cavafy only implicitly terms as a fall, remains the inevitable conclusion to a series of futile attempts to bypass τῆς τύχης τὴν καταφορά ("the course of fortune") through ἀπόφασι καὶ τόλμη ("brief outbursts of resolution and boldness"): Ὅμως ἡ πτῶσις μας εἶναι βεβαία ("Nevertheless, our fall is certain"; 60).

It is noteworthy that Hektor predicts the fall of Troy with the same certainty in the *Iliad* (6.448–49), during his last encounter with his wife and son. Though determined to fight Achilles outside the walls of Troy, Hektor undergoes a remarkable change of heart when he realizes that he was misled into making this decision by Athena, Achilles's patron goddess. Like Patroklos before him, Hektor is lured into a labyrinth of false expectations created by a god-antagonist. Although he capitalizes on the image of Hektor paralyzed with fear at the prospect of dueling with Achilles, Cavafy remains silent about the background of this astonishingly unheroic behavior. As in the "Horses of Achilles" and "Perfidy," his main preoccupation in "The Trojans" is the tragedy of death, which he approaches with the authorial intention of adding his voice to a diachronic poetic tradition. Thus, Cavafy's Homer elucidated for the class a poetics between *kleos* and *nostos*, where even a hero's νεκρώσιμος νόστος ("funerary *nostos*"; Maronitis 105), in all its splendor, falls short of giving a definitive answer to the dilemma of human existence.

In conclusion, Cavafy's Iliadic poems constitute a magnificent teaching tool for Homer's *Iliad* by inviting instructor and students to examine the ancient epic through the lens of reception. As their fellow reader of the *Iliad*, Cavafy introduces classes to an immediate yet complex hermeneutics centered on the existential challenges with which Homeric heroes are confronted throughout the poem. Shaped by the all-encompassing question of the inevitability of death, his choice of Iliadic characters engages the categories of animal, human, and divine within the mortal/immortal binary. By providing audiences with so insightful a dissection of the *Iliad*'s thematic layers, Cavafy's metapoetic perspicacity can also steer any in-class analysis toward a reader-response-oriented reading. While facilitating a direct look at the Homeric poem itself, this reading emerges as a brilliant guide to the *Iliad* and especially its discourse on mortality as articulated through the narratives of Sarpedon's, Patroklos's, and Hektor's heroic deaths.

NOTES

1. I am grateful to the editors of this volume for their insightful comments and to Carolyn Catherine Holder, Andreana Klein, Elias Pappas, and Anastasis Phyrillas—the students of The World of Greek Heroes—for their hard work in our fall 2018 class and for their kind permission to publish here excerpts from their papers.

2. Students were assigned Robert Fagles's translations of the *Iliad* and the *Odyssey*: see Homer. In addition, the course's reading list consisted of selections from Greek lyric poetry and Herodotus (read from *Perseus Digital Library*) as well as Aeschylus's *Oresteia*; Sophocles's *Oedipus the King*, *Oedipus at Colonus*, and *Antigone*; Euripides's *Alcestis*, *Hippolytus*, and *Helen* (Lefkowitz and Romm); and Plato's *Euthyphro*, *The Apology of Socrates*, *Crito*, and *Phaedo* (Rowe).

3. Two translations of Cavafy were used: Cavafy, *Canon* (2nd ed.); and Cavafy, *Collected Poems* (Keeley and Sherrard, 1975). Some students had advanced proficiency in Modern Greek (assessed by 2012 ACTFL proficiency guidelines) and were able to work with the original Greek as well. I borrow the term *Iliadic* from Paschalis.

4. The course, with an enrollment of four (two classics majors and two religious studies majors), was conducted as a seminar; special emphasis was placed on student participation in class discussions, which, along with reflection papers (two were required on Homer, one on Cavafy's reception of the *Iliad*, and one on his reception of the *Odyssey*) and term papers, constituted the course's main venue for the analysis of Cavafy's poetry.

5. To be distinguished from the παραιβάτης (*paraivatis*; "chariot fighter" or "warrior who stood beside the chariot fighter"); see Liddell et al. 132. In the absence of Achilles, Patroklos assumes the role of chariot fighter, with Automedon, who is also the groom, as chariot driver.

6. All translations are my own.

7. The artist, as noted on the museum's website, "wanted to give the picture a foretaste of disaster"; "Automedon." See also Jeffreys, *Reframing Decadence* 83.

8. On the similarity and antagonism between Apollo and Achilles, see Nagy 289–97; Rabel 430–40.

9. [Κ]ακῶν ἕταρ', αἰὲν ἄπιστε ("[Y]ou comrade of evildoers, ever untrustworthy"). The reference to evil may imply Apollo's connection to Paris. In the *Iliad*, the adjective ἄπιστος ("untrustworthy") is also employed by Menelaos to characterize the sons of Priam (3.106) and by Hecuba to describe Achilles (24.207).

10. In his prose piece Τὸ Τέλος τοῦ Ὀδυσσέως ("To Telos tou Odysseos"; "The End of Odysseus"), Cavafy entertains what-if scenarios for the Iliadic heroes we encounter in book 11 of the *Odyssey*: ὁ Ἀχιλλεύς, ἐὰν ἡ Μοῖρα δὲν εἶχεν ἀποφασίσει τὸν θάνατόν του ἐν Τροίᾳ, θὰ ἦτο ὁ εὐδαιμονέστερος τῶν ἀνθρώπων ζῶν τιμώμενος καὶ φοβούμενος ὑπὸ πάντων ἐν Θεσσαλίᾳ ("Achilles, if Fate had not decided his death in Troy, would have been the happiest of men, honored and feared by all in Thessaly"; *Ta peza* 224).

11. As Paschalis notes, "In his typical manner, Cavafy has turned particular events (the misfortunes of the Trojans) into a reflection on the universal (the fate of humanity)" (169).

Cavafy's Decadent Aesthetic

Peter Jeffreys

Readers of Cavafy often assume that he was a Greek poet writing in his national language and that he followed the path of many other modern Greek poets in adapting the Greek poetic tradition to encompass prevailing European literary influences. This is not quite the case. In his instance, we have an autodidact who received an unconventional education mostly from tutors employed sporadically during his peripatetic upbringing. Cavafy was indebted primarily to his own immersion in the British and French literary traditions rather than to any school of Greek poetry per se. Indeed, the early critic Glafkos Alithersis was quick to point out that Cavafy belongs more to English than Greek literature (qtd. in Malanos 218), and Timos Malanos noted that in the 1890s and early 1900s the poet was fully in thrall to French literary currents (221). In this sense, he stands at a slight angle to the modern Greek poetic tradition. Not that he ignored it—indeed his decision to write in Greek rather than in English necessitated that he engage in a linguistic dialogue with contemporary Greek writers in order to craft a style, which, ultimately, he did by creating his own Greek idiom, one that contained elements from both the puristic (*katharevousa*) and the colloquial (*demotiki*). Teaching Cavafy in the context of a broader transnational literary tradition such as decadence invites students to appreciate more fully his current global popularity;[1] it contextualizes him in the interrelated aesthetic and decadent movements that remained central to his evolution as a poet. Both would leave profound and indelible marks on his work.

    I include a section on Cavafy in an upper-level undergraduate class, Readings in Decadent Literature, which I teach regularly at Suffolk University. Enrollment usually consists of English majors and minors, but the idea of decadence proves attractive to many nonmajors. Most students are unaware that there was a cultural movement that would later be defined as decadent, and many are fascinated by the fact that Edgar Allan Poe's notion of the perverse and Théophile Gautier's slogan "art for art's sake" proved to be grounds for nineteenth-century culture wars that continue to resonate in discussions about art and literature. The class begins with the classic authors that are considered integral to the decadent canon—Poe (short stories and essays), Charles Baudelaire (*The Flowers of Evil, Poems in Prose*, and related essays), Joris-Karl Huysmans (*Against Nature*), Oscar Wilde (*The Picture of Dorian Gray, Salome*, and various essays)—and then veers in the direction of writers who have a more fluid relationship to the decadent tradition: Evelyn Waugh (*Brideshead Revisited*), Christopher Isherwood (*The Berlin Stories*), and Tony Kushner (*Angels in America*). This lineup of male writers is broken up by the inclusion of texts by women writers (short stories drawn from Elaine Showalter's anthology *Daughters of Decadence*) as well as poetry from Michael Field (the pseudonym adopted by Katherine Bradley and Edith Cooper) and H.D. Many of these writers are gay or queer authors who shaped and constitute the gay canon of literature, in which Cavafy now occupies a central position.

In the course I dedicate four classes to teaching Cavafy and read him in tandem with writers to whom he is both indebted and who mirror his decadent aesthetic, particularly its pictorial manifestations. For this reason, I organize a visit and guided tour of the Fogg Art Museum at Harvard University to view its Pre-Raphaelite canvases and works by Gustave Moreau and James McNeill Whistler. This tour constitutes an additional class session, and students are required to write a reflection on their experience and make intertextual connections between the paintings and the authors read in class.[2] I schedule this gallery visit the weekend prior to the four Cavafy sessions and structure my lectures and assignments around this pivotal pictorial experience. Among the holdings of the museum are the following relevant canvases that serve as informing images for our discussion of Cavafy within an aesthetic and decadent context: Thomas Couture's *Romans of the Decadence*, Moreau's *The Apparition* and *Jacob and the Angel*, Dante Gabriel Rossetti's *The Blessed Damozel* and *A Sea-Spell*, George Frederic Watts's *The Creation of Eve*, Edward Burne-Jones's *Flamma Vestalis*, and Whistler's *Nocturne in Blue and Silver*, *Nocturne in Grey and Gold: Chelsea Snow*, and *Green and Violet: Mrs. Walter Sickert*.[3]

Prior to their visit, students are assigned a reading on Cavafy and British aestheticism[4] that establishes a biographical background and outlines the Anglo-Greek connections of the Cavafy family to the significant coterie of artists, models, collectors, and patrons that constituted the Anglo-Greek community in London. The canvases we view thus offer a way for students to interact visually with this world of painters who were personally associated with the Cavafy family and their network of London commercial connections. Having already studied Huysmans's notorious ekphrasis on Moreau's Salome paintings in *Against Nature*, the class reads Cavafy's ekphrastic early poem "Oedipus" (*Complete Poems* [Dalven] 196), which is based on Moreau's canvas *Oedipus and the Sphinx*. This allows students a glimpse into Cavafy's interest in painting and the genre of the ekphrastic salon review[5] to which such poems are indebted. The museum visit allows us to explore Moreau's jeweled aesthetic, Burne-Jones's and Rossetti's Pre-Raphaelite faces and aesthetic poses, and Whistler's avant-garde impressionism.[6]

Building on this pictorial experience, the class proceeds to read select poems and prose works in dialogue with other texts from Poe, Baudelaire, and Huysmans, with a view to establishing Cavafy's debt to these writers and their shared aesthetic and decadent tastes. Our reading of Cavafy opens with a discussion of "I've Brought to Art," which serves as a touchstone for the aesthetic of art for art's sake that persists throughout Cavafy's oeuvre. Here the aesthete speaker "submits to Art" by bringing "desires and sensations," blending impressions, and shaping "forms of Beauty." This simple yet profound lyric illustrates how Cavafy set out in his work to imperceptibly "complete life" by aligning it with art and establishes fixed aesthetic criteria for his poetic approach that students can clearly grasp (*Collected Poems* [Keeley and Sherrard, 1992] 116). From here we analyze some early poems that foreground artifice and the decadent rejection of nature. In "Desires" we are presented with the metaphor of a beautiful body in a magnificent mausoleum "with roses at the head and jasmine at the feet," an image both aesthetic and decadent where dead youths are transformed into works of art whose desires pass "without fulfilment; without having achieved / a night of sensual delight, or a moonlit morn" (*Complete Poems* [Dalven] 3). The poem resonates with the fixation of many aesthetes of the period on unfulfilled sexual desire. A parallel poem is the brief "Forgetfulness," where flowers are entombed, "shut up in a greenhouse" where they forget "what the sun's brightness is / and how the dewy breezes blow when they pass" (244).

Closely related are the analogous poems "Artificial Flowers" and "For the Shop." In the former, early poem, natural flowers are replaced by artificial ones made of glass and metal, "never-wilting, never-spoiling, never-aging forms." These "genuine gifts of a genuine Art" are superior to natural forms, illustrating one of the central tenets of decadent aestheticism—the repudiation of nature—which we encounter in Huysmans and Wilde (Cavafy, *Complete Poems* [Dalven] 210). This scenario will be recast in the later canonical poem "For the Shop," where flowers made of jewels are carefully wrapped in costly green silk: "Roses of rubies, lilies of pearl / violets of amethyst: beautiful according to his taste." These artificial flowers are left in the safe by the jeweler-aesthete and not shown to anyone, recasting the idea of something lovely kept hidden (and entombed): "beautiful according to his taste, / to his desire, his vision—not as he saw them in nature" (*Collected Poems* [Keeley and Sherrard, 1992] 47). Rounding off these poems is Cavafy's first published poem, "Builders" (*Complete Poems* [Dalven] 176), which interrogates the idea of progress, a favorite target of many decadent writers, for whom progress is an illusion to be debunked.

We conclude the class with the early unpublished prose narrative "A Night Out in Kalinderi" (*Selected Prose Works* 73–76), which recounts Cavafy's stay in Istanbul as a young adult. The narrator is a flaneur who observes the people of this suburb of the Ottoman capital; the story closes with a macabre folk song about death that gives the text an almost gothic twist. Students are asked to make connections to the Poe-Baudelaire trajectory of the "Man of the Crowd" urban stroller who delights in observing yet whose fascination is interlaced with ambivalence and pessimism about progress and modernity.

Our second class begins with Cavafy's translation and rewriting of Baudelaire's classic poem "Correspondences" (*Flowers* 19). The unpublished "Correspondence according to Baudelaire" (*Complete Poems* [Dalven] 217–18) documents Cavafy's direct engagement with the French poet, and students are asked to compare the original poem with Cavafy's translation and additions on the theme of synesthesia as they assess its relevance to Cavafy's own burgeoning decadent aesthetics. Continuing along this Baudelairean trajectory, we read the three unpublished prose poems—"Garments," "The Pleasure Brigade," and "The Ships"

(*Selected Prose Works* 80, 81, 84–85)—in juxtaposition with their French analogues.

"Garments" is a brief meditation on the prospect of living a full life and storing and preserving life's garments: "I will look upon these clothes and will remember the great celebration which by then will be completely finished" (*Selected Prose Works* 80). Echoes of Baudelaire's poem "Spleen (II)" (*Flowers* 147) are evident here, and Cavafy finished off the piece with the familiar image of entombed somnolence: "A few weary people will be sitting all alone, like myself, inside dark houses—others who are even more weary will have gone to sleep" (*Selected Prose Works* 80).

"The Pleasure Brigade" begins with the following admonition: "When the Pleasure Brigade passes by with music and banners, when the senses pulsate and tremble, those who keep their distance and refrain from taking up the good cause and its march toward the triumph of pleasure and passion are foolish and vulgar" (*Selected Prose Works* 81). Cavafy's recherché aesthetic parable climaxes with a funeral procession that betrays its debt to Baudelaire's dialectic between melancholy and the ideal in *The Flowers of Evil*: "the young Olympian gods will lift you onto their shoulders and will bury you in the Cemetery of the Ideal where the mausoleums of poetry glisten in whiteness" (81).

The third prose poem, "The Ships," is Cavafy's most ambitious and is highly indebted to Baudelaire's prose poems "The Port" and "The Invitation to the Voyage" (*Poems* 167, 79), with which students are required to make thematic and stylistic comparisons. It opens by evoking the whiteness of the blank page as the speaker begins an imaginative journey. The poem expands into an extended metaphor for the artistic experience, whereby ships function allegorically as vehicles that carry precious cargo (thoughts and ideas) that is vulnerable to confiscation by customs agents (censors), damage (hostile critics), or stagnation owing to the shallow harbors (bourgeois values). The piece concludes with a nod to Homer: "and we recall that these strophes were part of the song sung by the sailors—sailors as beautiful as the heroes of *The Iliad*—when the great ships were passing us by, those sublime ships that were heading—who knows where" (*Selected Prose Works* 85). From "The Ships" we transition to two of Cavafy's best-known canonical poems, "Ithaka" and "The City." "Ithaka" (*Collected Poems* [Keeley and Sherrard, 1992] 36) picks up where "The Ships" leaves off with its Paterian seizing of the sensuous moment along with its foregrounding of the allure of luxury goods—a vestige of decadent materiality and aesthetic connoisseurship. "The City," in turn, offers a unique take on flânerie whereby the city actually stalks the flaneur: "You won't find a new country, won't find another shore. / The city will always pursue you" (28).

The third class session focuses on the pictorial dimension of Cavafy's poetry with a rereading of "Oedipus" and Huysmans's presentation of Moreau's two Salome paintings in *Against Nature* (50–57). We then consider how Cavafy adapts the Salome legend in his poem "Salome" (*Complete Poems* [Dalven] 245), which is a very different retelling of the story—where the Herodian princess is spurned by a Greek sophist rather than by John the Baptist. We proceed to analyze the impressionist poem "Morning Sea" (*Collected Poems* [Keeley and Sherrard, 1992] 58) and read it in juxtaposition with Whistler's *Harmony in Blue and Silver: Trouville*, a canvas that was owned by Cavafy's uncle George and which he would have seen in London during the time he resided there.

Cavafy applied Burne-Jones's androgenous visual aesthetic to poems that fixate on beautiful faces ("Days of 1903," "Gray," "I've Looked So Much . . ."; *Collected Poems* [Keeley and Sherrard, 1992] 80, 75, 78). We conclude with "Following the Recipe of Ancient Greco-Syrian Magicians," which dabbles in the occult fantasy of casting a spell to bring back youth and the specter of a lost love (174).

In the final class, we spend a generous amount of time on what is perhaps Cavafy's most influential and complex poem, "Waiting for the Barbarians" (18–19), which we initially compare to Paul Verlaine's decadent sonnet "Langueur" (Desmarais and Baldick 117). Our reading frames the poem thematically within the obsession of adherents of decadence with the Roman Empire's archetypal decline and fall—the so-called Matter of Rome.[7] The decadent dilemma proposed by the final line of the poem—"And now, what's going to happen to us without barbarians? / They were, those people, a kind of solution" (*Collected Poems* [Keeley and Sherrard, 1992] 19)—presents students with an interpretative challenge: how to reconcile the implied idea of cultural annihilation with the lingering exhaustion of cultural ennui and oversophistication. A more contemporary resonance of the poem is found in Ross Douthat's discussion in the chapter aptly titled "Waiting for the Barbarians" in his book *The Decadent Society* (155–75), where he reads the poem within the context of the current state of American cultural stagnation. Douthat problematizes the text by asking what it would mean "for decadence to continue despite recent disturbances, and, indeed, to gradually become universal; that might be what sustainable decadence would mean. . . . And it's more likely than you think" (175). This current iteration of the decadent discourse of civilizational exhaustion allows students a relevant reading of the poem and provides for stimulating discussion on the political debate surrounding cultural decline that dominates the critique of progress, cosmopolitanism, and globalization.

We conclude our unit on Cavafy with his short story "In Broad Daylight" (*Selected Prose Works* 86–93), which may be read as a gothic narrative indebted to Poe for its tone and narrative details, specifically its reliance on the doppelgänger and the motif of a buried treasure. The story's protagonist panics after three encounters with a ghost who asks that he retrieve a treasure of gold and jewels buried near Pompey's Pillar in Alexandria. The treasure is never retrieved, and the protagonist (Alexander A.) suffers a mental breakdown in the presence of a friend (G. V.) who happens to be well-versed in the occult and magical lore. The tale is written in a rather mannered purist Greek and is likely Cavafy's stylistic attempt to capture something of Poe's arabesque aesthetic. Students are invited to compare this narrative with Poe's short stories "William Wilson" and

"The Gold-Bug" (*Selected Writing* 216–32, 321–48) and assess how successful Cavafy is in adapting Poe's psychological use of the supernatural to achieve his lauded unity of effect.

The discourse of decadence has evolved in extraordinary ways since the fin de siècle and now assumes a "multidisciplinary dimension, broadening the concept beyond the field of cultural history alone into such areas as philosophy, sociology, psychology, and more" (Desmarais and Weir, Introduction 1). For the course I reserve or use electronically accessible versions of a number of recommended texts. Among the most relevant to Cavafy are three rather recent reappraisals of decadence. Two are fine collections of essays: *Decadent Poetics: Literature and Form at the British Fin de Siècle* (Hall and Murray) and *Decadence and Literature* (Desmarais and Weir, *Decadence*). The third is Matthew Potolsky's *The Decadent Republic of Letters: Taste, Politics and Cosmopolitan Community from Baudelaire to Beardsley*, whose assessment of the movement is particularly compelling. As Potolsky writes, the key figures in the decadent movement "conceived of their work as part of a larger project: the construction of a decadent republic of letters . . . made up of knowing readers and the privileged texts they produce, admire, and circulate, its bonds fashioned through a shared taste for the perverse and a common sense of alienation . . ." (172). Cavafy may surely be counted among this decadent republic's most notorious citizens.

NOTES

1. As Potolsky argues, decadent writings "move within a recognizable network of canonical books, pervasive influences, recycled stories, erudite commentaries, and shared tastes" (5).

2. Poe, Baudelaire, Huysmans, and Wilde were all highly pictorial in their aesthetic and foreground paintings in many of the texts that are assigned in class.

3. Since most of these paintings are available for viewing online, this visit could be easily replicated and augmented with additional relevant art works and worked into the syllabus as an asynchronous class assignment.

4. I explore these connections in detail in Jeffreys, *Reframing Decadence* 1–25.

5. Baudelaire and Huysmans were art critics and penned numerous salon reviews that students are encouraged to explore.

6. Students will have already read chapters from Cantalupo (49–85, 103–21). Chapters from Dijkstra are assigned that offer a decadent framework for many of these paintings (25–63, 83–108).

7. Our class reading includes the section on the Matter of Rome in Desmarais and Baldick (40–85).

Conversing with Cavafy through Music

Vassilis Lambropoulos

Cavafy's presence has been felt everywhere in our culture—in poetry, fiction, theater, ballet, painting, video, installation art, advertising, journalism, political discourse, and beyond. No wonder Cavafy is one of the most translated poets of the twentieth century. What is little known is that he is also one of the poets whose work is most often set to music. To date more than ninety Greek composers and more than forty non-Greek ones have composed some four hundred pieces of music based on his poetry. Close to two-thirds of his canonical poems—around one hundred—have been used in some twenty-five song cycles and 140 individual songs. The most popular poems among composers have been "The God Abandons Antony" and "Voices," both set about twenty times, followed by "Ithaca," "Candles," "The City," and "The Windows." This wealth of material may be activated and refunctioned in a broad range of courses (as well as related outreach activities) exploring topics such as Cavafy's work, Greek language, linguistic or intermedial translation, classical reception, the lyric, modernism and its precursors, poetry and music, the lied or art song, and gender. Since this musico-poetic material may be used in several courses and collaborations, I first indicate its pedagogical potential by describing the outcome of a specific research and performance project in which I have been involved, and then I suggest works and approaches for further classroom and public uses.

The project I was involved with produced and toured an evening-long event, C. P. Cavafy in Music, which was neither a concert nor a lecture but something different: A Recital of Songs and Reflections, according to its subtitle. The mezzo-soprano Alexandra Gravas, the pianist Pantelis Polychronidis, and I, as speaker and commentator, invited audiences to reflect with us in musical, poetic, scholarly, and philosophical terms on the art of song in the milieu of Cavafy's composed poems. Our innovative concept was to combine a recital and a lecture, with two musicians and a scholar continuously on the stage, into a program of wide-ranging reflections that provided an immersive survey of artistic trends and aesthetic issues.

Researching, acquiring, organizing, and selecting the material was particularly challenging since we had to find out what kind of music had been written by which composer and in which language, organize our findings, and compare settings in order to create a well-rounded yet exciting playlist. We wrote to publishing houses, consulted composers, pored over scores, arranged our own scores, debated meanings, rehearsed, and so on. The process itself was important to the project: it was an exhilarating and exhausting commitment for three collaborators working under different conditions and living in different countries!

This team project involving a singer-performer, a pianist-coach, and a scholar-critic was tremendously rewarding and enjoyable for all of us. The opportunity to present it in 2012 and 2013 at eight universities (six in America, one in Mexico, and one in Chile) and four cultural centers (in Brussels, London, Delphi, and Athens) encouraged us to explore many of its dimensions. The project was further enriched by additional cooperation between me and Polychronidis, the pianist friend who is my other self (to echo Aristotle). Together we did additional collaborative lecturing, interviewing, and publishing in the United States, Greece, and Austria. Thus, what was originally supposed to be a song recital developed into a three-year project on the stage, in the lecture hall, and in the media.

Taking into account questions of repertoire, canonicity, language, poetics, performance, and interpretive history, we drew on three major approaches to the art song—that of French theory (Roland Barthes and Gilles Deleuze and Félix Guattari [*Thousand Plateaus* 347–50] on Robert Schumann), American musicology (from Edward Cone to Lawrence Kramer), and Brill's book series Word and Music Studies—while also consulting current discussions of the lyric in English literary studies.

Contemporary musicology in particular helped us define our approach to the musical settings of Cavafy's poetry: musicology has a rigorous interest in the art song as a composed reading, specifically, a dramatic and interpretive reading that appropriates or recreates a poem rather than a literal, illustrative reading that serves a poem by imitating it. A mimetic musical setting imitates and repeats a poem, especially if it is a great one. In the mimetic composition, the music is acting out feelings and events. On the other hand, a dramatic composed reading does not set a poem to music but performs it; it does not supplement the poem but stages it. It works at the same time to dismember and transform the poem. According to Lawrence Kramer, such a song constitutes

> a reading, in the critical as well as the performative sense of the term. . . . On this view, the relationship between poetry and music in song is implicitly agonic; the song is a "new creation" only because it is also a de-creation. The music appropriates the poem by contending with it, phonetically, dramatically, and semantically; and the contest is what most drives and shapes the song. (127)

In such songs, poetry and music exchange positions, defer or displace one another, or write or sound above or below one another. The contest between verses and music in the art song foregrounds (or reenacts) the rhythmic contest between words and meter in the poem.

Historically, versification involves the harmonization of regular meter (the fixed norm of the verse line) and variable rhythm (the fluid modulation of speech). To review their combinations, we drew on the musical aesthetics of Deleuze and Guattari, who distinguish between ritornello (refrain) and variation, *aion* (transcendental time) and *chronos* (living time), repetition and difference, stratification or fixing and destratification or unfixing, Johann Wolfgang von Goethe and

Heinrich von Kleist. Refrains are regularized and relatively fixed patterns that emerge out of continuums of modulation, zones of flux. They are patterns of meter that organize a milieu, that regulate and restrict the metamorphic variation by territorializing it. The refrain is rhythm that has become expressive and has been territorialized (Deleuze and Guattari, *Thousand Plateaus* 317). Territorialized time is pulsed, chronological time that orders, marking the temporality of a form in development. Also, there is *chronos* when time measures and scans the formation of a subject, a *Bildung*, a sentimental education.

However, repetition is not the return of the same. Thus, ritornellos are traversed by nonpulsed time, which is a continuum of intensities, a conjugation of diverse fluxes. The deterritorialization of repetition releases this nonpulsed time. To deterritorialize refrains means to decode rhythmic patterns, to detach them from their ordered context, to give them new functions by putting them into a mutative process of becoming other. Let us now look at the selections for our event, which are merely indicative of the tremendous possibilities available for such a compilation, whether in a presentation or a course.

The first song in our Recital of Songs and Reflections was by Dimitri Mitropoulos,[1] the first composer to grapple with Cavafy's verse, who later became world-famous as a conductor. In 1925 he composed a song cycle using fourteen Cavafy poems, which he was planning to call "Hedonistic poems" (Sakallieros 165). Given their erotic content, one might have expected an expressionistic style close to Richard Strauss or an impressionistic one close to Debussy. Instead, Mitropoulos chose austere forms that he set to a generally atonal idiom, and he called his songs inventions, alluding to the contrapuntal compositions that J. S. Bach wrote in 1723. In the song Έτσι πολύ ατένισα ("Etsi poly atenisa"; "I've Gazed So Much"), he deploys the insistent pedal on the pianist's left hand, clusters on the right hand, and a musical recitation similar to *sprechgesang* that is mostly syllabic (one note to one syllable), favoring the projection of speech.

The next song was a very different setting of an erotic poem. Those familiar with the irresistibly melodic style of Manos Hadjidakis's work might expect a powerful Greek dance. Instead, in his Μέρες του 1903 ("Meres tou 1903"; "Days of 1903"; from the eleven-song cycle Ο Μεγάλος Ἐρωτικός [*O Megalos Erotikos*; *The Great Erotic*], opus 30, for string chamber orchestra, two voices, and mixed choir, composed in 1972), Hadjidakis devises a march that immediately recalls Gustav Mahler's combination of yearning and sarcasm. The poem expresses desire with several repeats (of words, syntax, and meter), which the composer intensifies with his repeats of the word ἤθελα (*ithela*; "I longed").

In the encounter of poetry with music, the outcome may be anything from a fusion of the two to a contest between the two. We hear both elements at work in the following two songs by American composers. William Bolcom, in "The Next Table" (from the seven-song cycle *Old Addresses*, for baritone and piano, composed in 2001), asks for a tone that is leisurely, with a hint of amusement. Leisure is generated by the twenty-two-year old man sitting at the next table, while amusement is derived from the fleeting memory of an old erotic encounter like so many others. There is swing in the right hand in the introduction as the piano triggers the voice to speak.

Ron McFarland uses "Windows" in the first movement of String Quartet No. 2 (*Windows*), for quartet and soprano, a suite of four songs or movements set to poems by Cavafy (composed in 1985). In reading the original poem, the reader often does not know what will rhyme with what. The composer creates a restless song with strange harmonies and dissonances, repetitive motives, and echoes that go nowhere. He also dramatizes the speaking "I" by putting in the very first vocal phrase all twelve chromatic pitches.

The dialectic between repetition and variation is obvious in the next song, by Ned Rorem, "Waiting for the Barbarians," from the cycle *Another Sleep* (composed in 2000), which includes nineteen songs for medium voice and piano on texts by fourteen authors. Here the composer's challenge is to set to music a poem written in dialogic form. Rorem gave a different articulation to each voice (staccato-like to the question, legato to the answer), and throughout his composition he repeated the tone of each voice while also varying it. The result is a highly dramatic song that may be approached as a lied, like Schubert's "Erlkönig" ("Erlking"). It starts with the ominous threat of a single line in the piano's lower register and ends stranded up in the higher register, off-key.

To give our audience a sense of the variety of musical approaches to Cavafy, we presented two different settings of two poems. First, we presented two settings of the poem "Voices," both compositions named Φωνές ("Fones"; "Voices") and composed in 1963: one by Christian Boissel, consisting of French recitation, vocalises, and Greek recitation; and another by Antiochos Evangelatos, third in a cycle of four songs set to Cavafy poems, for voice and piano. We invited our listeners to judge for themselves which setting they found more faithful to the original or more inventive. In the next song, by Boissel, Τείχη ("Tichi"; "Walls"), from the suite *Adieu Alexandrie* (*Farewell Alexandria*), the singer is caught in the piano ostinato of a 5/8 Greek dance as if closed off by musical walls.

When we read that somebody set a poem, any poem, to music, we may think that they took all the verses and words and used them with great respect and care. Often that is not the case. Composers may show their admiration for a poem by appropriating it, remaking it entirely, making it their own. Indeed, composers have been taking great interpretive liberties with Cavafy. Here is another example. In the second song of his cycle *Shades of Love* (completed in 2003), the composer David Gompper does something that purists of poetry would consider sacrilege: He starts with the first four lines of "I Went," continues with most of "One Night," returns to the rest of "I Went," and concludes with the last three lines of "One Night." In effect, he has written his own poem by combining verses from two Cavafy poems. This is how he describes his approach to Cavafy:

> I chose poems that stressed three voices—future, present and past, and unified them by highlighting three recurring themes: light/night, senses

(vision, body, lips, etc.), and memory. The basic theme is derived from his last name, Kabaphes (B-flat, A, F, E-flat), and the inward motion inherent in the voice leading (perfect fifth, major third) reflects in many ways the thrust of his poetry and his life: itself inward looking, solitary, personal and still.[2]

Gompper's setting of the last poem, "Far Off," was followed by a different setting of the same poem. The original poem is so thoroughly and elaborately punctuated that it reads like a score, its typography functioning like musical notation. And here is another challenge for composers: since so many of Cavafy's poems, despite their nonlyrical feel, are already composed, what can a composer add to them? Perhaps that is why Calliope Tsoupaki, the next composer to consider here, wrote to us that she only tried "to render in music the words of the poem as faithfully and deeply as possible." Her Μακρυά ("Far Off"), composed in 1999, comes from *The Face of Love*, a song cycle of nine Greek songs for alto soprano and piano about unrequited love.

The next two songs belong to a distinct and well-known tradition of Greek music: songs that draw on poetry and that can be hummed, whistled, sung to a lover, or danced to. This tradition began at the end of the 1950s with Mikis Theodorakis's cycle Ἐπιτάφιος (*Epitaphios*; *Epitaph*), based on the long poem by the Greek poet Yiannis Ritsos, and continues to our time. This kind of song is willing to ignore nuance and sacrifice complexity in order to reach the largest possible audience. It has to be something simple and catchy that people can make their own in their daily lives. Although Η Πόλις ("I Polis"; "The City"; from Symphony No. 3, for soprano, choir, and orchestra, completed in 1981), by Theodorakis, is a song in this tradition, it was originally part of a large-scale composition. The third movement of the symphony is based on the Good Friday Greek Orthodox hymns "My Sweet Spring" and "Life in the Tomb." Between them come two lines from Cavafy's poem "The City." The song we presented is based on that movement but is a reworking that quotes from the movement rather than being an excerpt of it. In terms of lyrics, it adds the opening two lines of the poem and also reverses the order of the lines in the symphony.

Dimitris Papadimitriou placed Δυνάμωσις ("Dynamosis"; "Fortification") as the first song in his song cycle *C. P. Cavafy: An Alexandrian Writing on an Alexandrian*, which consists of eighteen songs and six instrumental compositions for orchestra, eight singers, and two actors. According to the composer, these songs are "direct descendants of the Modern Greek Art Song. Still, they easily offer themselves to the International Symphonic Tradition as a variation of the genuinely Greek classical song through the folkloric idiom's development into Modern Greek melodism" (125). This piece is another simple, uncomplicated setting that one can hum or whistle, and it attempts to turn the poem into a popular song. It represents a special approach to Cavafy in that it sacrifices both form and content to make the poems as accessible as possible.

A song makes different sense when it is part of a larger whole as opposed to a stand-alone piece. Indeed, Theodorakis's "The City" is in every respect two different pieces, one as part of a symphony and the other as a single song. In the 1970s Mimis Plessas wrote a stand-alone song, Κεριά ("Keria"; "Candles"), for Irene Papas, the famous Greek actress. It consists of a musical recitation accompanied by sparse piano arpeggios. It has a very limited vocal range and few pitches, in order to foreground the text, to let the verses be heard clearly and without adornment.

Kostas Rekleitis placed his Όταν διεγείρονται ("Otan diegirontai"; "When They Come Alive"), composed in 2011 for orchestra, soprano, and female choir, as the third song in part 2 of the ninety-minute cantata *Cavafy Cycle*, composed in 2012 for symphony orchestra, forty-member mixed choir, seven solo voices, and two narrators. The cycle consists of a total of twenty-seven Cavafy poems, eighteen in Greek and nine in English translations. "When They Come Alive" consists in a mostly syllabic setting that may remind us of the Mitropoulos song. It has a rhapsodic quality, evident in the use of two harps in the original orchestration, which fits well with its topic.

Our recital concluded with the world premiere of a composition by Demosthenes Stephanidis that was completed in 2012. The German title of the piece, "Kavafis im Gedanken," means "Cavafy in Our Mind," and in his poem "Ithaca," Cavafy advises, "Always keep Ithaca in your mind." In his composition, which is based on the poem, Stephanidis advises, Always keep Cavafy in your mind. The piano part consists of a theme and twelve variations that are played in reverse order. That is, the journey back to Ithaca starts with the twelfth variation and moves back toward the theme. Pianists must play the last variation and the theme but are free to omit other variations if they like. Singers have no score and therefore improvise as they go on their own metaphoric journey to Ithaca. They can do whatever they like with the poem in one language or in many (our singer used three). Thus, the composition does not really set the poem to music. The voice does not sing the poem and the piano does not accompany the voice. Instead, singer and pianist are asked to stage an occasion. As the composer put it to us, the work consists of twelve events where verses, variations, ideas, and bodies interact and clash on their way to Ithaca, the ultimate πόθος (*pothos*; "desire"). This means that every interpretation of the piece is different, and its every performance is a world premiere—a unique performance, like every occasion when poetry and music meet. This is the open-ended conclusion of our recital.

Instructors can draw on a great number of pieces based on Cavafy's poetry to create their own courses or enrich existing ones. The variety of musical settings is impressive in every respect. Greek, American, British, German, Dutch, Catalan, Chilean, and other composers have been inspired by Cavafy to use classical, popular, rock, and other musical idioms, drawing on a varied combination of instruments, ensembles, and voices to compose individual pieces, cycles, and large-scale works. The case of this poet is particularly intriguing because composers repeatedly claim that he is too prosaic, too nonlyrical, to be set to music, yet they keep turning to him for inspiration. Cavafy's poems resist and attract μελοποίησις (*melopiisis*; "setting to music"), prompting composers to express both their inability and their determination to set him to music. Below I list several representative examples that show what may happen when poetry and music meet.

Some works aspire to a large scale: John Tavener's *Tribute to Cavafy* (composed in 1999), for soprano, narrator, percussion, and chorus, whose seven movements set to music four Cavafy poems as well as the genealogy of Christ and lines by Saint Gregory Nazianzen; Leo Cottakis's *The Last Voyage* (composed in 2003), for soprano, mezzo, four instruments, and electronics in ten movements, a requiem on death and regeneration; Gerhard Stäbler's *Afternoon Sun* (premiered in 2006), a chamber opera for baritone, violin, viola, cello, and tape; and Constantine Koukias's *The Barbarians* (premiered in 2012), an hour-long chamber opera. Other composers incorporate Cavafy verses in larger compositions: Theodorakis uses two lines from "The City" in the third movement of his Symphony No. 3, as mentioned above, while Haris Vrontos includes two of Cavafy's Julian poems in his seven-part stage cantata *Julian the Apostate* (premiered in 2002).

Some composers make their own translations, like Lou Harrison in his *Scenes from Cavafy* (1980), a cantata for male voice, chorus, and gamelan orchestra, in three movements, which uses paraphrases of four poems made with Harrison's shaky Greek. Others take a Cavafy poem and rewrite it or write their own version, like Hans Werner Henze, who drafted his own "Cäsarion" for the cycle *Sechs Gesänge aus dem Arabischen* (*Six Songs from the Arabian*), for tenor and piano (premiered in 1999), and Leonard Cohen, who included "Alexandra Leaving" on his disk *Ten New Songs*.

Other composers set poems to music without words: Yorgos Sicilianos wrote *Six Imaginary Pieces*, opus 54 (composed in 1992–93), for large orchestra, based on Cavafy poems; Michael Finnissy included Cavafy in the piece "Seventeen Immortal Homosexual Poets," section 6 of his eleven-section, five-and-a-half-hour solo piano cycle *The History of Photography in Sound* (composed in 1995–2001); Luke Parkin included "Waiting for the Barbarians" in his thirty-one-piece solo piano cycle *Things I Didn't Know I Loved* (recorded in 2006), inspired by several twentieth-century poets; Gilbert Biberian wrote his piano trio *Ithaca* in eight movements (composed in 2011); and Vangelis composed the soundtrack for the 1996 movie *Cavafy*, by Yiannis Smaragdis.

The exploration of this ever-growing musical corpus opens up several terrains of study. First, in drawing on Cavafy to write music, composers must consider the multiple translations involved: from Greek to another language, from poem to lyrics, from language to music, from poetry to song, from silent reading to voice or instruments, from word to pure sound (in the case of wordless settings), and from one genre to another. Second, there are multiple interpretations involved: musical settings aspire to throw new light on a poem, to uncover hidden meanings, to update the message, to transform a poem into an entirely different artwork or register. Third, there are multiple performances involved, by one or many voices or instruments, through reductions of the score, through different interpretations of the music, through theatrical or technical means. Fourth, there are multiple personas involved in these songs: the writer Cavafy, the "I" in certain poems, the omniscient narrator in other poems, the composer, the singer, the pianist, the "I" in the text sung, and the "I" in the song as it is performed.

As translations, interpretations, performances, and personas multiply (Lambropoulos, "Violent Power"), it seems that the territory of Cavafy's canonical poetry loses its concrete form and well-defined boundaries, begins to expand and dissolve (Lambropoulos, "Pos o Kavafis"), and becomes more of a "milieu," to use terminology from Deleuze and Guattari—a "vibratory . . . block of space-time constituted by the periodic repetition of the component. . . . Every milieu is coded, a code being defined by periodic repetition; but each code is in a perpetual state of transcoding or transduction. . . . The milieus are open to chaos, which threatens them with exhaustion or intrusion. Rhythm is the milieu's answer to chaos" (*Thousand Plateaus* 313). The rhythm of Cavafy's poetry intensifies and reverberates. As we approach it through its musical elaborations, we can see (and hear) Cavafy's poetry as a coded milieu that vibrates with rhythm, instigating and hosting the becoming of compositions until they settle in territories: "There is a territory precisely when milieu components cease to be directional, becoming dimensional instead, when they cease to be functional to become expressive. There is a territory when the rhythm has expressiveness. What defines the territory is the emergence of matters of expression (qualities)" (315).

Each course incorporating this material may have a substantial research and creative component. Students may be invited to contribute in several ways: by identifying and locating additional musical settings; by soliciting, composing, or performing new ones; by adding media to existing settings; or by translating poems into various media. It would be great for instructors to present their work in an evening-long collective recital of musical approaches to Cavafy, like the one that my two collaborators and I put together and presented twelve times. Also, colleagues specializing in fields such as composition, music history, gender, classics, Near Eastern literature, English literature, and creative writing may be invited to give presentations that may later develop into collaborations, like the several ones I had with the pianist Polychronidis.

Readers may treat our Recital of Songs and Reflections as a pilot program for ideas that may contribute to part of a course, an entire course, a public event, or a larger project, perhaps by drawing on the scholarly and artistic approaches suggested in this essay. One does not need to be musically trained to participate, though obviously such training helps. I, for one, cannot even read music, yet I have great enthusiasm for this work, and I am always eager to learn from musicians. The other factor that should encourage scholars to explore Cavafy-inspired music is its availability online.[3] I have also found that composers are excited to respond to requests and share with others their love for this particular poet. When it comes to Cavafy, once you start looking for works in dialogue with his, invariably you end up with more material than you ever imagined. Before you know it, you discover that the course of Western music over the last one hundred years may be traced through settings composed under the spell of the Alexandrian.

NOTES

This essay is dedicated to Pantelis Polychronidis.

1. On Mitropoulos's written exchanges with Cavafy and the composition of these inventions, see Sakallieros 147–85.

2. Personal communication with the author.

3. See *C. P. Cavafy Music Resource Guide*. The list of over one hundred bibliographic entries aspires to contain every composition (though not every version) performed in a public setting or recording in a printed score, whether the composition sets poetry to music or was inspired by Cavafy's life and work.

Digital Cavafy: Teaching Poetry through Connective Media

Foteini Dimirouli

Poetry's popularity among younger generations has seen a meteoric rise. Smartphones, social media, and a culture of connectivity are largely to be credited with this development. Access to verse online and sharing practices across platforms have led to the emergence of new poet-celebrities,[1] while also boosting printed poetry book sales.[2] Teaching is now called to ride the wave of poetry's revived relevance, by taking heed of the transfiguration of audiences' engagement with literature on digital media. This essay proposes that the integration of new media into teaching frameworks can assist educators to promote textual analysis, critical thinking skills, and creativity within the classroom; besides, it can prompt students to be more mindful of the nature of their digital activity outside the classroom. Research findings suggest that the extensive use of digital tools by young people has positive effects on their lives—including their sense of self, relationships, and overall well-being—that are strongly correlated with active engagement rather than passive observation (or lurking online; Roberts and David). With this correlation in mind, this essay presents ways to teach poetry that meet the university classroom's educational objectives, such as the refinement of close reading skills, while also fostering creative and aware forms of media intensity among students.

A culture of scrolling and ephemeral fandom, interactive shortcuts, and diversified visual content dominates literary afterlives on the Internet, especially those of revered authors who have long been at the epicenter of university education. C. P. Cavafy is such an author, and this essay offers suggestions about how to balance traditional and innovative methods in the teaching of his poetry at a time when the poet's popularity has accelerated in networked settings of sociality and connectivity. The assignments are also meant to encourage students to reflect critically upon the transformative social effects of their own digital literacy. The focus is placed on the platforms most popular in 2021, when this class was taught. However, the pedagogical logic of the assignments can be adapted to different digital environments that are bound to appear in the future.

Digital outlets, both social media and journalism platforms, have appropriated and reproduced Cavafy's authority in ways that derive from his preexisting reputation in print but produce it anew through tropes and modes that are specific to them. On the one hand, digital media have prompted a democratic and user-led evolution of Cavafy's popularity by freeing it from the authoritative voices of traditional literary criticism; on the other hand, these media have immersed the poet in a culture of connectivity that is predicated on a series of tools that shape interactions—a culture of tagging and sharing that informs practices of self-fashioning and expression of preference. The visibility of Cavafy's work today is subject to methods of online evaluation; by receiving generous star ratings, likes, and shares, the poet's importance is consolidated by the powerful currencies of online ranking and evidenced by *Google Trends* analytics.[3]

At a time of ebbs and flows, when literary stars rise and fall within a matter of hours, and what is trending today may disappear tomorrow,[4] the constancy of Cavafy's fame, and its steady enhancement, is a reminder of how firmly rooted his appeal is not only in times present but also in times past. The Alexandrian poet's survival is testament to the attention his poetry still commands, but also to a large audience's investment in a familiar authorial signature and corpus of work. His celebration by authors and critics around the globe, prior to the coming of age of the digital domain as a major player in the cultural field, secured the poet's future; the analogue Cavafy is integral to, and continuous with, the digital Cavafy that populates the web, where his popularity and symbolic value are at once affirmed and refashioned.

The poet's centrality in university curricula predates the digital era and constitutes one of the markers of Cavafy's long-standing canonicity. Accordingly, traditional teaching methods that rest on a combination of close reading, formal analysis, and sociohistorical contextualization in lectures, seminars, or tutorials have long dominated pedagogical approaches to Cavafy's work. In certain cases, these methods continue to exclude the live environments in which the poet garners his popular following today—be it *Instagram* posts and reels that transform Cavafy's verse into an opportunity for self-expression, *YouTube* videos inspired by Cavafy's life and work that reach millions of users, journalism that crafts allegories through his verse to illuminate current affairs, or even *Facebook* content leveraging colorful interpretations of his verse for comedic effect. This exclusion leads educators to bypass the opportunities that the poet's digital domestication introduces for the diversification of rehearsed practices in the teaching of Cavafy, or indeed of any comparable poet. If the departure from traditional textual forms is seen to endanger a meaningful and critical engagement with poetry—and this is a real concern for teachers of literature—then this essay argues not for losing sight of those goals but rather for better accomplishing them by leaning on the modalities of reading that online culture favors. This approach, which is additive rather than substitutive, promises to open up Cavafy's work to students in new and exciting ways that are participatory rather than passive, peer-engagement-centered rather than entirely instructor-led.

A teaching plan that tackles Cavafy's web presence addresses a crucial fact about higher education today: the research activity of those participating in university instruction and learning is inundated with digital media. It is as unlikely that a student would compose a term paper without consulting online sources as it is that a teacher would prepare for a class without also doing so. The integration of digital environments in the classroom therefore corresponds to the realities that permeate reading, researching, and engaging with literature today. Urging students, as it were, to take their phones out and use them as a tool in a lesson plan rather than to put them away is not to endorse gimmickry; rather, it is to acknowledge the networked environments that frame our social and cultural interactions and also to be selective about the ways in which digital tools infiltrate education at a time when "attention is in short supply" in the classroom (Turkle 213).

This essay puts forward a twofold proposal of, first, following a research-directed method premised on the collection and critical analysis of social media content related to Cavafy and, second, implementing a creative method through collaborative projects. In appealing to Cavafy's digital presence and its incorporation into university education, I revisit a question that is at the heart of Cavafy's new media presence: does Cavafy's "popular reception," which is now "pluriform, multi-layered and anarchic," constitute an "overappropriation" or an "undermining" of the poet's work (Papanikolaou and Papargyriou, "Cavafy Pop" 184)? This inquiry is central to a teaching plan that aspires not just to stay current or to highlight Cavafy's co-options as rich and diverse but also to foster a better understanding of the digital category as a historical successor of print media—and this is particularly pertinent to a generation of users who have naturalized "the ecosystem of connective media" (Van Dijck 21)—and therefore as game-changing for students' encounters with poetry.

For these reasons, I propose that students' final creative projects—including, for example, the creation of digital content that is shared on a dedicated class handle—are best prefaced by inviting students to survey digital content pertinent to Cavafy and to investigate what purpose it serves and how it relates to the user interface, interactivity model, and branding aesthetics of each platform. Students are directed toward the appropriation of Cavafy on *X* (previously *Twitter*) and *Instagram* as well as in journalism published online. On these platforms, social media users often rework Cavafy's poetry into captions, images, or quotations, whose effectiveness typically hinges on three key features: fragmentation, allusion or allegory use, and visual or multimodal interpretations. By placing emphasis on these features, the instructor can guide students to revisit Cavafy's poetry and to remain conversant with themes that go beyond Cavafy, such as the refashioning of literature at a time when audiences derive information online, the associative function of literary figures at crucial political and historical turning points, as well as the relationship between user-generated content and the business model of each platform.

One of the main platform sources of this classroom activity, *X*, has nourished a culture of short written forms inserted in a live stream of instant opinion. Here, poetic fragments are in vogue, lending themselves to the character limit that nudges users toward expressive minimalism. Cavafy's terse and recognizable poetic style lends itself to this world of condensed content, in which the retweet function embeds extracted parts of his poetry in new contexts—which can be political, social, personal, or quotidian. An all-time favorite, Cavafy's "Waiting for the Barbarians," with its "jaundiced appreciation of cultural torpor and political stagnation" (Mendelsohn, "Waiting"), has been a much-favored source of one-liners for posts commenting on twists of fate, disappointments, and failed ideals. Lines from Cavafy's erotic poetry, previously pushed to the margins by conservative criticism, have been appropriated by gay pride activists in tweets advocating social and political empowerment. Parts of his poems about stifling isolation and enclosure have come to resonate with the COVID-19 era of lockdowns and the anxieties it introduced.

On X, Cavafy's fragments fuse the voice of the poet with that of the user. This merging between authoritative content and appropriative agenda creates possibilities for a fresh outlook on poetry but also hosts tensions. In 2013 Cavafy's fragments became contested ground when an initiative meant to celebrate the acquisition of the Cavafy archive by the Onassis Foundation placed single lines extracted from the poet's verse on Athenian public transportation. The standalone lines sparked semiotic confusion, exacerbated by the disparity between Cavafy's idiom and the modern meaning of particular terms, such as βία (*via*, meaning "haste" when Cavafy was writing in 1928 but "violence" in today's vernacular), and by the misinterpretation of this disparity in the fraught social climate of the ongoing financial recession. A media frenzy of criticism against the foundation was triggered, on the grounds of the distortion and mutilation of the poetic whole for the sake of a nefarious political agenda. These reactions emphasized the need to safeguard Cavafy's authenticity from erroneous usage, but in actuality, Dimitris Plantzos argues, they queried what it means for "a familiar and usable cultural commodity" to "develop in rather unfamiliar ways" ("Perverse Fragments" 198).

Audiences' attachments to an author's monumentalized status can precipitate conflicts—between meaning proper and the meanings that emerge from readings or misreadings, between academic study in the ivory tower and the open engagement of a nonspecialist audience. This incident in Cavafy's afterlife illustrates the ways in which stakeholders of literary authenticity wage social wars in the name of high culture or, in this case, in the name of Cavafy. This is not a marginal incident that is merely relevant to the Greek Alexandrian poet. Rather, the challenge that platform-generated short forms of expression pose to conventional literary study brings forward continuities that are both contested and urgent and that revolve around a key question: what does a correct reading look like, who is entitled to it, and who is to deem it as such? As a first step toward acknowledging transformations in the reception of the poet's work before critically assessing what they may signify, instructors can invite students to employ the technogrammar of trending topics (prefaced by the # sign) and tagging (prefaced by the @ sign) to identify instances of Cavafy's co-option in fragmented form online and to share them in an online class group before the seminar.

Turning to fragments in the classroom is not an invitation to leave the poetic whole behind. Rather, it is a prompt to assess the dynamics that emerge from platforms that premise creativity on brevity and that therefore create new norms in the interpretation of literature. After collecting and sharing fragments online, students are expected to relate their chosen fragment to the original poem from which it was extracted and to share a commentary about the dialogue between the fragment and the poem. The exercise could take place either during contact time or after some preparation, and the instructor could act as facilitator of a student-led discussion on Cavafy's poetic nuances and the ways in which they complicate the stability of meaning. "The recent tendency to use phrases from Cavafy's poetry in (multi)media texts and contexts," Dimitris Papanikolaou and Eleni Papargyriou argue, "might have attracted the ire of traditional aficionados of poetry, yet it has also had the effect of showing, in practice, how Cavafian poetry functions at the level of the phrase, often creating sentences that work as good punchlines, that thrive on double entendres, interesting rhythmical effects or their dramatic irony." Ultimately, the "tendency to create phrases that work within and against the integrity of the poem, within and against dominant ideologies, within a deep historical context and actively disengaging from it" ("Cavafy Pop" 186) offers a powerful tool for guiding students toward deliberating the value of great originals, recognizing hegemonic ideology, and thinking about poetry's shifting affective impact. Peer-to-peer presentations based on comparisons between Cavafy's fragments drawn by students from social media and their corresponding original poems can steer students to consider the formal elements and content of poems through the prism of their adaptations. They can also prompt them to reckon with the process of poetry's transition from print to digital. What might be gained or lost in this process, and why does it matter? The meeting point between the fragment and the poem is bound to create frictions, but if the fragment can be best understood through knowledge of the poetic whole, then the poetic whole can also be approached in different ways through the imaginative reframing of its extracted parts.

The last part of this exercise calls on students to do some self-led research and select another poem by Cavafy that shares common ground with the poem already examined. In this way students are encouraged to research Cavafy's poetry beyond the handful of poems that microblogging relies on. Cavafy's work abounds in thematic cohesion: historical scenarios of rise and fall, ironic twists, cruel machinations of fate, or misguided human actions as well as themes of homoerotic love, memory, tenderness, and the fleeting nature of time. As the American poet James Merrill once put it, "[A]lways, in Cavafy, what one poem withholds the other explains" ("Marvelous Poet" 12), and this complementarity is useful in guiding students away from the dominance of Cavafy's "microcanon"—namely, the showcasing of his life's work through a small number of poems.

The fragmentation of Cavafy's verse online frequently overlaps with its allusive or allegorical uses. Fragments are often enlisted for the critique of political and social realities, providing opportunities for the instructor to engage students with questions that are latent in all teaching of literature: How is poetry relevant? What is it about the human condition that the study of poetry gives us access to, and how can it help us decipher the world around us? The meeting between the registers of poetry and news coverage is well suited to the exploration of such open-ended questions. By eschewing the conventions of reasoned argumentation or provision of evidence, poetry has the "capacity to offer emotional responses to current events in a different language than that of the daily news" (Houston 239).

In 2015 Daniel Mendelsohn noticed Cavafy's verse becoming a conduit to discussions about the Greek financial crisis, with *Twitter* users "trading screen shots of poems on Twitter, wondering which of [Cavafy's] disappointed lyrics about this or that failed regime is the 'right' poem for the current Greek crisis" ("Right Poem"). But apart from *Twitter* users, journalists across the globe also turned to Cavafy's poetic dealings with social inertia and imminent catastrophe to allegorize the country's predicament. A 2015 *Financial Times* article found in Cavafy's poem "Waiting for the Barbarians" themes of decline and decay that highlighted universal concerns arising from the Greek crisis; in the journalist's words, "the pervasive foreboding of doom depicted in Cavafy's masterwork should serve in 2016 as a wake-up call for Europe" (Barber). Similarly invoking the poet to criticize the handling of the Greek crisis, in 2013 the former editor in chief of the German newspaper *Die Zeit*, Theo Sommer, quoted the poem "In a Large Greek Colony, 200 BC" in its entirety, along with its German translation, urging readers to benefit from its message about external intervention and reform. The more prominent Cavafy's usage was on an international scale, the more dependable became the poet's authority as the guiding voice of the crisis; those navigating major online news sources and seeking information about, or analyses of, the crisis, encountered Cavafy's poetry, already trending on *Twitter*, inserted in daily news releases.

And yet, it is not solely culturally minded journalists that we should credit with augmenting Cavafy's metaphoric, allegorical, and allusive currency but also digital media themselves, which have breathed new life into the long-standing yet often overlooked encounters between news writing and poetry. As early as 1961, Maurice Bowra hailed Cavafy as a "prophet" who offered early "answers" to the questions dominating the 1960s Cold War landscape. He "is a poet of our age," Bowra asserts in an article published by *The New York Times*, for in his work's "dramatic contents" readers will be able to see with clarity "a sharp analysis of their own troubles" ("Answers"). Bowra's siding with the eye-opening potential of Cavafy's verse brings to mind Mendelsohn's similar observation in 2013, in an article for *The New Yorker*, about Cavafy's aptness for helping readers arrive at a better understanding of politics ("Waiting"). Both Bowra and Mendelsohn rehearse notions of Cavafy's timeless, timely, or relevant poetic diction, perhaps the most overused terms in cultural journalism inviting attention to Cavafy's overarching literary merits. However, the traction of an opinion piece such as Bowra's published in the pages of a daily newspaper in the sixties is limited compared to a piece available to subscribers to the online platform of *The New Yorker*. There, Mendelsohn's essay can be accessed as a stand-alone entry, separate from the rest of the issue, and shared as a link by users whose preferences have a cascading impact on those of affiliated users (their social media friends or followers), who are bound to share common educational backgrounds, cultural interests, and even political inclinations—a phenomenon aided by algorithmic grouping.

Similarly, Merrill's little-known "After Cavafy" (*Collected Poems* 853), written in 1994 in emulation of Cavafy's "Waiting for the Barbarians" to critique the dehumanizing forces of capitalism and globalization, was restricted to a significantly smaller audience compared to that of the extensively reshared "Waiting for Boris," a parody modeled on the same poem by Cavafy, written by Kevin Higgins, and published online in 2019 as a scathing review of the UK prime minister Boris Johnson's conservative policies. Such comparisons can serve to demonstrate to students how digital platforms and social media, rather than eradicating print culture, can expand the reach of journalism that was previously confined to print. Assigning selected journalism that draws on Cavafy's poetry as reading material can demonstrate to students the ways in which his poetic language has been deployed through time in attempts to seek solace or wisdom in literature. Additionally, journalism is subjected to editorial control, rather than being anonymously user-generated, and therefore lends itself to more comprehensive context analysis, especially in terms of the political and historical landscapes that Cavafy's work has inhabited through time.

To lose sight of these evolving landscapes amounts to an inability to comprehend fully key aspects of Cavafy's ascension in the ranks of literary acclaim. In this sense, providing students with subtexts to Cavafy's work or familiarizing them with the long history and tradition of Cavafian scholarship—be it biographical information, a historical navigation of twentieth-century Alexandria, an overview of Cavafy's intricate publishing practice, or a variety of critical perspectives on the poet—is also necessary and can be effectively accomplished by following a modified version of the flipped classroom. According to this pedagogical approach, lecture material and core information is offered to students as homework in digital forms, freeing up contact time for discussion, presentation, and assignments guided by the instructor. I propose here some preparation for assignments—through the collection of tweets and composition of commentaries—but the core questions surrounding them are intended for development during contact time. Essential information about Cavafy could be imparted in class but also provided outside contact time through short video lectures created by the instructor to communicate condensed critical insights about Cavafy or in the form of a playlist of relevant talks and lectures compiled by the instructor, in addition to selected reading material drawn from online or print sources. The emphasis on knowledge acquisition prior to contact time through material that can be paused, replayed, and saved for future reference enables students to pace learning to their own needs and to participate actively in the discussion during contact time.

Whereas *X* is a platform that lends itself to poetic fragmentation, and online journalism to extensive, allusive uses of poetry, *Instagram*, which is becoming popular among a wider demographic compared to *X*, is based on image sharing.

On *X*, too, poetic fragments accompany images as captions or are disseminated in image form, but *Instagram*'s entire business model is predicated on younger generations' preference for image sharing over microblogging and expression of opinion. Within *Instagram*'s universe, Cavafy is enmeshed in visual culture, and the mystique around his persona, which rests on the interplay between his poetry and life, is further fetishized and cultivated. The variety of Cavafy-themed content does not lend itself to summary: it ranges from new artwork or photographically captured street art and graffiti of the poet's image or his verse in slogan form to digitally manipulated stills of quotidian life alongside newly published Cavafy volumes and images of Cavafy's single-sheet manuscripts now widely accessible through the Onassis Foundation, which has digitized the poet's archive. *Instagram*'s editing tools, such as filters and frames, allow users to enhance such images in keeping with their personal aesthetics. Variable in their impact, these digital events converge on one point: Cavafy's verse, his portrait, and the materiality of his archive have a new life on *Instagram*, where sociality intersects with visual innovation and experimentation.

Prompting students to explore this environment and compile a database of Cavafy-themed images is meant as preparation for a classroom debate that will embark from any of the selected images to broach matters of broader relevance. What is compelling about the fusion of poetics and image—compelling enough to generate approval in the form of followers? How does the creativity surrounding Cavafy's portraits create a popularized image of the poet, and to what extent do contributions to this space interrogate the highbrow? Is a doctored image of Cavafy, however pop, vocal of users' willingness or intentions to ingratiate themselves in the selective realm of the so-called cultured? Does visual content relate to the act of reading—for example, does an image of a teacup diligently placed next to a volume of Cavafy's collected poems necessarily suggest textual engagement? Or can the symbols of literary engagement become mere simulacrum as Instagrammers aestheticize an action for the sole purpose of self-fashioning? And if they do come to supplant the actual reading of poetry, from where do these images derive their symbolic meaning and authority? Does visual grammar and online curation lose all contact with the substance of the writing itself? Is poetry's popularity meaningfully enhanced when a user's interest in Cavafy prompts the algorithm to feed the user additional poetic content or connect the user to other poetry enthusiasts? These questions are ideally placed to bind together students' previous textual and digital engagement with Cavafy's work (along with the reflection on the idioms of online connectivity that these engagements instigate), preparing them for the final stage of implementation of creative projects on the poet.

A first in-class group project could include editing the Cavafy *Wikipedia* page. This assignment relies on the platform's open editing policy and requires students to fill in omissions or gaps in existing information about the poet by writing new entries. These entries may be assessed both within the educational institution and outside it: *Wikipedia*, arguably the most democratic of platforms, invites users to create content that is then algorithmically checked for accuracy, citations, and footnotes (Van Dijck 140). Following the publication of research that compared *Wiki* with the *Encyclopedia Britannica*, *Wiki* was hailed as equally accurate as an encyclopedic source and thus revolutionary in its inclusive and participatory content creation paradigm (Giles). This student-led *Wikipedia* editing project resembles other collaborative class assignments but also grants students the liberty to choose an angle that they would like to disseminate to the public while adhering to an ethos of knowledge production that is "moored in the neutrality principle" (Van Dijck 133). A more expansive iteration of this project would call on students to organize a university-based *Wikipedia* editathon and invite users from all over the world to contribute collectively to the updating of Cavafy pages.

A second group project could entail the creation of a classroom handle on *X* or *Instagram* where students can share their own free associations and personal readings of Cavafy through a combination of words and images. The educational potential of this project depends on previous classroom sessions, such as the ones proposed in this essay, designed to integrate awareness of the medium and close engagement with Cavafy's poetic corpus. Young people, Helen Gregory argues, "were busy creating and disseminating digital art and forging online identities while many of us (teachers, scholars and poets) were still debating what digital literacy *meant*" (122); this discrepancy, however, need not be a roadblock to creativity. Rather, by utilizing the traditional tools of literary analysis, teachers are still able to harness the digital skills of students while steering them toward a critical evaluation of the multimodal environments in which poetry becomes remodeled, therefore guiding them to more sophisticated forms of digital expression. By bridging mainstream literacies with student agency to create digital content, and by encouraging students to survey digital rewritings of the original poetic text, this strategy nurtures reflective learners adept at remediating poetry in novel ways and teachers who step back to assume the role of facilitator.

The assignments proposed rely on students' familiarity with digital platforms and the revival of poetic forms through online sociality and digital interactions. To consider how digital tools enhance an author's talismanic status is also to appreciate the major impact that these tools have had on the shaping of literary traditions, new and old. If the process of canon formation has been scrutinized for its Eurocentric, male, and exclusionary articulation—and there is an argument to be made that Cavafy's stature and reputation were reliant on culturally dominant forces for their constitution—what does it mean for the poet to now be free from the control of the so-called great voices of literary modernism and sustained through practices that are geo-expansive, inclusive, and varied in their co-option of poetic discourse and that may be utilized to forge new identities and collective trajectories? Coursework that traces Cavafy's digital afterlives not only allows students to place the poet in history and approach his work through the lenses of current interpretations but also assists them in reflecting upon the realities of their own digital immersion, as users of environments that foster unprecedented identity plasticity and grant them the power to discover and understand poetry on their own terms.

NOTES

This research essay was supported by the Onassis Foundation (scholarship ID: R ZR 002-1/2021-2022).

1. The most preeminent example of this trend is Rupi Kaur, an India-born Canadian poet who started her career as a performing poet in 2009, eventually gaining millions of followers on *Instagram*. Her printed poetry collections were a commercial success, and she is today hailed as one of the most prominent Instapoets of her generation.

2. Poetry sales nearly doubled from 2012 to 2018. See Crown; Ferguson.

3. *Google Trends* analytics help to quantify interest taken in an author, both within a country and on a worldwide scale. In Greece, *Google* searches about Cavafy from 2015 to 2020 surpassed those about Dionysios Solomos (the country's national poet, who lent his verse to the national anthem) and George Seferis (a Nobel Prize winner). The discrepancy is even larger when the search terms are applied on a worldwide scale, indicating the extent to which Cavafy reigns relative to other prominent Greek figures as well as his centrality to the opening of modern Greek literature to the global digital arena.

4. Consider the transience of Instapoets and Twitlit, phenomena that rely on the convergence of popular platforms and the use of their microsyntax (hashtags and tagging) by aspiring authors and poets looking to acquire popularity; Van Dijck 77.

Digital Intertextuality and the Cavafy Archive

Takis Kayalis

The last decade or so has witnessed a remarkable rise of interest in the uses of primary material from writers' archives for postsecondary teaching and learning. This trend came as a response to "overarching pedagogical and disciplinary developments," including "a focus on active learning and the rise of book history" (Dean 40). It was made possible by the proliferation of digital literary archives, which allow effortless access to an unprecedented wealth of manuscripts and other documents to students and instructors alike. Surely the opportunity to glimpse into a favorite writer's private life and to look through rare documents, which until recently were exclusively reserved for advanced researchers, would please many students. But beyond this initial sense of excitement, any serious attempt to use digital archives in teaching is bound to face strong methodological challenges. What and how can we teach from a writer's archive once we rule out the use of these rare or unique documents as mere illustrations and without risking a retreat to antiquated pedagogies? Can archival material be meaningfully employed in undergraduate classrooms, or should its use be limited to the training of research students? How can we handle such material without conjuring old and familiar ghosts, like trivial biographism and the cult of personality? These questions are highly relevant today, as witnessed by the spread of related articles and other academic initiatives, including research projects (e.g., "Creating"), workshops and conferences,[1] and edited volumes (e.g., Cotton and Sharron; Greer and Grobman; Hackel and Moulton; Mitchell et al.; Smith and Stead) that try to address the theoretical and pedagogical challenges of teaching with literary archives.

Far from facilitating a nostalgic return to a pretheoretical state of affairs or retreating to obsolete pedagogical directions, like antiquarianism or biographical fetishism, the archival turn in contemporary literary studies seeks to open the domain of reading to a variety of new experiences and to strengthen our students' interpretative and creative skills. Exposure to archival documents may also help students gain a clearer understanding of important issues, such as the radical difference of past literary cultures from our own, the significance of the texts' materiality, the impact of historical changes in cultural technologies, and the role of networks and other cultural processes in arbitrations of literary value. Bringing students into immediate contact with "the context in which literature is created, circulated and consumed" (Dean 43), literary archives may foster a subtler understanding of the ecologies and economies of writing than any other instructional resource we may possess.

Despite the groundbreaking conceptual shift "from archive-as-source to archive-as-subject" (Stoler 44), manuscripts continue to be valorized as the most important contents of literary archives, largely for "the insights they give into the act of creation" (Sutton 295). Manuscripts, however, demonstrate little on their own and certainly do not teach by themselves. They are material traces for the weaving of stories, whose telling depends on the interpretative skills and inventive powers of the reader. In fact, even the work of professional archivists "does not consist solely of categorization and rule-enforcement, but also of the creation of pathways and narratives within the archive" (Kelly 173). Putting such stories together in the literature classroom is in itself a compelling experience and should always be our purpose, lest we end up teaching trivialities such as the aesthetics of authors' handwriting or shorthand styles (which have become engulfed in nostalgia because of the disappearance of handwriting from our culture; Kaplan 108). Similarly, it would not make much pedagogical sense to present an author's earlier or discarded drafts as stages in the creative journey toward completion and perfection. Such texts may be treated more profitably in the classroom as alternative versions, which allow us to trace options and possibilities that were ultimately supplanted by the finality of the printed format. Employed in this manner, as a source for fascinating specimens that defamiliarize teaching practices and enhance critical thinking, literary archives may create a valid opportunity for active learning and may also balance the somewhat trite experiential and affective response to certain literary texts, among which C. P. Cavafy's poems stand as a prime example.

The Onassis Foundation's launching, in March 2019, of the Cavafy Archive's digital collection ("Digital Collection"), which made freely available online the full contents of the poet's archive (including the Sengopoulos archive), was a major event not only for modern Greek literature as a field of study and research but also for everyone around the world who was interested in the poet's work.[2] Surely, digital archives "make documents more freely and readily accessible online." This is partly because of their architecture, which permits, "via hyperlinks, a document to straddle multiple categories or genres at once. The hyperlink also makes possible a multitude of new connections to other files and documents, forging pathways between objects that might otherwise not exist" (Kelly 173). Open access policies, like the one adopted by the Onassis Foundation, also set an archive free from the regulation of "the sentinels who control access to its interior" and who limit its users to "a coterie of privileged insiders" (Voss and Werner i). Yet for a digital literary archive to become fully open, it must also dare to imagine and project itself as "a conceptual space whose boundaries are forever changing" (i), one that, much like its contents, is "characterised by unfinishing, openness, and the contingency of meaning" (Kelly 173). To go beyond its use as an adjunct to scholarly research, a multifunctional digital archive needs to become the locus for new, imaginative, and plural pursuits, which will open it to new user communities and provoke fresh responses. This calls for the development of experimental and innovative educational initiatives aiming to take the digital archive out of the box and set it in cultural motion, preventing its fossilization into a digital silo. Apart from their beneficial impact on the digital archive's openness and usability, such initiatives may also contribute to the renewal of methods, practices, and goals of literary education toward active learning and fruitful interdisciplinary or cross-arts hybridization. In this spirit, under the auspices of the Onassis Foundation, I collaborated with Christos Dermentzopoulos, a professor of art anthropology and my colleague at the University of Ioannina, to develop and codirect an experimental extracurricular workshop program titled Cavafy Goes to College, which was first implemented at the university immediately after the online launch of the Cavafy Archive's digital collection, during the week of 18–22 March 2019. This program was jointly sponsored by the university's Modern Greek Literature Lab (in the Department of Philology) and the History of Art Lab (in the School of Fine Arts) and was attended by forty advanced undergraduate and graduate students. The program offered two workshops, which were run in parallel three-hour sessions every day for five days.

The aim of our workshops was to search for new theoretical insights and fresh responses to Cavafy by means of experimental and artistic methods. We attempted to set poetic texts in dialogue with unlikely artifacts from the digital archive and to transfer techniques and procedures from one artistic medium to another by means of digital tools and applications. We conceptualized the digital archive as a juncture in which the historical time of Cavafy's poetry becomes conflated with consecutive stages in the archive's processing, organization, and annotation of its contents to form a multilevel temporality, which in turn intersects with the timing of random visits, of systematic study, and of educational inquiry. We also approached the archive as a cultural edifice whose probing may facilitate renegotiations of important concepts, including the multiple facets of authorship, the archival collection as memory and as memorial to the self, its silences and exclusions, literary history as a volatile amalgam of microhistories, and conflicting narratives based on archival stories. Our workshops were provisional and heuristic; they invited students to work creatively, to pose extravagant questions to the Cavafy archive, and to freely experiment with its contents. In other words, we took seriously Aleida Assmann's conceptualization of the archive as "the storehouse for cultural relics. These are not unmediated; they have only lost their immediate addressees; they are de-contextualized and disconnected from their former frames which had authorized them or determined their meaning. As part of the archive, they are open to new contexts and lend themselves to new interpretations" (99).

One fifteen-hour workshop, favored mostly by literature students, included sessions on parody, imitation, and the phenomenal appropriation of verses and phrases by Cavafy in the public sphere, experimental uses of techniques from creative writing and rewriting, theoretical discussions, and the aesthetic and interpretative value of earlier and current musical adaptations of Cavafy's poems. The other workshop focused mainly on questions of visual culture and on interrogations of the archive from the viewpoints of photography, cinema studies, painting, and applied arts. The questions investigated here included cinematography as a source of poetic forms, the fluid and evolving nature of archives (literary and visual), their historicity, and their openness to artistic reworkings. In both workshops, topics were first introduced through seminar presentations and then probed through hands-on assignments and creative work by students. This was the first time the Cavafy archive's digital collection was a focal point in a Greek university and was employed as a paradigm for interdisciplinary and cross-arts queries and creative pursuits by means of academic workshops. In 1979, Philip Larkin famously discerned the "magical value" from the "meaningful value" of archival manuscripts, claiming that the former "is the older and more universal," whereas the latter "is of much more recent origin, and is the degree to which a manuscript helps to enlarge our knowledge and understanding of a writer's life and work" (99). Cavafy Goes to College may be described as a deliberate attempt to unearth, interrogate, and restore the "magical value" of the Cavafy archive in a contemporary academic setting and through current concepts, methods, and cultural idioms.

The success of any pedagogical experiment depends not only on its theoretical premises but equally on the carefully curated selection of documents and other material to be used. For this purpose, we needed to locate less-known material, free from strong canonical meanings, that could startle our student participants and inspire them to experiment. As Bianca Falbo suggests about the pedagogical value of sending students to the archives, when "confronted with the odd or unusual artifact, students must reconsider what they think they know about the work of reading and writing, about their experience making sense of a text" (34). I present here some of the documents from the archive that we selected and used in workshop sessions, in the hope that readers may be tempted to use similar specimens in their own teaching.

Texts

In the workshop sessions we made good use of Cavafy's own documents, including his handwritten rosters listing the recipients of his handmade poetry collections and the collections themselves. These provided an excellent opportunity to revisit Cavafy's fascinating publishing strategies but also broader questions of disclosure and concealment as manifested in the fluid domain of modern literary dissemination practices. But some of the archival documents most favored by our students were not written by the poet. One such example is "Keravnos," a long parody published on 7 January 1925 in the Athens newspaper *Politeia* (*The Republic*) by a twenty-one-year-old student of law who would later be recognized as the preeminent statesman of the Greek Left: Ilias Iliou. Iliou signed as K. Vafis and thinly masked his poem as a reaction of Cavafy's adversaries to the poet's tribute by the journal *Nea Techni* (*New Art*), which had come out just a few weeks earlier.[3] The poem is a political satire in which Iliou imitates Cavafy's style to scorch the then interior minister Georgios Kondylis, whom Iliou compares to Mussolini. ("Keravnos," meaning "thunderbolt," was a nickname attributed to Kondylis for his swift military actions.) This text is one of the earliest examples of Cavafy's writing style being used as a vehicle for topical political satire and may serve as an introduction to the legacy of the social and political appropriation of the poet's work in the public sphere, a legacy that is still strong in Greek culture. This text may also set us thinking about the significance Cavafy himself attributed to this publication and the reasons that made him keep it in his archive, in contrast to other parodies of his poems.

Another interesting poetic imitation is a handwritten manuscript entitled "Byzantine Philosopher in 396 A.D. to His Students" and signed with the poet's name.[4] Both the poem and the signature try to imitate Cavafy's handwriting. This is a text we know nothing about. And precisely for this reason, it can be used to stimulate speculation about its author and time of writing, the purpose it was meant to serve, the reason Cavafy or a later curator kept it in the archive, and other similar questions.

For a different viewpoint and as a token that reveals how early Cavafy gained international recognition, instructors may introduce students to *Spider Boy: A Scenario for a Moving Picture*, a 1928 book by the American novelist and photographer Carl Van Vechten. Students can be given time to conjecture how two copies of this early Hollywood satire may have found their way into the poet's library ("Cavafy Library") before the instructor reveals that Van Vechten used as an epigraph two lines from Cavafy's "The City," in George Valassopoulo's translation, probably quoted from E. M. Forster's *Pharos and Pharillon* (92–93).

Memorabilia

Like most personal archives, Cavafy's also contains a variety of textual and visual mementos that are not directly related to his art but may afford a subtler understanding of the quirkiness of the poet's life and times and are often touching in themselves, as unfamiliar or mysterious specimens of a bygone era. A case in point is a humoristic ink drawing showing a pharaoh sitting on a throne with an attendant kneeling in worship in front of him.[5] The piece bears a handwritten title, "An Ancient Sculpture Recently Discovered at Alexandria," whereas the note under the sketch reads "The scribe Fri-a implores King Ka-fafi to eat bread at his house." The handwriting on this well-drawn sketch is similar to that of the poet's brother and early translator, John Cavafy, and the specimen, which could be a handmade invitation to dinner, clearly converses with late-nineteenth-century Egyptomania.

Another interesting example from the same category is furnished by six printed menu cards from 1895 and 1896.[6] On rectos, menu dishes are listed in lavish handwriting, while versos bear the signatures of the poet and some of his closest male friends in his youth. These were probably occasions Cavafy enjoyed and whose memory he was eager to preserve.

A memento that is bound to attract students' interest is Cavafy's forty-five-page handwritten gambling ledger, which he ran from January 1887 to April 1893—that is, from his twenty-fourth to his thirtieth year.[7] In this handmade notebook,

Cavafy jotted down the amounts he gambled and those he won or lost per game and per month (and the total per year), revealing his full-blown impulse to archive as well as a type of sociability that sharply contrasts with the solitary pose projected in his verse and by his carefully staged portraits.

Music

A lot of time in our workshop sessions was devoted to cross-arts collaborations, through presentations and hands-on assignments. In this context, we unearthed and examined the handwritten musical scores of compositions for voice and piano based on three of Cavafy's poems ("Come Back," "To Pleasure," and "In Stock"), which were sent to the poet from Paris by the composer Georges Poniridy, probably in 1931.[8] An anonymous note in the journal *Alexandrini Techni* (*Alexandrian Art*) that year, probably written by Cavafy, mentions these unpublished compositions as "extraordinarily fine" ("Simeiomata" 302). Born in Istanbul, Poniridy studied and worked in France for many years before settling in Athens. He was a regular recipient of Cavafy's handmade poetry collections. But what really triggered our collective imagination was finding out that this violinist and composer was a close friend of George Seferis's during this poet's years as a student in Paris, and that Seferis was fond of taking long walks through the night with his musical friend discussing art, poetry, and, perhaps, Cavafy.[9]

By contrasting Poniridy's scores with the printed edition of Dimitri Mitropoulos's "Ten Inventions," also saved in the archive, and taking into account the famous composer and conductor's letters to Cavafy, we attempted to probe the early musical reception of Cavafy's poems and to discuss broader issues, including musical adaptations of poetic texts as acts of criticism, interpretation, and canonization.[10]

Cavafy's poetry is particularly well suited to this line of inquiry since there are other musical scores freely available online (e.g., those by Giannis Papaioannou for "The Funeral of Sarpedon" and by Theodoros Antoniou for "Morning Sea," at the Aristotle University of Thessaloniki Digital Archive)[11] and also many recorded adaptations that can easily be located and listened to online, by artists ranging from John Tavener (whose unpublished rendering of "In the Month of Athyr" features Paul McCartney as narrator) to the cyperpunk band Pornostroika Dadaifi ("'In the Month of Athyr'"; "Pornostroika Dadaifi").[12] Needless to say, students who can read or perform music may assume active roles in such collective cultural ventures, which may well lead to new trial settings of Cavafy's poems to music.

Photographs

A parallel line of cross-arts collaborations, presentations, and hands-on assignments in our workshop sessions focused on the study of photographs from the archive. These included the poet's seated portrait by Racine, which was probably taken around 1930 and which reveals aspects of the poet's private space, including the hanging tapestry that Kostis Kourelis has related to British aestheticism and James McNeill Whistler.[13] We also examined Apostolos Ververis's photographs of the room in which Cavafy died, at the Greek Hospital of Alexandria, and of the interior of the poet's flat, probably taken after his death.[14] These images triggered discussion of the alternative narratives we can read in photographic depictions of spaces, depending on the information we possess about their time frames and circumstances. Students were also encouraged to use photographs along with manuscripts and other texts from the archive to create their own visual and multimedia rematerializations of Cavafy's works and to experience the archive as a space for artistic revision and experimentation. A second iteration of Cavafy Goes to College, at Ionian University, in Corfu, in May 2020, was sadly postponed at the last minute because of the COVID-19 crisis. But some themes and ideas from our workshops resurfaced during the International Cavafy Summer School 2023 (on Cavafy across the disciplines and the arts), which was led by Peter Jeffreys and me ("Open Call").

As a response to the long quarantine, which in Greece rendered face-to-face teaching obsolete, the Cavafy Archive of the Onassis Foundation developed a new initiative, aiming to introduce students, instructors, and other interested individuals to the archive's wealth of resources and to provide stimuli for various educational uses through an online course, which has launched on the foundation's digital educational platform *Classroom Onassis Education*. Entitled Unlocking the Cavafy Archive: People—Images—Stories, this course consists of ten open online lessons (in Greek), which require a total of about thirty hours of independent study. This project was directed by me; instructional material was written by Angeliki Mousiou, Sofia Zissimopoulou, Alexandros Katsigiannis, and the project's director; an abundance of teaching aids and fully structured lesson plans were developed by Marili Douzina and Evangelia Moula; and Marianna Christofi served as project coordinator. The course includes the following lessons:

> Lesson 1: Using Literary Archives: From Research to Education
> Lesson 2: The Personal Archive of Cavafy: Reflections of the Poet's Life
> Lesson 3: Writing the Self: Diary Notes, Autobiographical and Biographical Texts in the Cavafy Archive
> Lesson 4: Visual Representations of Cavafy: Photographic and Painted Portraits in the Archive
> Lesson 5: The Poet's Personal Library: An Overview
> Lesson 6: The Poet at Work: Literary Manuscripts, Drafts, and Notes in the Archive
> Lesson 7: From Manuscript to Print: Cavafy's Publishing Tactics
> Lesson 8: Cavafy and the Greek Community in Egypt
> Lesson 9: The Poet among His Contemporaries: Intellectual and Artistic Networks in Greece
> Lesson 10: Cavafy in the English-Speaking World

This syllabus clearly reflects the main goals of educational and general presentations about literary archives, as recently proposed by Heather Dean: "Specifically, archivists can highlight how literary archives are a window into, firstly, the creative process, secondly, literary networks and intellectual circles, and thirdly, biographical details (which can reveal the ways in which an author's personal and professional life may—or may not—interplay with their writing)" (43). Each lesson is self-contained and may be consulted on its own, depending on users' interests and needs. As a complete educational tool kit that traverses the entire scope of the Cavafy archive and features original material developed for online learning, this resource is, to my knowledge, unique among digital literary archives internationally. It may be used equally well in the context of experimental and nonformal teaching practices and for the advancement of scholarly research. As such, the Cavafy archive's series of open online lessons highlights the dynamic and multifaceted potential of teaching with archives in the pedagogical landscape of the digital era.

NOTES

1. For example, the conference Reclamation and Representation (University of Exeter, 2010) and session 291 of the conference Manuscripts Still Matter (UK Literary Heritage Working Group, British Library, 2012). See also "Teaching"; Collins.

2. For further information on the digital collection, see Angeliki Mousiou's contribution to this volume.

3. See the *Onassis Cavafy Archive*: Cavafy, C. P. Fonds, sub-fonds SF02, series S02, file F25, sub-file SF007, item 0055 (https://doi.org/10.26256/ca-sf02-s02-f25-sf007-0055). Iliou's parody has often been misattributed to the poet and critic Nikos Karvounis. For its correct attribution, see Moschos 261–62; Nikolakopoulos 12–13.

4. See the *Onassis Cavafy Archive*: Cavafy, C. P. Fonds, sub-fonds SF01, series S01, file F01, sub-file SF001, item 0173 (https://doi.org/10.26256/ca-sf01-s01-f01-sf001-0173).

5. See the *Onassis Cavafy Archive*: Cavafy, C. P. Fonds, sub-fonds SF01, series S04, file F16, item 0019 (https://doi.org/10.26256/ca-sf01-s04-f16-0019).

6. See the *Onassis Cavafy Archive*: Cavafy, C. P. Fonds, sub-fonds SF02, series S02, file F25, sub-file SF006, item 0003 (https://doi.org/10.26256/ca-sf02-s02-f25-sf006-0003).

7. See the *Onassis Cavafy Archive*: Cavafy, C. P. Fonds, sub-fonds SF02, series S02, file F25, sub-file SF004, item 0001 (https://doi.org/10.26256/ca-sf02-s02-f25-sf004-0001).

8. See the *Onassis Cavafy Archive*: Cavafy, C. P. Fonds, sub-fonds SF01, series S04, file F15, item 0002 (https://doi.org/10.26256/ca-sf01-s04-f15-0002), item 0003 (https://doi.org/10.26256/ca-sf01-s04-f15-0003), and item 0004 (https://doi.org/10.26256/ca-sf01-s04-f15-0004).

9. On Poniridy, see Beaton, *George Seferis*.

10. See the *Onassis Cavafy Archive*: Cavafy, C. P. Fonds, sub-fonds SF01, series S04, file F15, item 0008 (https://doi.org/10.26256/ca-sf01-s04-f15-0008) and sub-fonds

SF02, series S01, sub-series SS01, file F18, sub-file SF003, item 0100 (https://doi.org/10.26256/ca-sf02-s01-ss01-f18-sf003-0100).

11. See digital.lib.auth.gr/record/132570 and digital.lib.auth.gr/record/132637.

12. For more examples, see *C. P. Cavafy Music Resource Guide*.

13. See the *Onassis Cavafy Archive*: Cavafy, C. P. Fonds, sub-fonds SF02, series S03, file F26, sub-file SF001, item 0013 (https://doi.org/10.26256/ca-sf02-s03-f26-sf001-0013).

14. See, for example, the *Onassis Cavafy Archive*: Singopoulo, Alekos / Singopoulo, Rica Fonds, series S01, file F04, item 0009 (https://doi.org/10.26256/sing-s01-f04-0009) and item 0002 (https://doi.org/10.26256/sing-s01-f04-0002).

CLASSROOM CONTEXTS

Teaching Cavafy to the *Instagram* Generation

Gregory Jusdanis

People around the world celebrate Constantine P. Cavafy for being ahead of his time, for predicting by a century many of our cultural, political, and social anxieties. They salute him for anticipating our ecumenical world of racial and ethnic mixing, ever-expanding diasporas, and more-permeable national borders. And they hail him for having had the courage to write frank verses about homoerotic desire when contemporaries, like E. M. Forster, sometimes skirted around the subject in their published work. In these panegyrics, however, critics fail to note that Cavafy also prophesied the dire situation of literature today. In their attempt to demonstrate the poet's prominence as a global writer, to reveal the so-called real Cavafy—as political, historical, gay, sexual, diasporic, transnational, and Greek—they overlook the fact that he was also a poet writing about poetry. Cavafy thought systematically about the place of poetry in a society not well disposed toward it, dramatizing in a way the ideological tensions between the uselessness of art and the utilitarian impulses of daily life. This aspect of his work can serve as a tool and a platform in the classroom. I argue that Cavafy's reflection on the relevance of poetry in his time and his use of the aesthetic to draw attention to life's insignificant moments can help students grasp the importance of noninstrumental, seemingly wasteful activities like reading poetry, watching the sun set, or telling a story.

I have in mind two classes I teach at Ohio State University that deal with literature and that at the same time constitute part of the general curriculum. That is to say, they satisfy literature requirements undergraduates have to fulfill for their majors. The first class, Introduction to Classical Literature, is a large lecture course of about two hundred first-year students. I assume that most students take the class because of the literature requirement. This is also true for my second example, a third-year course that focuses on modern Greek literature. Although our Modern Greek majors register for this particular course, most of the students in the class take it as a general education course. My challenge in both classes is to make literature relevant, especially to these students who might sign up for only one or two literature courses during their undergraduate career. I address this issue by arguing for the importance of literature as an activity valid on its own terms. Cavafy's poetry helps me demonstrate the efficacy of placing value on something for its own sake.

The position of poetry in the world constitutes one of the dominant themes of Cavafy's oeuvre, along with the themes of homosexuality, history, and transnationalism. As I have shown elsewhere, about one-third of the poems directly deal with poetry, and another third address secondary topics like artistic inspiration, artists, reading, and interpreting (Jusdanis, *Poetics*). Yet this significant theme continues to be overlooked by Cavafian criticism, as though Cavafy had not thought or written about poetry so profoundly. This attention he showed to all matters concerning poetic art is another sign of how Cavafy was ahead of his time. Of course, he was also a product of his own age. He grew out of a particular European literary tradition. Thus, his preoccupation with the creation and consumption of art can be seen as a manifestation of his poetic inheritance. Romantic artists, for instance, anxious about the loss of traditional patronage and reticent about finding new readers, feared that there would be no place for art in the new, industrializing society. Friedrich Hölderlin mourned that his age had lost the capacity for poetry. "Why be a poet in dead time?" he asked in his celebrated elegy "Bread and Wine" (91). The social transformations he saw taking place around him rendered the poetic art vulnerable and poets irrelevant.

Writers coming after Hölderlin, who witnessed the mass consumption of culture, began to bemoan the pressures placed on them by publishers seeking efficiency and profit. In *Lost Illusions*, Honoré de Balzac's great 1842 novel about the commercialization of life, Lucien Chardon, the young, idealistic poet arriving in flashy Paris, discovers that literature has been reduced to the cruel laws of commerce. Editors and publishers pursue the latest fad instead of aiming for poetic value. One day Lucien overhears a conversation between an editor and a publisher: "Will you take five hundred copies? If you do, I will let you have them at five francs and give you fourteen to the dozen" (203). Lucien feels disillusioned to see poems handled like fish. Similarly, the protagonist and novelist Edwin Reardon, in George Gissing's 1891 novel *New Grub Street*, grows disenchanted by writing fiction that has become a "trade" (36). Frustrated that he can't succeed in this new environment, he turns cynical about the new manufacturing techniques producing commodities rather than inspired novels (137).

A contemporary of Gissing's, Cavafy himself experienced similar challenges in Alexandria. While people celebrate his home city for its cosmopolitanism, they ignore the fact that it was a commercial center with a tiny minority of people who cared about art. Cavafy regularly complained about the lack of a market for poetry, and he grew disillusioned by his discovery that he could not make a living through his art. After all, he himself financed the printing and dissemination of his work, his personal study serving as a mini–publishing house, while the offices of the magazine Αλεξανδρινή Τέχνη (*Alexandrini Techni*; *Alexandrian Art*), one floor below his apartment, served as a distribution and marketing center for his poetry.

Although Cavafy faced unfavorable conditions for his poetry, neither in his life nor in his poems did he voice Gissing's despondency. Nowhere did Cavafy say that the time for poetry was over, that poetry was inconsequential, or that it had been overtaken by technological changes in printing. While in some of his poems, such as "Of the Shop" (*K. P. Kavafis: Ta piimata* 243),[1] he portrays alienated artists who keep their prized creations at home while selling baubles to the public, he did not exhibit this aestheticist attitude in real life. On the contrary, he advocated on behalf of his own work with all the means available, converting his self-promotion into a daily concern. At the same time, he displayed in his verses a willful defiance against the world's indifference to poetry and a spirited defense of the continued importance of art in life. As a modernist, Cavafy had an unshakable belief in art as an autotelic and autonomous entity, his work constituting a decades-long exploration of the meaning and power of poetry.

As a private individual, Cavafy invested most of his energy in writing poetry and becoming a global poet. After his early successes, the approbation he received during his 1901 trip to Athens from Gregorios Xenopoulos and other leading critics, and the growing number of supporters in Alexandria and Greece, he devoted himself unreservedly to his poetic mission at the expense of love and all intimate relationships. Cavafy is a rare example of a person who risked everything in his quest for fame and won magnificently. So it is not surprising that for both literary and personal reasons he wrote about poetry's triumphs and its vital presence in life. For a person who addressed the subject of civilizational lassitude in "Waiting for the Barbarians" (*K. P. Kavafis: Ta piimata* 200–01) and personal despondency in "The City" (216–17), he never once wavered in his belief that poetry was just as important as history. And indeed, he showed poetry waging war for survival if not cultural supremacy.

Of course, it is difficult to deal with these issues in class when I only have two weeks devoted to Cavafy. The challenge becomes almost insurmountable when we read historical poems that require much explanation of their references and prior reading. Even though I can't necessarily introduce these historical poems every time I teach Cavafy, I can delve into Cavafy's own life as a means of gaining access to his aesthetic pursuits. This is the advantage of a biography, which is much more graspable than poetics. By making reference to Cavafy's life and his absolute devotion to his craft, I can help students understand those poems that might seem abstract or inaccessibly historical. Biography, then, contrary to what I learned as a graduate student, can have its pedagogical usefulness.

In the third-year course on Greek literature, I assign one week to Cavafy's poetry with the intent of introducing students to a representative sample of his oeuvre. Depending on the interests of the students, we may read poems concerning poetic themes. Three major poems dramatize these poetic battles. In "Darius" (*K. P. Kavafis: Ta piimata* 308), an imaginary poet, Phernazis, of the royal court of Mithridates, the Persian king of Pontus in the Hellenistic period, is preparing an epic poem about the king's ancestor, Darius, the illustrious Persian emperor. Phernazis hopes that with this work he will silence his critics and curry favor with Mithridates. But at that moment, news arrives that the Romans have crossed the frontier and will conquer the kingdom. Dazed by what he hears, he wonders if the new rulers would be interested in poems about a Persian emperor. Understandably, he fears that they will install their own poets in the court. But in all his confusion and horror, he still can't abandon his task. "The poetic idea comes and goes" (308). Poetry refuses to subject itself to politics, tentatively affirming its autonomy even when it senses that its autonomy will be squelched.

While the position of poetry might be equivocal in Phernazis's situation, it is affirmed with vehemence in "Young Men of Sidon (A.D. 400)" (*K. P. Kavafis: Ta piimata* 305). Set in late antiquity, the poem answers Phernazis's doubts about the validity of the poet's efforts with a vigorous celebration of poetry. In the city of Sidon, perfumed young men are listening to an actor declaiming Hellenistic verses. But when the actor delivers the lines allegedly written by the tragedian Aeschylus as his epitaph (in which Aeschylus seeks to be remembered for his valor in the Persian Wars rather than for his tragedies), a young man, "fanatical for letters," jumps to his feet and chastises the great tragedian. Taking Aeschylus to task for undervaluing his illustrious works—such as *Agamemnon*, *Prometheus*, and *Seven against Thebes*—so as to boast that he too fought among the "herd" against the Persian foe, the youth encourages the great tragedian always to elevate poetry over history (305).

And this is the message the young man would deliver to the imaginary sophist in "Simeon," a poem set in 454 CE, five years before the death of Simeon Stylites, who had been living on a pillar for thirty-five years as an act of Christian devotion. But the theme of the poem is less Simeon's extraordinary sacrifice than how this act seems to trivialize poetry. In the speaker's eyes, the absoluteness of faith and self-abnegation of Simeon render poetry into a trifling preoccupation. Finding himself in an unpoetic time, an age when people prefer creed to art, the speaker can't continue his conversation with Mevis about the best poet in Syria. Not having "the spiritual calm" of the Christians, he "shook completely and suffered" below Simeon's column (*K. P. Kavafis: Ta piimata* 548). Confronted by the magnitude of history and the certainty of religion, the speaker loses faith in poetry's promise to entertain, represent, and make strange. But in the end, he can't really dismiss poetry either and returns to the conversation, saying that Lamon is the foremost poet in Syria. The conclusion, like that in "Darius," is ambiguous.

In its ambivalence, this text and so many of Cavafy's other poems can open up discussions in class not only about the relevance of art today but also more widely about the place of nonproductive experiences in an age that glamorizes goal-directed thinking and reduces all value to economic ends. These conversations are essential now, especially when literature, in particular, and the humanities, in general, find themselves in a crisis. Preoccupied with their non-humanities majors and worried about their financial futures, students in my classes do not always see the point in taking courses about literature, let alone Greek poetry.[2] So how does one teach Cavafy for the general curriculum in a time of dwindling resources, enrollments, and interest in literature? I would recommend adopting a Cavafian posture. Against those who shout about literature's inutility, we should argue that the relevance of art lies exactly in its uselessness. Cavafy's unbending belief in his own poetry when those around him mocked its merit and his indefatigable defense of the poetic act against historical forces could serve as a teaching strategy in today's classroom.

Let me offer an example by way of another poet. Before I begin teaching the *Iliad* in Introduction to Classical Literature, I introduce Mary Oliver's "The Summer Day." Oliver, an Ohio State alumna, best-selling author, and former poet laureate, addresses in her poem a tiny grasshopper, a subject seemingly unbefitting of Homer. But in another respect, her text is very Homeric, piercing through the confusion of the world to focus on one small creature, as Homer does when he shines a light on human encounters, like the last conversation between Hector and his wife, Andromache. The speaker in Oliver's poem has spent the whole day ambling through a field, until she takes a break and lets a grasshopper jump on her hand and then observes the creature moving "her jaws back and forth" and gazing "around with her enormous and complicated eyes." After a while, foretelling perhaps that she would soon be censured by the working world for wasting her time, for being "idle," for just strolling "through the fields," she asks defiantly: "Tell me, what else should I have done?" (316). This simple question overturns the running assumptions of our ostensibly productive lives and certainly resonates with students, who are rushing to the next seminar, worrying about their exams, and anxious about their future employment. Before dismissing that particular class on Oliver, I suggest that students try to spot something beautiful outside, something that they linger over before turning to their next task. The best things in life, I add, are useless.

This is the lesson of all poetry—the necessity of inutility, the primacy of inefficiency, the obligation to idleness. And it is certainly one of the most prominent themes in Cavafy's poetry, a topic that may be important in the classroom. Although Cavafy addresses many subjects in his work, one of his most benevolent acts is to invite us to pause, take time, and pay attention to the beats, signs, and impulses of life. It was the Russian formalists who first proposed that literature's capacity to intensify our awareness of the world helps us look at this world with fresh perspectives. Literature for them burnished the tarnish off their experience. Romantic writers also wrote on the creative, synthetic powers of the imagination, and on poetry's facility to highlight the insignificant. As Percy Bysshe Shelley writes, "[P]oetry lifts the veil from the hidden beauty of the world, and makes familiar objects be as if they were not familiar" (13). In its basic form, this is a Kantian idea, namely that beauty has value for itself and need not be demoted to economic or political ends.

This revolutionary concept, filtered to Cavafy through the aestheticist movement in Europe, motivates his poetics and underwrites all his mature poems. And it is what Cavafy must have repeated to himself the day he rejected the offer by the Benaki family for a more lucrative job that would have tied him to the metronome of mercantilism. He wanted time not only to write but also to promote his poetry despite those influential early voices ridiculing it. Alexandria was a metropolis of flashing lights, cinemas, café music, honking cars, and advertisements on walls. He understood the myriad stimuli that Georg Simmel had identified as the hallmark of modern life. But he did not advocate an escape from the urban environment and would have had no patience for Oliver's nature poem.

His discomfort in the natural world becomes apparent in the poem "Morning Sea." Despite trying, the speaker can't grasp the seaside. "Let me stand here," he says, adding, "And let me also behold nature for a while / morning sea and cloudless sky." His efforts yield only literary clichés—the outlines of landscape all "beautifully illuminated." Although he cannot communicate the tropes of the sea, he does convey to us what interests him—internal life, his memories, and the visions of his pleasure (*K. P. Kavafis: Ta piimata* 254). That is, what he chooses to endow with aesthetic attention is not the natural world but the society of individuals residing in Alexandria. After his trip to Athens in 1905, Cavafy rarely left his city, even to go to Cairo. His life was circumscribed by European Alexandria: the fifteen-minute jaunt to his office located on the quay, the brief walk to the offices of the magazine Γράμματα (*Grammata*; *Letters*), visiting his friends along Rue Rosette, daily visits to his favorite cafés, or the odd excursion by tram to the Ramleh Casino. But he used his poetry to highlight these places of quotidian inconsequentiality. In his daily strolls through the streets of Alexandria, he would stop at a shop, talk briefly to its owner, peek into a café, get a glimpse of a handsome face, or rest on a park bench, setting his newspaper down beside him and playing with his κομπολόι (*komboloi*; "worry beads").

These outings illustrate the practice of emphasizing something for its own worth. Just as Cavafy would dawdle briefly at a storefront or by the cinema, his poetry encourages students to linger, take note, and observe. What else should they be doing, to recast Oliver's question, other than devoting a little time to life's impractical suggestions? What seemed self-evident to Cavafy—not reducing every act and experience to its instrumental value—is perhaps not apparent to us. In Cavafy's poem students witness the validity of the aesthetic—the importance of doing nothing, the power of resisting the sirens of utility and function. They may discover this in the poem "From Nine O'Clock," where the speaker sits for three hours "without reading, without speaking." But far from killing time, he has been reminiscing, recalling his past lovers, transformed neighborhoods, deaths in the family. As he looks at his watch, he realizes that he has been in this position for over three hours: "Half past twelve. How time has passed. / Half past twelve. How the years have passed" (*K. P. Kavafis: Ta piimata* 291). Again, what else should he have been doing? Cavafy teaches us how to waste time purposefully. In the poem "In the Evening," the speaker is lost in thought after reading a letter. So preoccupied has he been that he has not noticed that his lamp has gone out. So, in his sadness, he steps out onto the balcony "to change my thoughts by briefly catching / my beloved city for a while, a slight movement of the street and the shops" (271).

What the speaker is doing in this and in other poems is spelled out poetically in "I Have Gazed So Much," a poem that dramatizes Cavafy's poetics. The speaker tells us how he has "gazed very much at beauty," looking at "lines of the body. Red lips. Sensual bodies. / Hair as if taken from Greek statues" (*K. P. Kavafis: Ta piimata* 256). And he has brought them to his art, as Cavafy says in "I Brought to Art," a similar poem. Here again the speaker is in reverie: "I sit and daydream." He thinks about how he created his poetry by bringing in "half-seen faces or lines of unfulfilled loves" (317). Cavafy's poetry is full of these moments when the poet stops to endow an otherwise nameless person, moment, or building with aesthetic value, retrieving it from memory's trash bin. In "In the Café Entrance," someone sitting next to the speaker brings his attention to the café door, where he looks at the "beautiful body" of someone he neither knows nor will probably ever meet but whose face and body he notices and then records in poetry (251). In "Days of 1908," the sea and sky delight at the poor, unemployed youth who comes to the shore every week, casts off his worn-out clothes, and dives naked into the sea. The days of 1908 aesthetically preserve the handsome "faultlessly beautiful" figure, before he puts on again the "unworthy" garments and returns to his tedious habits (392).

This indeed is the central task of Cavafy's poetics: to linger, to take notice, to rescue from historical indifference. Poetry not only draws away the cobwebs of deadening routine—according to the formalist notion of defamiliarization—but also brings attention to things for what they are. This mission is dramatically enacted in "Caesarion," which Cavafy wrote in 1914 and published four years later. Ostensibly about Caesarion (meaning "little Caesar"), the son of Julius Caesar and Cleopatra, who was born in 47 BCE and killed on the orders of Octavian, the future Augustus, because Octavian did not want any pretenders to the throne, the poem details how the poet rescues Caesarion from history's indifference. The speaker-poet, finding himself perusing volumes of Ptolemaic inscriptions, is bored by the inflated epithets attached to every ruler: "all are brilliant, glorious, powerful, beneficent." As he is about to put these texts away, he lets his attention pause over a mention of Caesarion, the little-known, last pharaoh. And then in the dim light of the room, he lets this young prince enter his room, appearing "pale and weary." Because history had preserved only "a few lines" about him (*K. P. Kavafis: Ta piimata* 280), the poet fashions him more freely through his imagination and, in so doing, rescues this minor figure from the oblivion of historiography.

Caesarion mirrors the anonymous figure at the café door and the many other young men in Cavafy's funerary poems about antiquity and in the "Days" poems of modern Alexandria, all of whom Cavafy pauses over to delineate. Cavafy does not describe this Alexandria with any realism, as, for instance, Joyce did with Dublin. Cavafy's verses contain no real street names, actual buildings, or references to the large Muslim population that kept European Alexandria running. But Cavafy still was a poet of the urban scene and would have understood the power of the city, its capacity to fluster us by its sounds, signs, and promises. But not even he could have imagined the stimuli we experience: the pings our phones make and the endless stream of tweets and posts. Although he could not have foreseen the distractions of social media, Cavafy's work helps counteract them by bringing attention to beauty as a reflection on the thing for its own sake. Critics have been understandably reluctant to consider the social significance of the aesthetic for fear of resurrecting nineteenth-century aestheticism, the artistic and literary movement that elevated aesthetic value over all other values. To be sure, aestheticism overemphasized art's role in social change while minimizing the power of the economy and politics. We can be mindful of these dangers while we try to understand what the aesthetic uniquely renders, that is, the necessity of not subjecting all experiences to efficiency, productivity, and economic profit.

The omnipresence of the Internet in students' lives and the precarious economic conditions that students face undermine the aesthetic while lionizing a ruthless utilitarianism. Much alarm has been raised—most recently by Jaron Lanier, a founder of virtual reality, and Roger McNamee, a venture capitalist and early investor in Facebook—about the role of social media in creating a surveillance culture, fostering addiction, and subverting democracy. But ignored in these critiques is the tendency of social media to devalue experience for the sake of experience—in other words, the aesthetic impulse in life. I have found that students appreciate being informed of this. They wish to know that there exist other domains of life, such as poetry, that have a long history and that provide some space outside of reductive, means-oriented thinking. Cavafy's poetry can be used as a corrective here in two ways. More than most poets, Cavafy explores the multifaceted dimensions of poetry in his verses, championing art against the unjust accusation of being historically inconsequential. And in a Wildean move, he reverses this argument of art's detractors by making uselessness the central ploy in his defense. At the same time, he shows how poetry encourages us to tarry and take notice of exactly those aspects of life that social media devalue—the morning glow over a lake, a chat with a friend, sauntering through city streets, or reading a letter.

We can teach Cavafy for many reasons: the beauty of his language, his terse poetics, his representation of homoerotic desire, his reflection on the power of identity, his description of racial and ethnic mixing in antiquity. There is no one, definitive Cavafy. But one of the most urgent insights he can offer students is the splendor of life's ineffectual moments. In today's hyperbolic, speedy, and work-obsessed world, this might be the most profitable lesson of all.

NOTES

1. All translations from Cavafy's poetry are my own. In my class on modern Greek literature I use *The Complete Poems of Cavafy*, translated by Rae Dalven.

2. Harris examines the economic precarity that preoccupies the generation of our current students.

"Dangerous Things"? Cavafy in the Modern Greek Language Classroom

Elsa Amanatidou

Curriculum design in foreign language education has traditionally been driven by a twofold question: what to teach and how to teach it. The ebb and flow of trends in teaching approaches notwithstanding, the challenge of what to teach has dominated the discussion around curriculum configuration, especially when it comes to the integration of language and culture and the complicated relationship between language and literature in particular. This essay presents my position in this debate, as seen through the lens of teaching Modern Greek with Cavafy.

The pedagogical rationale for teaching language through Cavafy's poetry is to enable my students to develop proficiency in the Greek language, mastery of content, and critical thinking abilities. My experience of teaching language with Cavafy has shown, and continues to reveal, that in guiding students to an understanding and appreciation of Cavafy's poems, I can create conditions for language use that range from the everyday and colloquial to the creative and poetic, and I can cultivate critical reflection on ideas that touch on many of the concerns that students nowadays bring to class: from the plurality of identities to perspectives on love, memory, religious affiliation, patriotism, disintegration, and stability. A textbook cannot afford me these opportunities and cannot provide an entry point into worldviews that have the same currency as the poetry.

This is not to say that the process does not come with challenges—depending on whether the poems are taught in a high school or collegiate setting, such challenges mostly stem from commonly held views about the role of poetry in the moral edification of the young or the place of literature in foreign language education. The decision to place Cavafy at the center of the modules that constitute language students' introduction to literature in Greek is not only grounded in the pedagogical reasons stated earlier but also has to do with the recognizability of Cavafy's cultural capital across continents and instructional contexts. In the United Kingdom, for example, high school students, mostly heritage speakers of Greek, study the poems as part of the A-level examination for Modern Greek that will qualify them to be admitted to a university of their choice.

In a collegiate setting, the inclusion of poetry in the foreign language curriculum comes with its own challenges and is not without controversy. Freda Mishan is correct in pointing out that a language-based approach to poetry has often been seen, especially to all the Leavisites out there, as a practice of trivializing an "elite canon" that represents *Culture* with a capital *C* (100). Even now, after thirty years of teaching, in my effort to make the poem Ιθάκη ("Ithaki"; "Ithaca") accessible and enjoyable to undergraduates who are beginning their journey into Modern Greek, I occasionally feel I am committing an irreverent act. The same feeling happens when I ask them to read Εν Σπάρτη ("En Sparti"; "In Sparta") and identify the instances of the imperfect tense in order to reinforce their knowledge of linguistic structures, rather than to discuss, in deserving detail, how the imperfect underscores King Cleomenes's weakness and indecisiveness.

This controversy, or at least unease, about poetry being an appropriate linguistic and cultural expression in the foreign language classroom is not only linked to a perceived violation of literary sensibility and worth. We also see this unease emerge in scholarly work and teachers' perspectives in the field of foreign language education itself. The preoccupation with the representation of language in living social contexts, and its use to describe the real world and carry out real-life tasks, assumes that poetic language lacks the currency and authenticity to provide models of what the learners can do with the language. The language of poems is simply, in this view, not natural enough. This distinction has a limiting effect on my teaching practice and my intention to introduce undergraduates to the imagined and imaginary landscapes of poetry and the linguistic hybridity of the Greek language in order to fill the cultural void created by the referential and transactional language of textbooks.

But the tide has turned. Over the last thirty years or so and in response to the dominance and infantilizing tendencies of the communicative language teaching approach, second language acquisition scholars and education reports by professional organizations have underscored the importance of moving away from a primarily skills-based, instrumentalist view of language, issuing a call to situate foreign language education within the broader humanistic endeavor. What is likely the most publicized and quoted example of this reform to date remains the 2007 MLA report "Foreign Languages and Higher Education: New Structures for a Changed World," which calls for "a broader and more coherent curriculum in which language, culture, and literature are taught as a continuous whole" (Ad Hoc Committee). There are pedagogical, intellectual, and pragmatic reasons why Cavafy's poetry lends itself to the realization of this goal as an effective and affective teaching tool.

For example, a poem like Τα επικίνδυνα ("Ta epikindyna"; "Dangerous Things"), in addition to serving as fertile ground for the exploration of discourse features and the role of word order in underscoring meaning, consistently gives rise to affective responses that betray the students' engagement with their learning. As students move from surface analysis of linguistic features to a deeper comprehension that allows them to explore values, compare them, and organize them in order of priorities, they progress through the activities of what Bloom's taxonomy identifies as the affective domain (Bloom). Students go from receiving knowledge (listening to and reading the poem, identifying words, and selecting and naming the structures that challenge comprehension) to responding (participating in teams to carry out comprehension tasks or respond to questions in writing), to organizing (explaining the ideas in the poem, differentiating between positions and tendencies), and to reflecting critically (questioning established values and belief systems, including their own). In the section that follows,

I explain the rationale for including a selection of Cavafy's poems in language classes that include undergraduate students from all over the world in addition to the occasional heritage speaker, outline some of the processes of teaching and learning Greek through Cavafy with the help of emerging instructional technologies, and demonstrate the value of this selection in achieving my intended learning outcomes, namely the development of communicative competence, symbolic competence,[1] and critical literacy in an environment of affective learning.

Cavafy in the Undergraduate Curriculum

Teaching and learning Modern Greek with Cavafy cannot be viewed separately from ongoing scholarly discussions about the complicated relationship between literature and modern foreign language education in the undergraduate curriculum in universities and colleges in the United States. Instructors face practical and methodological challenges when pondering the contribution of literary study to their students' language abilities, and these challenges have as much to do with governance structures as with the perceived objectives of foreign language education.

First, the bifurcation that exists in modern foreign language, literature, and culture departments not only reflects institutional hierarchical divisions but also curricular ones between lower- and upper-level courses. The former are traditionally conceived of as skills-focused; they prioritize oral, vernacular discourse and aim to cultivate communicative competence while preparing undergraduates for the more demanding literary material that awaits them later on in their academic trajectory. The latter are knowledge-based, with sophisticated learning objectives and literacy-oriented academic tasks such as the critical interpretation of texts. This two-tiered structure has for some time now defined the boundaries between language study and the study of literature in no uncertain terms. Engagement with literary texts and the higher-order thinking skills associated with it is considered appropriate for the upper-level courses, where the focus is no longer on language learning. This, in my view artificial, barrier is responsible for the lamentable fact that undergraduates who complete two, sometimes three, years of language study are often inadequately prepared to tackle the challenge of reading literary texts and engaging with them meaningfully and critically in the target language. In addition, Modern Greek programs are faced with a conundrum, one that affects most commonly taught languages. Unlike the governance structures of other more commonly taught foreign languages, which have in place a professorial rank that teaches the upper-level literature courses in the language, modern Greek literature offerings in the United States are usually taught in translation and in comparative literature departments. In this respect, unless Cavafy is somehow included in the language-based courses, many undergraduates might never engage with his work, in Greek, in an instructional setting.

Second, there is a disconnect between theory and practice, that is, between the objectives of foreign language education and the way they have been traditionally manifested in textbooks and classroom practices dominated by communicative language teaching in the last fifty years or so. The prioritization of language as a tool for oral communication—and the organization of textbooks around negotiations, information-gap activities, and transactions of cultural currency—paints the profile of a beginner student of Modern Greek as someone who is only interested in navigating the Greek landscape as a tourist or study-abroad student. And although this assumption may be partly true, it does not define the full range of their interests nor does it do justice to their intellectual profile. When a typical American student brings into the beginners' Greek class their concerns related to the academic discourses of gender, LGBTQ, postcolonial, and cultural studies, they are often appalled by what they perceive as linguistic homogeneity, infantilizing exercises, and the presentation of culture as binary categories or as a national collective and often self-exoticized imaginary. The inclusion of Cavafy, a recognizable literary figure who is at once canonical and contemporary, together with examples of other authentic multimodal forms of culture, bridges the gap between an instrumentalist and a constitutive view of language and affords students the opportunity to engage with intellectual content from the early stages of the proficiency continuum "for a more unified discussion of relations between readers, writers, texts, culture and language learning" (Kern 43).

Third, language and discourse in Cavafy's poems lend themselves well to the type of grading of difficulty that applies to various levels of language proficiency, from novice to advanced. A poem such as Μονοτονία ("Monotonia"; "Monotony") is often discussed in my first-year Greek course, which is built around the concept of self. With its relatively simple vocabulary, low conceptual challenge, high-frequency verbs—perhaps not including εικάζει (*ikazi*; "to guess")—and familiar tense structures, Μονοτονία can serve as an example of the type of useful and natural syntactical arrangements that are not often found in a textbook. The placement of object before subject in the opening line, Την μια μονότονην ημέραν ("One monotonous day"; Cavafy, *Piimata*, A' 22), usually stumps students and forces them to apply their knowledge of grammatical cases to decode meaning and notice its importance in action. Once the layers of meaning have been peeled off and the anxiety of comprehension has receded, students are able to notice the significance of rhyme and how repetition serves to underscore the subject matter. The poem has served the purpose of stimulating the development of language skills, as the students read, listen, and deploy communicative strategies in guided activities, which include dismantling the poem and putting it together again and visualizing its content by finding or drawing images that best correspond to certain verses. In addition to tangible pedagogical outcomes, however, the poem gives students (whose proficiency, in contrast with their intellectual ability, is a work in progress) the opportunity to work with content that is cognitively challenging, interesting, and therefore motivating.

Strategies for the Classroom

Now I wish to discuss the practicalities of implementation and what classroom practice focused on Cavafy looks like. For a less commonly taught language such as Modern Greek, which is a category 3 language in the language difficulty ranking created by the Foreign Service Institute,[2] the challenge of reading, interpreting, and enjoying a poem at beginner and intermediate levels is not negligible. When a beginner in their first year of learning Greek cannot even sustain a conversation, how can they engage with "Ithaca" in a meaningful way without being demotivated by the unknown vocabulary and grammatical structures that they encounter? The answer is to be found in a series of implementation strategies that draw from the corpus of second language acquisition research, the multiliteracies framework,[3] and the world readiness standards.[4] Even though the steps below are illustrated with the poem "Ithaca," which we discuss at the end of first-year Greek, they are applicable to other poems or any multimodal authentic content.

The first strategy is an effective syllabus design that ensures that the literary text fits within the broader thematic modules and learning outcomes of the class. The poem in question, "Ithaca," is selected to promote interpersonal, interpretive, and presentational communication goals in relation to the theme of travel as a literal and metaphorical concept, the communicative purpose of giving advice and talking about the future, and aspects of language use that include tense (the future) and aspect (the subjunctive). In addition, because of its Homeric elements and symbolic value in world literature, this particular poem lends itself well to the activation of prior knowledge and establishing valuable comprehension links.

The second strategy is effective lesson sequencing that ensures that the content is scaffolded and does not place undue pressure on the students' cognitive processes, which might demotivate them. Based on the multiliteracies framework, the scaffolding includes situated practice, overt instruction, critical framing, and transformed practice.

Situated practice allows students to gain familiarity with the text through initial exploration. This may include writing out on the board words they associate with Ἰθάκη (*Ithaki*; "Ithaca").[5] The instructor contributes to the scaffolding of information by providing vocabulary that the students identify but do not possess in Greek. As a follow-up to the brainstorming of words, students have the chance to complete an inventory of vocabulary as they listen to a recording of the poem being recited (e.g., by the Greek actress Ellie Lambeti ["'Ithaca,' by K. P. Kavafis"]), while jotting down known words they hear or by ticking words on a list they have been given. A final activity at this stage allows the students to work closely on the poem, thanks to the affordances of digital social reading platforms such as *Perusall* or *eMargin*. These Internet-based activities provide important scaffolding. They diffuse the cognitive load of solitary reading and cement team building and a supportive learning environment.

Students respond to guided questions by the instructor, create hyperlinks to research place names or proper nouns, tag words and provide definitions or principal parts (in the case of verbs), and generally read as they annotate a shared document and support each other while connecting with the content.

Overt instruction is instructor-driven and focuses students' attention on discourse: not only what words mean but also how meaning is created and how inflected, subjunctive verb forms (e.g., να σταματήσεις [*na stamatisis*; "you should stop"]) are used in the target language when in English an infinitive would be employed ("stop"). Translingual comparisons are often a feature of this stage, and explicit metalanguage and literary terms are necessarily employed. Therefore, for this step to be executed smoothly, students should already be in possession of a core vocabulary or glossary of terms (e.g., ρήμα [*rima*; "verb"], δεύτερο πρόσωπο [*deytero prosopo*; "second person"], αφηγητής [*afigitis*; "narrator"], στροφή [*strofi*; "stanza"], etc.) that allows them to identify parts of speech or words. Whether students build on something they already know or encounter a structure for the first time, what is important is that grammar is presented in context, that it is grounded in meaning, and that students understand what they can do with this form. Even though overt instruction is instructor-driven, it does not need to be instructor-dominated. Students can contribute to the building of explicit knowledge by applying rules of syntax and morphology in activities such as matching nouns with adjectives or participles (e.g., συγκίνησις, πρωιά πραγμάτειες [*synginisis, proia pragmaties*; "excitement, mornings, things"] and εκλεκτή, καλοκαιρινά, καλές [*eklekti, kalokairina, kales*; "rare, summer, fine"]), completing the second half of the many *if* clauses in the poem, reordering a jumbled sentence, and so on. Educational software such as the program *Hot Potatoes* offers an effective tool for creating web-based tasks of this nature.[6]

Critical framing is the most challenging stage in the multiliteracies framework, in the context of beginner learners engaging with a literary text. This is where their intellectual capabilities as literate subjects are far superior to their ability to express themselves in the target language. The challenge lies precisely in this conundrum. The contexts prescribed by communicative language teaching for language practice fall within the parameters of the students' linguistic competence, but these contexts do not do justice to the critical literacy students already possess. To enable students to apply and enhance their skills of reflection and analysis and to add the value of literature to their learning, we may need to abandon the immersive atmosphere of the classroom and accept contributions in English, particularly when a student is clearly struggling to express in Greek a concept that is already perfectly formulated in their head in English. The social, collaborative reading platforms that invite annotations and comments (including the instructor's) have proved to be an effective tool for building the required competences for this stage, as well as for developing the kind of digital literacy that is now an important transferable skill. When I teach "Ithaca," my text annotation directs students' attention to the second stanza and asks a question that encourages students to articulate the ideas and forms of happiness and fulfillment entailed in the journey that the poem describes: "Ένα από τα θέλγητρα του ταξιδιού είναι 'να μπαίνεις σε λιμένας πρωτοειδομένους.' Ποιες άλλες εικόνες ευτυχίας παρουσιάζονται; Πρόσεξε ιδιαίτερα τις φράσεις που αρχίζουν από 'να' και την επανάληψη ορισμένων λέξεων" ("One of the journey's attractions is to 'come into harbors seen for the first time.' What other images of happiness are included in the poem? Pay particular attention to phrases beginning with 'to' and the repetition of certain words"). Students take turns annotating the relevant verses with their observations, commenting on previous threads and contributing to the creation of a new text with their readings inscribed and shared. A tolerance for errors is important when the students prioritize communication over accuracy.

Transformed practice is where the students apply what they have learned in ways that may involve creative writing, a digital product, a discursive piece of work, or even a performance. Students who have spent a week rolling about in Cavafy's "Ithaca" may decide to compare translations of the poem, produce a digital story about a meaningful personal journey, perform a recitation, or even think transculturally by bringing in poetry that is written in another language and that is in dialogue with "Ithaca." The most palpable benefit of this last stage of the sequence is the increase in motivation and affect, as evidenced by the agency that students exercise in producing work meaningful to them.

The multiliteracies model has proved to be an effective pedagogical tool for teaching with Cavafy in the undergraduate curriculum in multiple ways. In addition to facilitating access to the indisputable value of literature, a pedagogy of multiliteracies addresses an important requirement in modern foreign language education. From situated practice to the redesigned product of transformed practice, the pedagogical activities around a poem underscore the students' development in response to the requirements of the world readiness standards, or five C's, as they have come to be known. By the end of the course, all the students have participated in interpersonal, presentational, and interpretive communicative acts, accessed the diverse genres and perspectives available in Greek, reflected on the grammatical forms of Modern Greek in hybrid variations, made comparisons with English, reflected on the concept of the journey through transcultural comparisons, and used Greek not only to perform functions but also for enjoyment and their own intellectual development. In this respect, we have gone beyond the achievement of learning goals that require students to "engage critically with intellectually stimulating materials, developing an appreciation of sophisticated and creative uses of Greek"; students' curiosity has also been piqued, and the road has been paved for further study and exploration of Cavafy's work.

NOTES

1. Symbolic competence, as defined by the linguist Claire Kramsch, refers to a more nuanced understanding of cultural products and "the ability to read and interpret

spoken and written discourse, identify the symbolic value of words and metaphors, grasp their social and historical significance, contrast them with metaphors in one's own language, and reframe one's interpretation of events" (24).

2. The Foreign Service Institute ranks foreign languages by their difficulty for native speakers of English. The order of difficulty begins at 1 (easiest and needing the fewest hours of study) and goes up to 4 (most difficult and needing the most hours of study).

3. A pedagogy of multiliteracies scaffolds learning around four key stages: situated practice, critical framing, overt instruction, and transformed practice. Cope and Kalantzis have expanded the multiliteracies model and reconceptualized it as "Learning by Design" (35).

4. The world readiness standards for learning languages provide a road map for the development of linguistic and cultural competence by outlining five key goal areas: communication, cultures, connections, comparisons, and communities. See "World-Readiness Standards."

5. These invariably include ταξίδι (*taxidi*; "journey"), Οδυσσέας (*Odysseas*; "'Odysseus"), θάλασσα (*thalassa*; "sea"), Πηνελόπη (*Pinelopi*; "Penelope"), Σειρήνες (*Sirines*; "Sirens"), δρόμος (*dromos*; "road"), and πόλεμος (*polemos*; "war").

6. The *Hot Potatoes* suite was developed by the University of Victoria in Canada and includes six applications that enable the creation of interactive multiple-choice, short-answer, jumbled-sentence, crossword, matching or ordering, and gap-filling exercises.

Cavafy as a Bridge
from Classics to Modern Greek Studies

Johanna Hanink

As an undergraduate classics student at the University of Michigan, Ann Arbor, I had my first encounter with Modern Greek at the 2002 exhibition *Cavafy's World: Ancient Passions* at the Kelsey Museum of Archaeology. The exhibition, curated by Lauren Talalay and Artemis Leontis, featured manuscripts of poems and photographs of C. P. Cavafy and his family, but it also "invite[d] the visitor to contemplate a dialogue between modern poetry and archaeology" ("What"). The Kelsey houses several artifacts from Egypt, and the temporary exhibition endeavored to cast the permanent collection, and the antiquity for which it stands as synecdoche, in a new light. "Through Cavafy's eyes," the exhibition materials suggested, "the viewer can reconsider the museum's collection of mummy masks, Fayoum portraits, funerary steles, jewelry, textiles, coins, and objects from everyday life" ("Cavafy's World").

The Kelsey Museum is on the university campus, directly across from Angell Hall, where the Department of Classical Studies is located. That department also houses an interdisciplinary program in Modern Greek. This nexus of physical proximity—of autographs of Cavafy's poems and "Fayoum portraits" in the same exhibition space, of the Kelsey Museum and the classics department on the same street, and of the offices of the C. P. Cavafy Professor of Modern Greek Studies and the D. R. Shackleton Bailey Professor of Greek and Latin in the same hallway—became important to my trajectory of study. The setting was what first allowed me, a traditional Homer-and-Virgil American student of classics, to see that Greece's story had not ended with the advent of Christianity, that classicism was flexible and dynamic, and that there was such a concept (however complex and contested) as Hellenism.

These ideas had begun to take root in my thinking and reshape my view of classics when I read *"What These Ithakas Mean": Readings in Cavafy* (Leontis et al.), which was published in conjunction with the exhibition. The volume prints facing texts of poems by Cavafy in Greek and English translation and is illustrated with images of materials from the exhibition and artifacts from the Kelsey collection. Two aspects of the book intrigued me most: that I could mostly work out Cavafy's Greek by triangulating it through the English translations and my knowledge of ancient Greek, and that some of the response pieces accompanying Cavafy's poems had been written by my own classics professors. I became curious to learn why a turn-of-the-twentieth-century poet was so important to those classicists and why they saw his poetry as somehow bearing on their own field.

Cavafy has long been a meeting point for classics and Modern Greek studies. In this essay, I explore how his writings, both poems and prose essays, can serve as an accessible and attractive introduction to Modern Greek studies for students of classics. It also outlines ways that Cavafy's work might help reshape how classicists view the relationship between their field and modern Greece.

Cavafy among the Classicists

The fascination that many classicists have with Cavafy is owed in part to the notion that he represents, paradoxically, a modern yet authentic witness to a lost Greek antiquity. This perception was articulated in the mid–twentieth century by the Oxford classicist and literary critic Maurice Bowra, who cast Cavafy as a relic of an ancient Greek past: "What was for Solomos and Palamas an irrecoverable past was for Cavafy a reality not merely of the imagination but of his own blood and bones. He felt at home in this past, because he knew that ultimately he belonged to it, that he spoke its language, that he shared its sun and air, that his stock was its stock" (*Creative Experiment* 32). Today Cavafy's poems on themes drawn from antiquity—poems such as "Ithaca," "Waiting for the Barbarians," "The God Abandons Antony," and "Young Men of Sidon (A.D. 400)"—regularly supply epigraphs and flourishes to the pages of classical scholarship. Many classicists have also published articles on Cavafy, and two of the most recent English editions of poems by Cavafy are by translators trained primarily in the study of Greek antiquity: the late Alan Boegehold (Cavafy, *One Hundred Sixty-Six Poems*), who was professor emeritus of classics at Brown University, and Daniel Mendelsohn (Cavafy, *Collected Poems* [Mendelsohn] and *Unfinished Poems*), an author and literary critic who holds a position in the Department of Classical Studies at Bard College.[1]

Cavafy is held especially dear by scholars of the Homeric and Hellenistic poetic traditions. In the first case, this is because the early decades of his poetic activity were marked by repeated returns to stories from Homer and the Trojan cycle: "Priam's Nocturnal Journey," from 1893, and "Ithaca," from 1911, bookend some ten poems on these subjects. After 1911, Cavafy largely abandoned themes of ancient mythology—the timing of "The God Abandons Antony," also from 1911, almost seems programmatic in retrospect—and came to redirect his imagination to pockets of, as he puts it in his poem "200 BC," a "new world that was Greek, and great" (*Collected Poems* [Mendelsohn] 172): a wide and cosmopolitan world forged by Alexander the Great and his successors. Perhaps counterintuitively, this embrace and promotion of an expansive Hellenism is one of the characteristics of Cavafy's poetry that most attracts and fascinates scholars of postclassical ancient Greek literature. It is no coincidence that Cavafy's poetic career coincided with an era in which classical scholars were themselves developing an appreciation and taste for Greek works composed after the fourth century BCE.[2]

Cavafy's friend and literary associate E. M. Forster was influential in informing the anglophone world about Cavafy's radical redefinition of Greek antiquity (radical, at least, for northern European classical scholarship). In "The Poetry of C. P. Cavafy," an essay in his Alexandria-themed collection *Pharos and Pharillon*, Forster famously remarks on how much Cavafy's imagination of the ancient Hellenic world differed from "an Englishman's": "Athens and Sparta, so drubbed into us at school, are to him two quarrelsome little slave states, ephemeral beside the Hellenistic kingdoms that followed them, just as these are ephemeral beside the secular empire of Constantinople. He reacts against the tyranny of Classicism—Pericles and Aspasia and Themistocles and all those bores." Forster goes on to pronounce that Cavafy's "literary ancestor if he has one is Callimachus" (94). It happens that *Pharos and Pharillon* was published in the same year that Rudolf Pfeiffer, the first modern scholar to establish a career on the study of Hellenistic poetry, was recognized for his work on Callimachus with an appointment to a professorship at Berlin's Humboldt University. Pfeiffer was also the first major scholar to edit the fragments of Callimachus's literary output: the first truly ancient artifacts of Callimachus's poetry (tablets and papyri, as opposed to copied manuscripts) had only started coming to light in the last years of the nineteenth century.[3] Among certain classicists whose work continues to react "against the tyranny of Classicism" (to borrow Forster's motto), Cavafy is still received as an inheritor of the Callimachean tradition, a "modern Alexandrian" (Schein, "Cavafy") who is sometimes even hailed in positive terms as an honorary Hellenistic poet: "in his allusivity, his engagement with a distant and largely mythical past, his oblique perception of figures, his emphasis on the refined and intricate, Cavafy epitomizes many of the qualities Classicists associate with 'Hellenistic poetry'" (Acosta-Hughes 82). Thus, it is by a kind of transitive equation (Hellenistic poetry is the purchase of classicists, Cavafy is a Hellenistic poet, therefore Cavafy is the purchase of classicists) that the study of Cavafy has, in at least the Anglo-American context, been enfolded into the modern, institutionally supported and authorized study of Mediterranean antiquity. But while Neohellenists and other scholars of modern literature might object to this appropriation—do classicists not claim enough territory as it is?—Cavafy's unique canonical status among both classicists and Neohellenists is precisely what renders his work a uniquely traversable bridge between the two fields.

From Ancient to Modern (Greek Studies)

Cavafy's "Ithaca" is standard fare in American undergraduate literature courses that cover Homer's *Odyssey*. Yet, in my experience, selections from Cavafy's less-read prose have proved capable of prompting richer and more probing discussions in classes populated by students with interests in antiquity. Today, undergraduate classics courses increasingly incorporate content related to antiquity's legacy in the modern world, from instances of classical reception to current sociopolitical engagements with (and so-called appropriations of) imagined classical pasts. In my own such courses, I have used Cavafy's journalistic interventions in the perennial Elgin marbles debate to introduce the contours of the controversy itself but also to help orient students toward a nexus of questions about the role that (fantasies of) antiquity has played in the formation of, and discourses around, the Greek nation-state.

I first assigned Cavafy on the Elgin marbles in my undergraduate seminar Old News: Antiquity and Current Events. The seminar ran under the auspices of Brown University's Cogut Institute for the Humanities, but about half of the students in the course were classics majors. Part of the course description read as follows: "Antiquity is often invoked to manipulate how we view current events. This course . . . will interrogate questions of 'who owns the past?' and of how we reckon antiquity's value." Students were introduced (or reintroduced) to Cavafy about midway through the course, in a unit called The Parthenon Marbles and Greece's Fragmented National Body. The seminar was designed for advanced undergraduates with strong critical and interpretive skills; the reading load was heavy. For this unit, I asked students to read three categories of material: position statements, theoretical frameworks, and recent news articles. Reading in the first category included excerpts from the 1816 *Report from the Select Committee of the House of Commons on the Earl of Elgin's Sculptures Marbles &c.* (in which Parliament recommended the British state's acquisition of the Parthenon marbles in Lord Elgin's collection) as well as various historical opinion pieces on the debate. Among these was Cavafy's essay "Give Back the Elgin Marbles" (*Selected Prose Works* 21–22), which he published in 1891 in the Alexandrian journal *Rivista quindicinale*.

In "Give Back the Elgin Marbles," Cavafy offers an English version of the first of two pieces that he had published in the 30 March and 29 April 1891 editions of the Athens newspaper *Ethniki (National)*. His impetus was a brief paper war being fought in British literary periodicals: in December 1890, Frederic Harrison fired the first shot in *Nineteenth Century* with a piece also titled "Give Back the Elgin Marbles"; James Knowles, the magazine's editor, replied in the March 1891 issue with his scathing and sarcastic "The Joke about the Elgin Marbles." Harrison's reply to Knowles's reply ("Editorial Horseplay") then appeared in the 1 April 1891 issue of *Fortnightly Review*, at about the time that Cavafy's first piece was published in *Ethniki*.[4] Like Harrison, whom he calls "learned and eloquent," Cavafy supported the return of the Elgin marbles to Greece and was outraged by Knowles: "He extols the vandalic act of Elgin. . . . He vilifies Byron" (*Selected Prose Works* 21).

As we discussed Cavafy's essay in class, we circled around one particular point. In a sentence lambasting Knowles's prose style, Cavafy offers an incidental yet significant characterization of those on the side of repatriation: "Aridity in style and prolixity of cheap wit render its [i.e., Knowles's essay's] perusal a heavy task even for those to whom the restitution of the Elgin Marbles is of direct interest,—I mean the true friends of Hellas and of the unity of the Hellenic tradition" (*Selected Prose Works* 21). Here we were able to use Cavafy's invocation of the "unity of the Hellenic tradition" as an inroad to a reading from our second category, theoretical frameworks. One of the pieces that I had asked students to read under that rubric was "Nostalgia for the Whole: The Parthenon (or Elgin) Marbles," chapter 7 in Yannis Hamilakis's influential monograph *The Nation and Its Ruins: Antiquity, Archaeology, and National Imagination in Greece* (243–86). In that chapter, Hamilakis develops an argument that he introduces toward the start of the book, namely that "the marbles today stand as the exiled and imprisoned members of the national body, and they personify a key feature of the national imagination, *nostalgia for the whole*" (32).

By juxtaposing the pieces by Cavafy and Hamilakis, we were able to open a discussion that departed from a familiar icon of classical Greek antiquity—the Parthenon and its sculptural program—and pursue a set of issues centered on the construction of a lost Greek wholeness. Cavafy's appeal to the "unity of the Hellenic tradition" was illuminated by Hamilakis's analysis of discourses that lament the fragmentation of Greece and its people: so-called historically Greek territories (homelands) lie outside the artificial national borders, the *omogeneia* ("diaspora") counts millions of members, and Greece's imagined mutilation is nowhere so literalized as in the case of the Parthenon marbles, which were hewn from the Parthenon and largely dispersed to foreign collections. "Seen in that light," Hamilakis writes, "the marbles are . . . members of the national body in exile," a "material manifestation of fragmentation and dismemberment" (32). Students in the class who were familiar with Cavafy's poems—poems such as "Ithaca"—expressed surprise at the stance the poet had taken in favor of the marbles' repatriation. This was a modern and political Cavafy, not the poet they thought they knew (see Peter Jeffreys's discussion in Cavafy, *Selected Prose Works* xiv). No one in the class had even been aware of these complexities of contemporary Greek national discourse. Mindful of my own early experiences as a classics undergraduate, I could empathize.

I was then able to pursue these issues in greater depth with the graduate students who participated in the Onassis Foundation's 2018 International Cavafy Summer School on the theme Cavafy and Antiquity. My session for the seminar was called Shades of Antiquity in Cavafy's Prose, and "Bring Back the Elgin Marbles" was just one of five prose works by Cavafy that we discussed. The others were "Professor Blackie on the Modern Greek Language," which appeared on 30 December 1891 in *Telegraphos* (*Telegraph*; *Selected Prose Works* 31–35), the Alexandrian daily at which Cavafy had been a correspondent in 1885–88, and three unpublished essays: "The Last Days of Odysseus" (103–11), from 1894; "A Few Pages on the Sophists" (112–15), from 1893–97; and "Greeks, Not Romans" (128), from 1901.

In "Professor Blackie on the Modern Greek Language," Cavafy praises a piece, "Shakespeare and Modern Greek," which John Stuart Blackie, a Scottish classical scholar and advocate of Modern Greek, published in the December 1891 issue of the *Nineteenth Century*.[5] Cavafy begins his response by asserting that "[f]oreigners discard our language a great deal. They separate it, so to speak, from ancient Greek. They deny or ignore the tradition of its continuity. They disregard its pronunciation" (*Selected Prose Works* 31). He is heartened by Blackie's essay, with its emphasis on the historical continuity of the Greek language, and by "the efforts of enlightened men who study the Greek language as it should be studied, in other words, not as a dead language but as a living one in its prime" (35). In the Onassis seminar, this piece inspired conversations about Cavafy's engagement with both the so-called Continuity Thesis, the much-disputed notion that Hellenism has maintained an unbroken character since antiquity, as well as with the Greek Language Question, whose contours were shifting in this era with the programmatic wave of new literary production in demotic Greek (as opposed to the archaizing Katharevousa) by the literary generation of the 1880s and their immediate successors. But the essay also served as a reminder of how avid a follower Cavafy was of British literary culture in this period. Blackie's piece appeared in the *Nineteenth Century* not long after the Harrison-Knowles exchange ran on its pages. As Peter Jeffreys notes, "The list of articles featured in the *Nineteenth Century* and the *Fortnightly Review* in the prolific year 1891 reveals a significant thematic overlap between Cavafy's reading and writing interests" (*Reframing Decadence* 42).[6]

Cavafy's consumption of and engagement with British intellectual culture wove through our discussions of other essays as well. In "The Last Days of Odysseus," Cavafy celebrates an innovation by Dante with respect to the Homeric tradition. Ancient sources held that Odysseus died in Ithaca, but the Odysseus of the *Divine Comedy*—who speaks to Virgil and Dante in hell (*Inferno* 26.90–142)—was in old age "urged on by a thirst for travel and exploration" to set sail once more and met his end in a storm at sea (Cavafy, *Selected Prose Works* 103). To Cavafy's mind, this fate was more in tune with the spirit of the ancient epic, for "when [Odysseus] eventually reaches his homeland, he finds that . . . his homeland is no longer there but rather in the great expanses with which his vision is filled. This is the conclusion that emanates psychologically from *The Odyssey*" (107). Cavafy here also expresses admiration for Alfred Tennyson's "Ulysses": though Dante had been responsible for the "raw material" of this new departure, Tennyson "reworked it like a skilled artist" (109). I had asked students to reread Cavafy's "Ithaca" (*Collected Poems* [Mendelsohn] 13–14), penned some fifteen years after "The Last Days of Odysseus," in conjunction with that essay. Few classicists, I would wager, realize that the reflections on *nostos* ("homecoming") in "Ithaca," a work by a poet whom Bowra claims "ultimately belonged" to the ancient Greek past (*Creative Experiment* 32), bear traces of Italian and British receptions of Homer.

Likewise, I find it unlikely that many classical scholars who celebrate Cavafy for his expansive vision of Hellenic antiquity realize that he ascribed, in "A Few Pages on the Sophists," his "great sympathy for the much-despised sophists of the ancient world" in part to George Grote's "masterpiece of a chapter in *A History of Greece*" (*Selected Prose Works* 112). That chapter, chapter 67 of Grote's epoch-making twelve-volume work, proved an immensely influential rehabilitation of the early sophists from the view that they "were either the cause or manifestation of the decay of late-fifth century Athenian history" (Turner 287). Cavafy's greater interest in the later sophists (i.e., of the Second Sophistic) is manifest in such poems as "But Wise Men Apprehend What Is Imminent" and "Herodes Atticus," which in different ways take cues from Philostratus's ancient *Lives of the Sophists*. Yet it was thanks in part to a British ancient historian that Cavafy formulated his sympathy with the sophists, which in the essay he casts in aestheticist terms: "These people lived solely for Art's sake" (*Selected Prose Works* 112). Like Grote, Cavafy argues—explicitly in his prose, implicitly in his poetry—that "[t]hey deserved a better fate" (115).

Prospectus for a Classics Proseminar

The students in the Onassis Foundation's Cavafy Summer School were informed and insightful interlocutors on all these matters. This was unsurprising, given that many were doctoral students with research interests in Cavafy, several held philology degrees from Greece, and most of the non-Greek participants had considerable experience in Modern Greek studies. Yet what I learned from our session, and from the experience of my undergraduate course, was that Cavafy's prose presents a unique means by which to challenge typical classicist assumptions about Cavafy's poetry, the continuity of Greek antiquity, and the authenticity of certain of its relics, such as the Athenian acropolis. Cavafy's impassioned participation in the Elgin marbles controversy (a debate that remains ongoing), his work as a reader and critic of European literature (including modern literary receptions of ancient Greek works), and his consumption of British classical scholarship all work against the grain of the notion that Cavafy was a living relic of the Greek past, a past that for him was a reality "of his own blood and bones," as Bowra had put it (*Creative Experiment* 32).

Most American universities that offer a PhD in classics provide some form of proseminar to new graduate students; typically, these consist in brief units on various subfields of classical studies (epigraphy, numismatics, papyrology, paleography, literary theory, etc.). These courses are an ideal forum for introducing classics students to Modern Greek studies, and Cavafy's writings supply an archive uniquely suited to the purpose. Many classics graduate students will be familiar with poems such as "Ithaca" and "Waiting for the Barbarians" (*Collected Poems* [Mendelsohn] 192–93), but directed study of these in conjunction with Cavafy's prose works will allow them to encounter, often for the first time, certain key concepts of Modern Greek studies, such as the following: "nostalgia for the whole" (Hamilakis's formulation), *ethnos* (a word that signifies both the nation as nation-state and as a people), *omogeneia*, the Continuity Thesis, and the Greek Language Question. In particular, Cavafy's essay in praise of Blackie might serve as a prompt for discussion of Modern Greek's curious second-class status as a research language in the field of classics (Hanink). That discussion could then easily move to the contentious politics of the relationship between classics and Modern Greek studies in American universities (see, e.g., Jusdanis, "Introduction"; Lambropoulos, "'Modern'"; Anagnostou).

Such a proseminar module would also help students recognize the roles that classical archaeology and scholarship have played in shaping ideas about what is authentically of the past. Cavafy was, strictly speaking, an Alexandrian poet, but if classicists recognize him as a Hellenistic one it is because, in approaching Cavafy, they are often gazing at a version of their own reflection. Both Cavafy and his intellectual world in Alexandria were molded by developments in European, and especially British, classical archaeology and scholarship. The *Rivista quindicinale*, in which Cavafy published his 1891 essay "Give Back the Elgin Marbles," was a publication of the Alexandrian Athenaeum presided over by Charles Cookson, a graduate of Oriel College, Oxford, and the British Consul General in Alexandria. The athenaeum was formed for the purpose of establishing in Alexandria a library dedicated to Greco-Roman antiquity and a museum to house Greco-Roman relics discovered in Egypt. Those aims were accomplished in 1892, and on 12 July of that year Cavafy wrote a piece, "Our Museum," for *Telegraphos* in celebration of the museum's opening (*Selected Prose Works* 41–42). In April 1893, at a meeting held at Cookson's home, the athenaeum was reinaugurated as the Archaeological Society of Alexandria (Reid, *Contesting Antiquity* 233).

Cavafy's career also coincided with the early scramble to recover literary papyri from the sands of the poet's native Egypt. A first transcription of "Mimes of Herodas"—an Alexandrian work from around the third century BCE, from a papyrus roll excavated in the El Fayoum oasis and purchased by the British Museum—was published by F. G. Kenyon in 1891; within months there followed a more complete edition prepared by W. G. Rutherford. The discovery was much discussed in European literary periodicals, and an encomium of the poems by Charles Whibley ran in the November 1891 issue of *Nineteenth Century*, just a matter of months after the Harrison-Knowles exchange. In 1892, Cavafy composed "The Mimiambs of Herodas," one of his so-called hidden poems. (Mimiambs were short comedic scenes in verse.) It begins with a reflection on how the mimiambs have long been buried (and bored) in the Egyptian desert, waiting for millennia to be discovered: "But now those times have passed away, / from the North have come savants; . . ." (*Collected Poems* [Mendelsohn] 263). Just a few years later, in 1895, the British Egypt Exploration Fund expanded its remit to include Greco-Roman antiquity; in the winter of 1895–96, Arthur Hunt and David Grenfell first set out for the El Fayoum oasis in search of papyri. Their efforts over several seasons would lead to the export from Egypt of many tens of thousands of scraps of papyri, the basis for the University of California's Tebtunis and Oxford University's Oxyrhynchus papyrus collections. The turn of the twentieth century thus marked not only the period of Cavafy's poetic engagement with Greek mythical themes but also an era in which "Europeans brought classical fashion to Alexandria" (Reid, *Contesting Antiquity* 231; see also Reid, *Whose Pharaohs?*).

The paradox of Cavafy's reputation as an authentic Hellenistic poet, on the one hand, and the poet's engagement with European "classical fashion," on the other, is an instantiation of the paradox that sits at the heart of the modern antiquity industry. The archaeological park of the Athenian acropolis, for example, is also presented as an authentic relic of a particular Greek past (in this case, Periclean Athens), yet its restoration and curation have, since the early nineteenth century, been driven by Western European classical fantasies (see Plantzos, "Behold"). Classicists are now beginning to make, en masse, the long-overdue move of engaging in critical self-reflection about their field's centuries-long implication in the construction and authorization of systems of racism, colonialism, and other entrenched violent societal structures. Against that background, the study of Cavafy offers a promising opportunity for students of classics to rethink common assumptions about their own discipline— and to use the tool kit of Modern Greek studies to do so.

The Cavafy exhibition that I visited as an undergraduate invited museumgoers to reconsider, "through Cavafy's eyes," the "museum's collection of mummy masks, Fayoum portraits, funerary steles, jewelry, textiles, coins, and objects from everyday life" ("Cavafy's World"). The provenance of many of the artifacts in the Kelsey Museum is the site of ancient Karanis (modern-day Kom Aushim), Egypt, where a University of Michigan team began to excavate in 1924. Karanis had first become the object of archaeological study in 1895, when Grenfell, Hunt, and D. G. Hogarth identified the site of the ancient town (Hessenbruch 10). What, then, would Cavafy have seen in such objects, at once ancient and new? And why, as Hala Halim has pointed out, did Cavafy—who so fervently supported the return of the Elgin marbles to Greece—not regard the "mimiambi" as "a heritage that should remain in the country where they were found" (*Alexandrian Cosmopolitanism* 78)?

In considering the complex ways in which Cavafy was influenced by the antiquity industrial complex, classics students might well be reminded that a collection such as the Kelsey Museum's is—in many ways like Cavafy's poetry—as much a product of a specific turn-of-the-twentieth-century context as it is of any ancient one. This paradox, which, again, is at the heart of the field of classical studies, is a version of the broader one on which classicism itself hinges: the classical is simultaneously ancient and new, archaic but perpetually fresh.[7] Cavafy's prose in part serves to expose the mechanics of that paradox by revealing the modern European intellectual formation that buttresses the classical facade of his poetry. Given the unique reputation that Cavafy enjoys among classicists, his prose essays can serve as a relatively inviting gateway from classics to Modern Greek studies, a field that is largely concerned with classical reception but also with classicism's constructedness, contingency, and consequences in the modern world. Or, better yet, the essays might become the groundwork for a stronger bridge between the two fields: a point of crossing, facilitating traffic and exchange on both of its sides.

NOTES

My thanks to Anna Uhlig for helping me work out several of the ideas proposed here and to the editors of this volume for their comments on and corrections of earlier drafts of this essay.

    1. For an illuminating comparative appraisal of Cavafy translations published in the first decade of the twenty-first century, see Ekdawi, "Definitive Voice."

    2. Klooster provides a useful overview of the development of modern scholarship on Hellenist poetry.

    3. On both the nineteenth-century tablet and papyri finds and Pfeiffer's contribution to Callimachean scholarship, see Lehnus 26–29.

    4. An account of the back-and-forth is provided by Fraser, who claims to have discovered Cavafy's English-language essay in a friend's personal library and provides a transcription of the piece.

    5. On Blackie's efforts in 1890–91 to reform the teaching of classical Greek in Britain, in part by incorporating instruction in the modern language, see Stoddart 418–20.

    6. Jeffreys identifies several articles from the two magazines that prompted some form of engagement from Cavafy; see *Reframing Decadence* 42.

    7. The locus classicus for the articulation of this paradox of classicism is Plutarch's *Life of Pericles* 13.5; see Porter 48–54.

NOTES ON CONTRIBUTORS

Elsa Amanatidou is distinguished senior lecturer and director of Modern Greek studies at Brown University. She has served as director of the Center for Language Studies at Brown and as executive director of the Consortium for Language Teaching and Learning. Amanatidou is an associate for the Chartered Institute of Educational Assessors and Pearson's chief examiner for national and international examinations in Modern Greek in the UK. Her research interests include testing and evaluation, curriculum development, the integration of literature and the arts in foreign language curricula, multiliteracies, critical literacies, inclusive and engaged pedagogies, and technology-assisted and technology-mediated language learning. She has been elected to the executive board of the Modern Greek Studies Association several times and serves as chair of its Undergraduate Studies Committee.

Foteini Dimirouli is Research Fellow in English at Keble College, University of Oxford. Her research interests span English, Greek, and comparative literature of the twentieth century. Dimirouli's monograph, *Authorising the Other: C. P. Cavafy in the English and American Literary Scenes*, contracted with Oxford University Press, investigates the role of renowned authors such as E. M. Forster, Lawrence Durrell, W. H. Auden, Joseph Brodsky, Stephen Spender, and James Merrill in establishing the global fame of Cavafy. Dimirouli's other publications explore the topics of canon formation, the uses of literature in contexts of authoritarianism, and the reframing of the literary category in the digital arena.

Stamatia Dova is professor of classics and Greek studies at Hellenic College. She teaches and publishes on archaic and classical Greek poetry, ancient Greek athletics, and the concept of the hero in ancient Greece. Her research interests also include Greek language pedagogy, gender studies, and the reception of the ancient Olympics in the modern world. She is the author of *The Poetics of Failure in Ancient Greece* (2020) and *Greek Heroes in and out of Hades* (2012), the editor of *Historical Poetics in Nineteenth and Twentieth Century Greece: Essays in Honor of Lily Macrakis* (2012), and a coeditor of *Homer in Sicily* (2023). Dova is also the director of the Kallinikeion Institute at Hellenic College Holy Cross.

Sarah Ekdawi is a faculty research fellow at the University of Oxford and reviews editor of the journal *Byzantine and Modern Greek Studies*. Her teaching career spans thirty years and includes university teaching; syllabus, course, and materials design; school management; and teacher training. She is a qualified technical translator and practicing literary translator and has many publications to her name.

Karen Emmerich is associate professor of comparative literature at Princeton University. Her monograph *Literary Translation and the Making of Originals* (2017) contains a chapter on the translation of Cavafy's unfinished poems. She is also a translator of modern Greek poetry and prose and has translated over a dozen book-length works of literature.

Hala Halim is associate professor of comparative literature and Middle Eastern studies at New York University. Her book *Alexandrian Cosmopolitanism: An Archive* (2013) received an honorable mention for the Harry Levin Prize, sponsored by the American Comparative Literature Association. *Clamor of the Lake* (2009), Halim's translation of a novel by Mohamed El-Bisatie, won an Egyptian State Incentive Award.

Johanna Hanink is professor of classics at Brown University. Her publications include *The Classical Debt: Greek Antiquity in an Era of Austerity* (2017) and a translation of Andreas Karkavitsas's The Archeologist *and Selected Sea Stories* (2021).

Peter Jeffreys is associate professor of English at Suffolk University. He has written and edited a number of books on C. P. Cavafy: *Eastern Questions: Hellenism and Orientalism in the Writings of E. M. Forster and C. P. Cavafy* (2005), *The Forster-Cavafy Letters: Friends at a Slight Angle* (2009), E.M. Forster–Κ.Π. Καβάφης αλληλογραφία: Φίλοι σε ελαφρήν απόκλιση (2013), *C. P. Cavafy: Selected Prose Works* (2010), *Reframing Decadence: C. P. Cavafy's Imaginary Portraits* (2015), Στο κάδρο της παρακμής: Φανταστικά πορτραίτα του Κ.Π. Καβάφη (2024), and *Constantine Cavafy: A New Biography*, cowritten with Gregory Jusdanis (2025). He is a member of the international Cavafy Archive Academic Committee at the Onassis Foundation and served as a consultant for the exhibits at the Cavafy House in Alexandria and the Cavafy Archive space in Athens.

Gregory Jusdanis is distinguished humanities professor at Ohio State University, where he teaches courses in Modern Greek and comparative literature. He is the author of *The Poetics of Cavafy: Eroticism, Textuality, History* (1987); *Belated Modernity and Aesthetic Culture: Inventing National Literature* (1991); *The Necessary Nation* (2001); *Fiction Agonistes: In Defense of Literature* (2010); and *A Tremendous Thing: Friendship from the* Iliad *to the Internet* (2014). His books have been translated into Arabic, Polish, Spanish, and Turkish. His book *Constantine Cavafy: A New Biography*, cowritten with Peter Jeffreys, will be published in 2025.

Takis Kayalis is professor of Modern Greek literature and director of the MA program in creative writing at the Hellenic Open University. He has previously taught Modern Greek and comparative literature at Queens College, City University of New York; the University of Crete; the University of Cyprus; and the University of Ioannina. His research focuses mainly on nineteenth-century prose, modernist poetics, cultural theory, digital humanities, and literary pedagogy. He is a member of the international Cavafy Archive Academic Committee at the Onassis Foundation, where he has also coedited the Cavafy Archive's digital collection and directed several other projects. He is the author of an extensive study of Cavafy's uses of material antiquity vis-à-vis colonial culture, *Cavafy's Hellenistic Antiquities: History, Archaeology, Empire* (2024).

Cat Lambert is assistant professor of classics at Cornell University. She works on ancient Greek and Latin literature and its reception through the lenses of book history, gender and sexuality, and queer studies. Her current book project traces how the cultural category of the bad reader intersects with discursive constructions of power, embodiment, and identity in imperial Rome.

Vassilis Lambropoulos is the C. P. Cavafy Professor Emeritus of Classical Studies and Comparative Literature at the University of Michigan. His main research interests are modern Greek culture, classical reception and the classics, civic ethics and democratic politics, tragedy and the tragic, and words and music. He is the author of *Literature as National Institution* (1988), *The Rise of Eurocentrism* (1993), and *The Tragic Idea* (2006). He coedited the volumes *The Text and Its Margins* (1985) and *Twentieth-Century Literary Theory* (1987) and two special issues of academic journals: *The Humanities as Social Technology* (October, 1990) and *Ethical Politics* (*South Atlantic Quarterly*, 1996). He has served on the editorial board of several international journals. His websites are *Tragedy of Revolution: Revolution as Hubris in Modern Tragedy* and the blog *Piano Poetry Pantelis Politics*.

Martin McKinsey teaches at the University of New Hampshire. He specializes in contemporary British, Irish, and anglophone literature, modernist cultures, multilingual poetry, and translation theory. Among his books are *Hellenism and the Postcolonial Imagination: Yeats, Cavafy, Walcott* (2010) and *Clearing the Ground: C. P. Cavafy: Poetry and Prose, 1902–1911* (2015). He has translated stories, novels, and poetry from Modern Greek into English. In 1996, he received a Special Greek State Prize for his translation of Andreas Franghias's *The Courtyard*.

Natalie Melas teaches comparative literature at Cornell University. She is the author of *All the Difference in the World: Postcoloniality and the Ends of Comparison* and coeditor of *The Princeton Sourcebook in Comparative Literature*. She is slowly finishing a manuscript titled "Modern Lyric and Racial Time around Aimé Césaire and C. P. Cavafy." Her most current research involves a transmedial inquiry into Caribbean environments through poetic and audiovisual registers, which has led to the award-winning short experimental film *We Love We Self Up Here* (2021), made with the documentary filmmaker Kannan Arunasalam and the architect and spatial theorist Tao DuFour.

Angeliki Mousiou studied Modern Greek literature at the Aristotle University of Thessaloniki and the University of Oxford. From 2017 to 2024 she was employed at the Onassis Foundation as the Cavafy Archive researcher. As a member of the Cavafy Archive team, she coordinated the archival and literary documentation that led to the publication of the archive's digital collection in early 2019 and the publication of the Cavafy library in 2024.

Kelly Polychroniou is master lecturer and head of Modern Greek in the Department of Classical Studies at Boston University, where she teaches courses in Greek language, literature, and culture. She is the founder of the Boston University Philhellenes Project, through which over one hundred students have visited Greece to study Hellenic culture, ancient and modern. In 2020–21 Polychroniou was a visiting fellow at Harvard's Center for Hellenic Studies in Nauplia, and she is currently engaged in a project on polyglossia in Cavafy's poetry.

Panagiotis Roilos is the George Seferis Professor of Modern Greek Studies and professor of comparative literature at Harvard University and the president of the European Cultural Center of Delphi. He is also a member of the Standing Committee on Medieval Studies and the Steering Committee on Byzantine Studies as well as faculty associate of the Weatherhead Center for International Affairs at Harvard, where he has established the Seminar Series on Cultural Politics. He is the founder and director of the Delphi Academy of European Studies. His books include *Towards a Ritual Poetics*, with Dimitrios Yatromanolakis (coauthor, 2003); *Amphoteroglossia: A Poetics of the*

Twelfth-Century Medieval Greek Novel (2005); *C. P. Cavafy: The Economics of Metonymy* (2009); *Imagination and Logos: Essays on C. P. Cavafy* (editor, 2010); *Neomedieval Postcapitalism* (forthcoming); and *From Byzantium to the Early Greek Enlightenment: Books, Readers, Ideologies in Early Modern Greek Contexts—Late Fifteenth to Early Eighteenth Century* (editor, forthcoming).

Loren J. Samons is professor of classical studies at Boston University and chief academic advisor and executive director of the Institute for Hellenic Culture and the Liberal Arts at The American College of Greece in Athens. Samons's most recent book, *Pericles and the Conquest of History*, appeared in 2016. His current research focuses on the origins of classical Athenian culture and government, Cavafy's historical poetry, and the historian Herodotus.

Demetres P. Tryphonopoulos is professor of English at the University of Alberta, Augustana campus. He is the author, editor, coeditor, or translator of sixteen volumes, including *The Celestial Tradition: A Study of Ezra Pound's* The Cantos, *"I Cease Not to Yowl": Pound's Letters to Olivia Rosetti Agresti*, *The Ezra Pound Encyclopedia*, an annotated scholarly edition of H.D.'s *Majic Ring*, a second annotated scholarly edition of H.D.'s *Hirslanden Notebooks*, and *Approaches to Teaching Pound's Poetry and Prose*.

SURVEY RESPONDENTS

Jonathan A. Allan, *Brandon University*
Elsa Amanatidou, *Brown University*
Thodoris Chiotis, *Onassis Cavafy Archive, Onassis Foundation*
Maria I. Cipriani, *Hofstra University*
Foteini Dimirouli, *Oxford University*
Mark Doty, *Rutgers University*
Stamatia Dova, *Hellenic College*
Anthony Dracopoulos, *University of Sydney*
Sarah Ekdawi, *Oxford University*
Joanna Eleftheriou, *Christopher Newport University*
Karen Emmerich, *Princeton University*
George Fragopoulos, *Queensborough Community College*
Liana Giannakopoulou, *Cambridge University*
James Gifford, *Fairleigh Dickinson University*
Maria Hadjipolycarpou, *University of Illinois, Urbana-Champaign*
Hala Halim, *New York University*
Johanna Hanink, *Brown University*
Antony Hirst, *Trinity College Dublin*
Kenneth David Jackson, *Yale University*
Gregory Jusdanis, *Ohio State University*
Nikolas Kakkoufa, *Columbia University*
George Kalogeris, *Suffolk University*
Vrasidas Karalis, *University of Sydney*
Takis Kayalis, *Hellenic Open University, Athens*
Martha Klironomou, *San Francisco State University*
Vassilis Lambropoulos, *University of Michigan*
Martin McKinsey, *University of New Hampshire*
Natalie Melas, *Cornell University*
Eftihia Mihelakis, *Brandon University*
Angeliki Mousiou, *Onassis Cavafy Archive, Onassis Foundation*
Dimitris Papanikolaou, *Oxford University*
Salvatore Pappalardo, *Towson University*
Eleni Philippou, *Oxford University*
Kelly Polychroniou, *Boston University*
Gary Reger, *Trinity College, Hartford*
Panagiotis Roilos, *Harvard University*
Loren J. Samons, *Boston University*
Jason Schneiderman, *Borough of Manhattan Community College, City University of New York*
William Stroebel, *Princeton University*
George Syrimis, *Yale University*
Karen Van Dyck, *Columbia University*

WORKS CITED

'Abd al-Sabur, Salah [Salah Abdel Sabour]. الأعمال الشعرية الكاملة. حياتي في الشعر. الدواوين الشعرية [*Al-A'mal al-Shi'riyya al-Kamila: Hayati fil-Shi'r: Al-Dawawin al-Shi'riyya*; *The Complete Works: My Life in Poetry: The Poetry Collections*]. General Egyptian Book Organization, 1993.

———. "The Hanging of Zahran." Translated by Omar Sabry. *Afro-Asian Poetry: An Anthology*, edited by Edward al-Kharrat and Nihad Salem, Permanent Bureau of Afro-Asian Writers, 1971, pp. 72–74.

"About the BA." *Bibliotheca Alexandrina*, www.bibalex.org/en/Page/About. Accessed 9 Sept. 2024.

Aciman, André. *Find Me*. Farrar, Straus and Giroux, 2019.

Acosta-Hughes, Benjamin. "The Prefigured Muse: Rethinking a Few Assumptions on Hellenistic Poetics." *A Companion to Hellenistic Literature*, edited by James J. Clauss and Martine Cuypers, Wiley-Blackwell, 2010, pp. 81–91.

Ad Hoc Committee on Foreign Languages. "Foreign Languages and Higher Education: New Structures for a Changed World." 2007. *Modern Language Association*, www.mla.org/Resources/Guidelines-and-Data/Reports-and-Professional-Guidelines/Foreign-Languages-and-Higher-Education-New-Structures-for-a-Changed-World.

Al-Asyuti, Darwish. أشكال العديد في صعيد مصر [*Ashkal al-'adid fi sa'id Misr*; *Forms of the Lament in Upper Egypt*]. Al-Hay'a al-'Ama li-Qusur al-Thaqafa, 2006.

Alexander, Meena. *Quickly Changing River*. TriQuarterly, 2008.

Alexiou, Margaret, editor. *C. P. Cavafy*. Special issue of *Journal of the Hellenic Diaspora*. Vol. 10, nos. 1–2, spring-summer 1983.

———. Introduction. Alexiou, *C. P. Cavafy*, pp. 7–9.

———. *The Ritual Lament in Greek Tradition*. Revised by Dimitris Yatromanolakis and Panagiotis Roilos, 2nd ed., Rowman and Littlefield, 2002.

Alexiou, Margaret, and Vassilis Lambropoulos, editors. *The Text and Its Margins: Poststructuralist Approaches to Twentieth-Century Greek Literature*. Pella, 1985.

Alfano, Mélanie. *La lanterne sourde, 1921–1931: Une aventure culturelle internationale*. Éditions Racine, 2008.

Al-Imam, Muhammad Rif'at. حكاية اليوناني المتمصر [*Hikayat al-Yunani al-Mutamassir*; *The Story of Egyptiotes Ellin*]. Al-Hay'a al-'Amma li-Qusur al-Thaqafa, 2012.

Al-Kharrat, Edwar. *City of Saffron*. Translated by Frances Liardet, Quartet Books, 1989.

———. *Girls of Alexandria*. Translated by Frances Liardet, Quartet Books, 1993.

Al-Masadi, Muhammad Jamal al-Din 'Ali. دنشواي [*Dinshiwai*]. General Egyptian Book Organization, 1974.

Al-Naqqash, Raja'. ثلاثون عاما مع الشعر والشعراء [*Thalathun 'aman ma' al-shi'r wal-shu'ara*'; *Thirty Years with Poetry and Poets*]. Dar Su'ad al-Sabbah, 1992.

Al-Sayyid, Marsot Afaf Lutfi. *Egypt and Cromer: A Study in Anglo-Egyptian Relations*. John Murray, 1968.

———. *A History of Egypt: From the Arab Conquest to the Present*. Cambridge UP, 2007.

Anagnostou, Giorgos. "Speaking Greek at the American University over the Last Two Centuries." *Vimeo*, uploaded by UM Classical Studies, 2017, vimeo.com/221459248.

Anton, John P. *The Poetry and Poetics of Constantine P. Cavafy: Aesthetic Visions of Sensual Reality*. Harwood, 1995.

"'Archive of Desire': A Festival Inspired by the Poet C. P. Cavafy." *Onassis*, Onassis Foundation, www.onassis.org/whats-on/cavafy-festival. Accessed 1 Apr. 2024.

"An Archive of Incalculable Value: An Archive Open to All." *Onassis*, Onassis Foundation, www.onassis.org/initiatives/cavafy-archive/cavafy-archive. Accessed 20 Dec. 2020.

Aristotle. *Politics*. Translated by H. Rackham, Harvard UP / William Heinemann, 1944.

'Ashmawi, Sayyid. الإقتصادي-السياسي ۱۸۰۵-۱۹۵٦ اليونانيون في مصر: دراسة تاريخية في الدور. [*Al-Yunaniyyun fi Misr: Dirasa tarikhiyya fi al-dawr al-iqtisadi-al-siyasi, 1956–1805; The Greeks in Egypt: A Historical Study of the Political Economy of Their Role, 1805–1956*]. Ayn, 1997.

Assmann, Aleida. "Canon and Archive." *Cultural Memory Studies: An International Interdisciplinary Handbook*, edited by Astrid Erll et al., De Gruyter, 2008, pp. 97–107.

Auden, W. H. *Collected Poems*. Edited by Edward Mendelson, Vintage Books, 1991.

———. Introduction. Cavafy, *Complete Poems of Cavafy*, pp. xv–xxiii.

"Automedon with the Horses of Achilles." *MFA Boston*, collections.mfa.org/objects/31014. Accessed 8 Jan. 2023.

Balzac, Honoré de. *Lost Illusions*. Translated by Kathleen Raine, Random House, 1997.

Barber, Tony. "The Decline of Europe Is a Global Concern." *Financial Times*, 21 Dec. 2015, ft.com/cms/s/0/ddfd47e8-a404-11e5-873f-68411a84f346.html.

Barnstone, Willis. *The Poetics of Translation*. Yale UP, 1993.

———. "Real and Imaginary History in Borges and Cavafy." *Comparative Literature*, vol. 29, no. 1, 1977, pp. 54–73.

Barthes, Roland. "Loving Schumann." *The Responsibility of Forms*, translated by Richard Howard, U of California P, 1991, pp. 293–98.

Bataille, Georges. *The Accursed Share: An Essay on General Economy*. Zone Books, 1988–93. 3 vols.

Baudelaire, Charles. *The Flowers of Evil*. Translated by James McGowan, Oxford UP, 1993.

———. *The Poems in Prose*. Translated by Francis Scarfe, Anvil Press Poetry, 2004.

Beaton, Roderick. "C. P. Cavafy: Irony and Hellenism." *Slavonic and East European Review*, vol. 59, no. 4, 1981, pp. 516–28.

———. *George Seferis: Waiting for the Angel: A Biography*. Yale UP, 2003.

———. *Greece: Biography of a Modern Nation*. Penguin Books, 2019.

———. *An Introduction to Modern Greek Literature*. Clarendon Press, 1999.

Beckett, Samuel. *Molloy*. Translated by Beckett and Patrick Bowles, Galder and Byoyars, 1966.

Bhabha, Homi K. *The Location of Culture*. Routledge, 1994.

Bien, Peter. *Constantine Cavafy*. Columbia UP, 1964.

Bien, Peter, et al., editors. *A Century of Greek Poetry, 1900–2000*. Bilingual ed., Cosmos Publishers, 2004.

Bishop, Elizabeth. *Selected Poems*. Chatoo and Windus, 1967.

Bloom, Benjamin, et al. *Taxonomy of Educational Objectives: The Classification of Educational Goals: Handbook 1: Cognitive Domain*. David McKay, 1956.

Blunt, Wilfrid Scawen. *Atrocities of Justice under British Rule in Egypt*. T. Fisher Unwin, 1907.

Boghiguian, Anna. *A Poet on the Edge of History (Constantine Cavafy)*. 1995–2017. Sharjah Art Foundation, sharjahart.org/sharjah-art-foundation/publications/anna-boghiguian.

Boletsi, Maria. Review of *"Made Just Like Me": The Homosexual Cavafy and the Poetics of Sexuality*, by Dimitris Papanikolaou. *Journal of Modern Greek Studies*, vol. 31, no. 1, 2016, pp. 198–203.

———. *Specters of Cavafy*. U of Michigan P, 2024.

Boustani, Rafic, and Philippe Fargues, editors. *The Atlas of the Arab World: Geopolitics and Society*. Facts on File, 1991.

Bowersock, G. W. "Cavafy and Apollonius." *Grand Street*, vol. 2, no. 3, 1983, pp. 180–89.

———. *From Gibbon to Auden: Essays on the Classical Tradition*. Oxford UP, 2009.

———. "The Julian Poems of C. P. Cavafy." *Byzantine and Modern Greek Studies*, vol. 7, 1981, pp. 89–104.

———. *Julian the Apostate*. Harvard UP, 1989.

Bowra, C. M. "The Answers of a Prophet." *The New York Times*, 28 May 1961, p. BR4.

———. *The Creative Experiment*. Macmillan, 1949.

Brodsky, Joseph. *Less than One: Selected Essays*. Farrar, Straus and Giroux, 1986.

Brown, Peter. *The World of Late Antiquity*. W. W. Norton, 1971.

Burgess, Jonathan S. *The Death and Afterlife of Achilles*. Johns Hopkins UP, 2009.

———. "Untrustworthy Apollo and the Destiny of Achilles: 'Iliad' 24.55–63." *Harvard Studies in Classical Philology*, vol. 102, 2004, pp. 21–40.

Cachia, Pierre. *Popular Narrative Ballads of Modern Egypt*. Oxford UP, 1989.

Calinescu, Matei. *Five Faces of Modernity: Modernism, Avant-Garde, Decadence, Kitsch, Postmodernism*. Duke UP, 1987.

Calotychos, Vangelis. *Modern Greece: A Cultural Poetics*. Berg, 2003.

Cantalupo, Barbara. *Poe and the Visual Arts*. Penn State UP, 2014.

Capri-Karka, C. *Love and the Symbolic Journey in the Poetry of Cavafy, Eliot, and Seferis: An Interpretation with Detailed Poem-by-Poem Analysis*. Pella Publishing, 1982.

190 WORKS CITED

Carson, Anne. *If Not, Winter.* Vintage, 2003.

Casanova, Pascale. *The World Republic of Letters.* Translated by M. B. DeBevoise, Harvard UP, 2004.

Catraro, Atanasio. Ο φίλος μου ο Καβάφης. [*O filos mou o Kavafis*; *My Friend Cavafy*]. Ikaros, 1970.

Cavafy, Constantine P. [Konstantinos P. Kafafis]. Ανεκδοτά Πεζά Κείμενα [*Anekdota peza keimena*; *Unpublished Prose Texts*]. Edited by Michalis Peridis, Fexis, 1963.

———. Ανέκδοτα Ποιήματα, 1882–1923 [*Anekdota piimata, 1882–1923*; *Unpublished Poems, 1882–1923*]. Edited by George P. Savidis, Ikaros, 1968.

———. Ανέκδοτα Σημειώματα Ποιητικής και Ηθικής [*Anekdota simiomata piitikis kai ithikis*; *Unpublished Notes on Poetics and Ethics*]. Edited by George P. Savidis, Hermes, 1983.

———. Άπαντα τα δημοσιευμένα ποιήματα [*Apanta ta dimosieumena piimata*; *Complete Published Poems*]. Edited by Renos Apostolidis et al., Ta Nea Ellinika, 2002.

———. Άπαντα τα Ποιήματα [*Apanta ta piimata*; *The Complete Poems*]. Edited by Sonia Ilinskagia, Narkissos, 2003.

———. Αποκηρυγμένα Ποιήματα και Μεταφράσεις, 1886–1898 [*Apokirygmena piimata kai metafrasis, 1886–1898*; *Repudiated Poems and Translations, 1886–1898*]. Edited by George P. Savidis, Ikaros, 1983.

———. Ατελή Ποιήματα, 1918–1932 [*Ateli piimata, 1918–1932*; *Unfinished Poems, 1918–1932*]. Edited by Renata Lavagnini, Ikaros, 1994.

———. *Before Time Could Change Them: The Complete Poems of Constantine P. Cavafy.* Translated by Theoharis C. Theoharis, Harcourt, 2001.

———. *The Canon: The Original One Hundred and Fifty-Four Poems.* Translated by Stratis Haviaras, Hermes, 2004.

———. *The Canon: The Original One Hundred and Fifty-Four Poems.* Translated by Stratis Haviaras, 2nd ed., Center for Hellenic Studies, Harvard UP, 2007.

———. *Clearing the Ground: C. P. Cavafy: Poetry and Prose, 1902–1911.* Translated by Martin McKinsey, Laertes, 2015.

———. *Collected Poems.* Translated by Edmund Keeley and Philip Sherrard, edited by George P. Savidis, Hogarth Press, 1975.

———. *Collected Poems.* Translated by Edmund Keeley and Philip Sherrard, edited by George P. Savidis, rev. ed., Princeton UP, 1992.

———. *Collected Poems.* Translated by Edmund Keeley and Philip Sherrard, edited by George P. Savidis, bilingual ed., Princeton UP, 2009.

———. *Collected Poems.* Translated by Daniel Mendelsohn, Alfred A. Knopf, 2009.

———. *The Collected Poems: A New Translation.* Translated by Evangelos Sachperoglou, edited by Anthony Hirst, Oxford UP, 2007.

———. *The Collected Poems of C. P. Cavafy: A New Translation.* Translated by Aliki Barnstone, W. W. Norton, 2006.

———. *Complete Plus: The Poems of C. P. Cavafy in English.* Translated by George Economou with Stavros Deligiorgis, Shearsman Books, 2013.

WORKS CITED 191

———. *Complete Poems*. Translated by Daniel Mendelsohn, Alfred A. Knopf, 2009.

———. *The Complete Poems of Cavafy*. Translated by Rae Dalven, Harvest, 1989.

———. "Constantinopoliad an Epic." Edited by Diana Haas. Ζητήματα Ιστορίας Των Νεοελληνικών Γραμμάτων [*Zitimata Istorias ton Neoellinikon Grammaton; Issues in the History of Greek Letters*], 1994, pp. 281–304.

———. *The Greek Poems of C. P. Cavafy*. Translated by Memas Kolaitis, Aristide D. Caratzas, 1989. 2 vols.

———. *Historical Poems: A Verse Translation with Commentaries*. Translated with commentaries by J. Phillipson, AuthorHouse, 2013.

———. Κ.Π. Καβάφη: Επιστολές στον Μάριο Βαιάνο [*K. P. Kavafi: Epistoles ston Mario Baiano; C. P. Cavafy: Letters to Marios Vaianos*]. Edited by E. N. Moschos, Estia, 1979.

———. Κ.Π. Καβάφης: Ποιήματα [*K. P. Kavafis: Piimata; C. P. Cavafy: Poems*]. Kastaniotis, 2005.

———. Κ.Π. Καβάφης: Τα ποιήματα δημοσιευμένα και αδημοσίευτα [*K. P. Kavafis: Ta piimata dimosieumena kai adimosieuta; C. P. Cavafy: The Published and Unpublished Poems*]. Edited by Dimitris Dimiroulis, Gutenberg, 2015.

———. Κρυμμένα Ποιήματα, 1877;–1923 [*Krymmena piimata, 1877?–1923; Hidden Poems, 1877?–1923*]. Edited by George P. Savidis, Ikaros, 1997.

———. Το λεξικό παραθεμάτων [*To lexiko parathematon; Dictionary of Citations*]. Edited by Michalis Pieris, Ikaros, 2015.

———. *One Hundred Sixty-Six Poems*. Translated by Alan L. Boegehold, Axios, 2008.

———. Πεζά [*Peza; Prose Works*]. Edited by George A. Papoutsakis, Fexis, 1963.

———. Ποιήματα [*Piimata; Poems*]. Edited by Dimitris Eleftherakis, Patakis, 2011.

———. Ποιήματα [*Piimata; Poems*]. Edited by Rika Sengopoulos, 1935.

———. Ποιήματα Α΄, 1896–1918 [*Piimata, A', 1896–1918; Poems 1, 1896–1918*]. 1963. Edited by George P. Savidis, Ikaros, 1991.

———. Ποιήματα Β΄, 1919–1933 [*Piimata, B', 1919–1933; Poems 2, 1919–1933*]. 1963. Edited by George P. Savidis, rev. ed., Ikaros, 1991.

———. *Poems*. Translated by John Mavrogordato, Grove Press, 1952.

———. *The Poems of the Canon*. Translated by John Chioles, Harvard Early Modern and Modern Greek Library, Department of the Classics, Harvard U, 2011.

———. *Poesie e prose*. Edited by Renata Lavagnini and Christiano Luciani, Bompiani, 2021.

———. "Professor Blackie on the Modern Greek Language." Cavafy, *Selected Prose Works*, pp. 31–35.

———. *Prose Works, 1882–1931*. Edited and translated by Michalis Pieris, Ikaros, 2003.

———. Σχόλια του Καβάφη σε ποιήματά του ["Scholia tou Kavafi se piimata tou"; "Comments on Cavafy's Poems"]. Edited by Diana Haas. Κύκλος Καβάφη [*Kyklos Kavafi; Cavafy's Circle*], Society of Neohellenic Culture and General Education, 1983, pp. 83–109.

———. *Selected Poems*. Translated by David Connolly, Aiora, 2013.

---. *Selected Poems*. Translated by Avi Sharon, Penguin Books, 2008.

---. *Selected Prose Works*. Edited and translated by Peter Jeffreys, U of Michigan P, 2010.

---. *Sixty-Three Poems*. Translated by J. C. Cavafy, introduction by Manuel Savidis, Ikaros, 2003.

---. Τα Πεζά, 1882–1931 [*Ta peza, 1882–1931; The Prose Works, 1882–1931*]. Edited by Michalis Pieris, Ikaros, 2003.

---. Τα Ποιήματα [*Ta piimata; The Poems*]. Edited by George P. Savidis, vol. 1, Ikaros, 1991.

---. *The Unfinished Poems*. Translated and introduced by Daniel Mendelsohn, Alfred A. Knopf, 2009.

---. "Yussef Hussein Selim, 27 June 1906 2 P.M." *Onassis Cavafy Archive*, Onassis Foundation, https://doi.org/10.26256/ca-sf01-s01-f01-sf001-0162.

"Cavafy Archive: An Archive Open to All." *Onassis*, Onassis Foundation, onassis.org/initiatives/cavafy-archive/. Accessed 20 Dec. 2020.

"Cavafy Goes to School: Workshop for Educators." *Onassis*, Onassis Foundation, onassis.org/whats-on/cavafy-goes-school-workshop-educators. Accessed 20 Dec. 2020.

"Cavafy Library." *Onassis Cavafy Archive*, Onassis Foundation, cavafy.onassis.org/cavafy-library/.

"Cavafy Script: Cavafy on Your Finger Tips." *Onassis*, Onassis Foundation, www.onassis.org/initiatives/cavafy-archive/cavafy-script.

"Cavafy's World: Ancient Passions." *Kelsey Museum of Archaeology*, U of Michigan, 2024, lsa.umich.edu/kelsey/exhibitions/special-exhibitions/past/cavafys-world.html.

"Cavafy's World: Hidden Things." *Kelsey Museum of Archaeology*, U of Michigan, 2024, exhibitions.kelsey.lsa.umich.edu/galleries/Exhibits/cavafy/hiddenthings.html.

Celan, Paul. *Selected Poems*. Penguin Classics, 1996.

Census of Modern Greek Literature. Boston College, censusofmoderngreekliterature.org/.

Césaire, Aimé. *Une tempête*. Présence Africaine, 1968.

Χρονολόγιο ["Chronologio"; "Chronology"]. Χάρτης [*Chartis; Map*], nos. 5–6, Apr. 1983, pp. 514–25.

Classical and Modern Literature. Special issue, vol. 23, no. 2, fall 2003.

Clogg, Richard. *A Concise History of Greece*. 2nd ed., Cambridge UP, 2002.

Coetzee, J. M. *Waiting for the Barbarians*. Penguin Books, 1980.

Cohen, Leonard. "Alexandra Leaving." *Ten New Songs*, Columbia, 2001. CD.

Collins, Kate. "Teaching with Archives: Duke Summer Doctoral Academy." *The Devil's Tale*, 26 Apr. 2019, blogs.library.duke.edu/rubenstein/2019/04/26/teaching-with-archives-duke-doctoral-summer-academy/.

Cone, Edward T. *The Composer's Voice*. U of California P, 1974.

Cope, B., and M. Kalantzis, editors. *Multiliteracies: Literary Learning and the Design of Social Futures*. Routledge, 2000.

"Copyright and Terms of Use." *Onassis Cavafy Archive*, Onassis Foundation, cavafy.onassis.org/policy/. Accessed 20 Dec. 2020.

Cotton, Justine, and David Sharron. *Engaging Students with Archival and Digital Resources*. Chandos Publishing, 2011.

"C. P. Cavafy." *Academy of American Poets*, poets.org/poet/c-p-cavafy.

"C. P. Cavafy." *Poetry Foundation*, www.poetryfoundation.org/poets/c-p-cavafy.

"C. P. Cavafy: Anthology of Readings." *Centre for Neo-Hellenic Studies*, www.snhell.gr/lections/writer.asp?id=60.

"C. P. Cavafy Forum." *LSA*, U of Michigan, lsa.umich.edu/modgreek/window-to-greek-culture/c-p--cavafy-forum.html.

C. P. Cavafy Music Resource Guide: Song and Music Settings of Cavafy's Poetry. Version 3, 3 Mar. 2022, lsa.umich.edu/content/dam/modgreek-assets/modgreek-docs/CAVAFY/Cavafy%20Song%20Bibliography_Version3_3-3-22.pdf.

"Creating a Literary Commons: Engaging Students in Digital Archives." *Center for the Humanities*, City U of New York, centerforthehumanities.org/programming/creating-a-literary-commons-engaging-students-in-digital-archives.

Crispin, Matt. *Cavafy: Anatomy of a Soul*. Crescent Moon, 1993.

Crown, Sarah. "Generation Next: The Rise—and Rise—of the New Poets." *The Guardian*, 16 Feb. 2019, www.theguardian.com/books/2019/feb/16/rise-new-poets.

Damrosch, David. *What Is World Literature?* Princeton UP, 2003.

Dante. *Divine Comedy*. Translated by Henry Cary, Everyman, 1994.

Daruwalla, Keki N. *Collected Poems, 1970–2005*. Penguin Books, 2006.

Daskalopoulos, Dimitris. Βιβλιογραφία Κ.Π. Καβάφη, 1886–2000 [*Bibliografia K. P. Kavafi, 1886–2000; Bibliography of C. P. Cavafy, 1886–2000*]. Kentro Ellinikis Glossas, 2003.

———. "C. P. Cavafy." Translated by Karen Emmerich. *Onassis Cavafy Archive*, Onassis Foundation, cavafy.onassis.org/creator/cavafy-c-p/. Accessed 20 Dec. 2020.

———. Ελληνικά καβαφογενή ποιήματα, 1909–2001 [*Ellinika Kavafogeni piimata, 1909–2001; Greek Cavafian Poems, 1909–2001*]. U of Patras P, 2003.

———. Introduction. Τριάντα Παρωδίες Ποιημάτων του Κ.Π. Καβάφη [*Trianta parodies piimaton tou K. P. Kavafi; Thirty Parodies of C. P. Cavafy's Poems*], by X. A. Kokolis, Kastaniotis, 2007, pp. 9–17.

———. Παρωδίες καβαφηκών ποιημάτων, 1917–1997 [*Parodies Kavafikon piimaton, 1917–1997; Parodies of Cavafy Poems, 1917–1997*]. Patakis, 1998.

———. Προσθήκες στη βιβλιογραφία Κ.Π. Καβάφη, 1886–2000 ["Prosthikes sti bibliografia K. P. Kavafi"; "Addendum to the Bibliography of C. P. Cavafy"]. Κονδυλοφόρος [*Kondylophoros; Penholder*], vol. 11, 2012, pp. 165–233.

Daskalopoulos, Dimitris, and Maria Stasinopoulou. Ο Βίος και το Έργο του Κ.Π. Καβάφη [*O vios kai to ergo tou K. P. Kavafi; The Life and Work of C. P. Cavafy*]. Metaichmio, 2013.

Dean, Heather. "Learning and Teaching with Literary Archives." *Comma*, no. 1, 2017, pp. 37–48.

Deleuze, Gilles, and Félix Guattari. *Kafka: Toward a Minor Literature*. U of Minnesota P, 1987.

———. *A Thousand Plateaus: Capitalism and Schizophrenia*. Translated by Brian Massumi, U of Minnesota P, 1987.

"Denishwai M.P.'s Sentimentalism: Questions in the House." *The Egyptian Gazette*, 5 July 1906.

Derrida, Jacques. *Given Time: I. Counterfeit Money*. Translated by Peggy Camuf, U of Chicago P, 1992.

Desmarais, Jane, and Chris Baldick, editors. *Decadence: An Annotated Anthology*. Manchester UP, 2012.

Desmarais, Jane, and Paul Weir, editors. *Decadence and Literature*. Cambridge UP, 2019.

———. Introduction. Desmarais and Weir, *Decadence*, pp. 1–11.

Dhomhnaill, Nuala Ní. *Selected Poems: Rogha Dánta*. Translated by Michael Hartnett, New Island Books, 1993.

Diamantopoulou, Lilli, and Zyranna Stoikou. "Cavafy Reanimated: Intermedial Transformations in Comics and Animation." *Journal of Greek Media and Culture*, vol. 1, no. 1, 2015, pp. 299–319.

Di Canzio, William. *Alec*. Farrar, Straus and Giroux, 2021.

"The Digital Collection of the Cavafy Archive." *Onassis Cavafy Archive*, Onassis Foundation, cavafy.onassis.org/.

"Digital Material: Creative Educational Approaches to Literary Archives and Research Libraries: The C. P. Cavafy Archive and Onassis Library." *Onassis*, Onassis Foundation, www.onassis.org/initiatives/cavafy-archive/digital-material-creative-educational-approaches-literary-archives-and-research-libraries-c-p-cavafy-archive-and-library-and-onassis-library. Accessed 20 Dec. 2020.

Dijkstra, Bram. *Idols of Perversity: Fantasies of Feminine Evil in the Fin-de-Siècle Culture*. Oxford UP, 1896.

Dimaras, C. Th. *A History of Modern Greek Literature*. Translated by Mary P. Gianos, State U of New York P, 1972.

Dimirouli, Foteini. *Authorising the Other: C. P. Cavafy in the English and American Literary Scene*. Oxford UP, forthcoming.

———. "C. P. Cavafy in the World: Origins, Trajectories and the Diasporic Poet." Lecture. *British School in Athens*, 1 Feb. 2021, bsa.ac.uk/videos/foteini-dimirouli-cp-cavafy-in-the-world/.

Dinshaw, Carolyn. *Getting Medieval: Sexualities and Communities, Pre- and Postmodern*. Duke UP, 1999.

Doty, Mark. *My Alexandria*. U of Illinois P, 1993.

Douthat, Ross. *The Decadent Society: How We Became the Victims of Our Own Success*. Avid Reader Press, 2020.

Dova, Stamatia. *Greek Heroes in and out of Hades*. Lexington Books, 2012.

———. *The Poetics of Failure in Ancient Greece*. Routledge, 2020.

Dowling, Linda. *Hellenism and Homosexuality in Victorian Oxford*. Cornell UP, 1994.

Durrell, Lawrence. *Baltazar*. Faber and Faber, 1958.

———. *Clea*. Faber and Faber, 1960.

———. *Justine*. Faber and Faber, 1957.

———. *Mountolive*. Faber and Faber, 1958.

Eaves, Morris. "Graphicality: Multimedia Fables for 'Textual' Critics." *Reimagining Textuality: Textual Studies in the Late Age of Print*, edited by Elizabeth Bergmann Loizeaux and Neil Fraistat, U of Wisconsin P, 2002, pp. 99–122.

Economou, George. *Unfinished and Uncollected: Finishing the Unfinished Poems of C. P. Cavafy and Uncollected Poems and Translations*. Shearsman Books, 2015.

Edelman, Lee. *No Future: Queer Theory and the Death Drive*. Duke UP, 2004.

Edwards, Jason. *Queer and Bookish: Eve Kosofsky Sedgwick as Book Artist*. Punctum Books, 2022.

Ekdawi, Sarah. "'Definitive Voice of the Loved Dead': Cavafy in English." *Journal of Modern Greek Studies*, vol. 30, no. 1, 2012, pp. 129–36. *Project Muse*, https://doi.org/10.1353/mgs.2012.0000.

———. "The Erotic Poems of C. P. Cavafy." *Kambos: Cambridge Papers in Modern Greek*, vol. 1, Faculty of Modern and Medieval Languages, U of Cambridge, 1993, pp. 23–46.

Ekdawi, Sarah, and Anthony Hirst. "Left Out, Crossed Out and Pasted Over: The Editorial Implications of Cavafy's Own Evaluations of His Uncollected and Unpublished Poems." *Modern Greek Studies (Australia and New Zealand)*, vol. 5, 1999, pp. 79–132.

Eliot, T. S. *The Waste Land*. *The Waste Land: Authoritative Text, Contexts, Criticism*, edited by Michael North, W. W. Norton, 2001, pp. 3–20.

———. *What Is a Classic?* Faber, 1944.

Έλληνες του πνεύματος και της τέχνης: Κωνσταντίνος Καβάφης [*Ellines tou pneumatos kai tis technis: Konstantinos Kavafis; Greeks of the Life of the Spirit and Art: Constantine Cavafy*]. Directed by Dimitris Lignadis, SKAI, 2012. *YouTube*, uploaded by SKAI.gr, 6 Dec. 2012, www.youtube.com/watch?v=BPZ4HVkcoYU.

Emmerich, Karen. *Literary Translation and the Making of Originals*. Bloomsbury, 2017.

Errington, R. Malcolm. *A History of the Hellenistic World*. Blackwell, 2008.

Esmeir, Samera. *Juridical Humanity: A Colonial History*. Stanford UP, 2012.

"Exhibition 'C P. Cavafy "Painted"–Forty Contemporary Greek Artists.'" *European Cultural Centre of Delphi*, 2024, eccd.gr/en/events/events-archive/exhibition-c-p-cavafy-painted-40-contemporary-greek-artists/.

Fahmy, Ziad. "Francophone Egyptian Nationalists, Anti-British Discourse, and European Public Opinion, 1885–1910: The Case of Mustafa Kamil and Ya'qub Sannu'." *Comparative Studies of South Asia, Africa and the Middle East*, vol. 28, no. 1, 2008, pp. 170–83.

Falbo, Bianca. "Teaching from the Archives." *RBM: A Journal of Rare Books, Manuscripts, and Cultural Heritage*, vol. 1, no. 1, 2000, pp. 33–35.

WORKS CITED

Ferguson, Donna. "Poetry Sales Soar as Political Millenials Search for Clarity." *The Guardian*, 21 Jan. 2019, theguardian.com/books/2019/jan/21/poetry-sales-soar-as-political-millennials-search-for-clarity.

Forster, E. M. *Alexandria: A History and a Guide*. 1922. Oxford UP, 1986.

———. *Pharos and Pharillon*. Hogarth Press, 1923.

———. "The Poetry of C. P. Cavafy." Forster, *Pharos*, pp. 91–97.

Foucault, Michel. "The Art of Telling the Truth." *Critique and Power: Recasting the Foucault/Habermas Debate*, edited by Michael Kelly, MIT Press, 1994, pp. 139–48.

———. *An Introduction*. Translated by Robert Hurley, Vintage Books, 1980. Vol. 1 of *The History of Sexuality*.

Fraser, P. M. "Cavafy and the Elgin Marbles." *The Modern Language Review*, vol. 58, no. 1, 1963, pp. 66–68.

Freccero, Carla. *Queer/Early/Modern*. Duke UP, 2006.

Freeman, Elizabeth. *Time Binds: Queer Temporalities, Queer Histories*. Duke UP, 2010.

Friar, Kimon, editor and translator. *Modern Greek Poetry: From Cavafis to Elytis*. Simon and Schuster, 1973.

Friel, Brian. *Translations: A Play*. Faber and Faber, 1995.

Gallant, Thomas W. *The Edinburgh History of the Greeks, 1768 to 1913: The Long Nineteenth Century*. Edinburgh UP, 2015.

Gav. "Ithaka: A Poem by Constantine P. Cavafy." *Zen Pencils*, 25 Sept. 2013, zenpencils.com/comic/131-c-p-cavafy-ithaka/.

General International Standard Archival Description. 2nd ed., International Council on Archives, 2000, ica.org/sites/default/files/CBPS_2000_Guidelines_ISAD%28G%29_Second-edition_EN.pdf.

Genette, Gérard. *Paratexts: Thresholds of Interpretation*. Translated by Jane E. Lewin, Cambridge UP, 1997.

Georganta, Konstantina. *Conversing Identities: Encounters between British, Irish and Greek Poetry, 1922–1952*. Rodopi, 2012.

Ghika, Katerina. "Ideal Library." *Onassis Cavafy Archive*, Onassis Foundation, cavafy.onassis.org/el/ideal-library/. Accessed 30 July 2020.

Gibbon, Edward. *The Decline and Fall of the Roman Empire, 1776–1789*. Modern Library, 2003.

Giles, Jim. "Internet Encyclopaedias Go Head to Head." *Nature*, no. 438, Dec. 2005, pp. 900–01, nature.com/articles/438900a.

Ginsberg, Allen. *Selected Poems, 1947–1980*. Harper Perennial, 1988.

Gissing, George. *New Grub Street*. Penguin Classics, 1976.

"The God Abandons Anthony." *Onassis Cavafy Archive*, Onassis Foundation, cavafy.onassis.org/?s=The+God+abandons+Antony.

Gorman, Anthony. "Repatriation, Migration or Readjustment: Egyptian Greek Dilemmas of the 1950s." *Greek Diaspora and Migration since 1700*, edited by Dimitris Tziovas, Routledge, 2009, pp. 61–72.

Gourgouris, Stathis, editor. *The Cavafy Dossier*. Special issue of *Boundary 2*. Vol. 48, no. 2, May 2021.

———. "Cavafy's Debt." *Boundary 2*, vol. 44, no. 3, 2017, pp. 129–57.

———. *Dream Nation: Enlightenment, Colonization and the Institution of Modern Greece*. Stanford UP, 2021.

"G. P. Savidis Historical Catalogue." *Onassis Cavafy Archive*, Onassis Foundation, cavafy.onassis.org/savvidis-catalogue/. Accessed 20 Dec. 2020.

Green, Peter. *The Hellenistic Age*. Modern Library Chronicles, 2008.

Greer, Jane, and Laurie Grobman, editors. *Pedagogies of Public Memory: Teaching Writing and Rhetoric at Museums, Memorials, and Archives*. Routledge, 2016.

Gregory, Helen. "Youth Take the Lead: Digital Poetry and the Next Generation." *English in Education*, vol. 47, no. 2, summer 2013, pp. 118–33.

Grote, George. *A History of Greece*. John Murray, 1846–56. 12 vols.

Haag, Michael. *Alexandria: City of Memory*. Yale UP, 2004.

———. *Vintage Alexandria: Photographs of the City, 1860–1960*. American U in Cairo P, 2008.

Haas, Diana. Ανέκδοτο Αυτοσχόλιο στο Ποιήμα "Η Ναυμαχία" ["Anekdoto autoscholio sto piima 'I naumachia'"; "Unpublished Self-Commentary on the Poem 'The Naval Battle'"]. *Logeion: A Journal of Ancient Theatre*, vol. 2, 2012, pp. 200–15, logeion.upatras.gr/sites/logeion.upatras.gr/files/pdffiles/HAAS_Logeion_2_0.pdf.

———. Ανέκδοτο Αυτοσχόλιο στο Ποιήμα 'Τὰ δ' ἄλλα ἐν Ἅδου τοῖς κάτω μυθήσομαι' ["Anekdoto autoscholio sto piima 'Ta d'alla en Adou tis kato mythisomai'"; "Unpublished Self-Commentary on the Poem 'The Rest I Will Tell to Those Down in Hades'"]. *Logeion*, vol. 3, 2013, pp. 132–45, logeion.upatras.gr/sites/logeion.upatras.gr/files/pdffiles/HAAS_2013Final_0.pdf.

———. "Cavafy's Reading Notes on Gibbon's 'Decline and Fall.'" *Folia Neohellenica*, vol. 4, 1982, pp. 25–96.

———. Κ.Π. Καβάφης: Ανέκδοτο Αυτοσχόλιο στο ποιήμα "Φωνές" ["K. P. Kavafi: Anekdoto autoscholio sto piima 'Fones'"; "C. P. Cavafy: Unpublished Self-Commentary on the Poem 'Voices'"]. Κονδυλοφόρος [*Kondylophoros; Penholder*], vol. 14, 2015, pp. 101–30.

———. Κ.Π. Καβάφης: Αυτοσχόλια στα ποιήματα "Δημητρίου Σωτήρος (162–150 π.Χ.)" και "Η Δυσαρέσκεια του Σελευκίδου" ["K. P. Kavafi: Autoscholia sta piimata 'Dimitriou Sotiros (162–150 p. CH.)' kai 'I Dysareskia tou Seleykidou'"; "C. P. Cavafy: Self-Comments on the Poems 'Demetrios Sotir (162–150 BC)' and 'The Displeasure of Selefkidis'"]. Κονδυλοφόρος [*Kondylophoros; Penholder*], vol. 16, 2018, pp. 97–140.

———. Κ.Π. Καβάφης: Αυτοσχόλια στα ποιήματα "Η Συνοδεία του Διονύσου" και "Τυανεύς Γλύπτυς" ["K. P. Kavafi: Autoscholia sta piimata 'I synodia tou Dionysou' kai 'Tyaneus glyptis'"; "C. P. Cavafy: Self-Comments on the Poems 'The Retinue of Dionysus' and 'The Sculptor of Tyranna'"]. Κονδυλοφόρος [*Kondylophoros; Penholder*], vol. 17, 2019, pp. 63–121.

Haas, Diana, and Michael Pieris, editors. Βιβλιογραφικός Οδηγός στα 154 Ποιήματα του Καβάφη [*Bibliografikos odigos sta 154 piimata tou Kavafi*; *Bibliographic Guide to the 154 Poems of Cavafy*]. Hermes, 1984.

Hackel, Heidi Brayman, and Ian Frederick Moulton, editors. *Teaching Early Modern English Literature from the Archives*. Modern Language Association of America, 2015.

Hadjikyriakos-Ghikas, Nikos, illustrator. Ποιήματα, 1896–1933 [*Piimata, 1896–1933*; *Poems, 1896–1933*]. By C. P. Cavafy, Ikaros, 1966.

Halberstam, Jack. *In a Queer Time and Place: Transgender Bodies, Subcultural Lives*. New York UP, 2005.

———— [published as Judith Halberstam]. "Queer Temporality and Postmodern Geographies." *Caring Labor: An Archive*, 30 July 2010, caringlabor.wordpress.com/2010/07/30/judith-halberstam-queer-temporality-and-postmodern-geographies/.

Halim, Hala. *Alexandrian Cosmopolitanism: An Archive*. Fordham UP, 2013.

————. "C. P. Cavafy as an Egyptiote." *Boundary 2*, vol. 28, no. 2, 2021, pp. 123–60.

————. "C. P. Cavafy the Egyptiote." International Cavafy Summer School, 12 July 2019, Onassis Foundation, Athens, vimeo.com/489375942/f14f68adb1.

Hall, Jason David, and Alex Murray, editors. *Decadent Poetics: Literature and Form at the British Fin de Siècle*. Palgrave Macmillan, 2013.

Hamilakis, Yannis. *The Nation and Its Ruins: Antiquity, Archaeology, and National Imagination in Greece*. Oxford UP, 2009.

Haninnk, Johanna. "On Not Knowing (Modern) Greek." *Eidolon*, 8 Sept. 2016, eidolon.pub/on-not-knowing-modern-greek-8611bc8151eb.

Haqqi, Mahmud Tahir. عذراء دنشواي [*'Adhra' Dinshiwai*; *The Maiden of Dinshway*]. Ministry of Culture, 1964.

————. *The Maiden of Dinshway*. *Three Pioneering Egyptian Novels*, translated by Saad El-Gabalawy, York, 1986, pp. 17–48.

Hardwick, Lorna, and Christopher Stray. *A Companion to Classical Receptions*. Blackwell, 2008.

Harris, Malcolm. *Kids These Days: Human Capital and the Making of Millennials*. Little, Brown, 2017.

Harrison, Frederic. "Editorial Horseplay." *Fortnightly Review*, vol. 49, Apr. 1891, pp. 642–55.

————. "Give Back the Elgin Marbles." *Nineteenth Century*, vol. 28, no. 166, Dec. 1890, pp. 980–87.

Harvey, Denise, editor. *The Mind and Art of C. P. Cavafy: Essays on His Life and Work*. Denise Harvey, 1983.

Heaney, Seamus. *Opened Ground: Selected Poems, 1966–1996*. Farrar, Straus and Giroux, 1998.

Hennessy, Christopher, editor. "Mark Doty." *Outside the Lines: Talking with Contemporary Gay Poets*, U of Michigan P, 2005, pp. 74–91.

Herzfeld, Michael. *Ours Once More: Folklore, Ideology, and the Making of Modern Greece*. Berghahn, 2020.

Hessenbruch, Carolyn. "Karanis: The Town, the People, and the Excavations." *Guardians of the Nile: Sculptures from Karanis in the Fayoum (c. 250 BC—AD 450)*, edited by Elaine K. Gazda, U of Michigan P, 1978, pp. 9–10.

Higgins, Kevin. "Poem: Waiting for Boris." *The Platform*, 21 June 2019, platformonline.uk/posts/poem-waiting-for-boris.

Hirst, Anthony. Note on the Greek text. Cavafy, *Collected Poems: A New Translation*, pp. xxxiv–xxxix.

———. "Philosophical, Historical, and Sensual: An Examination of Cavafy's Thematic Collections." *Byzantine and Modern Greek Studies*, vol. 19, 1995, pp. 33–93.

Hirst, Anthony, and Sarah Ekdawi. "Hidden Things: Cavafy's Thematic Catalogues." *Modern Greek Studies*, vol. 4, 1996, pp. 1–34.

Hirst, Anthony, and Michael Silk, editors. *Alexandria, Real and Imagined*. Ashgate, 2004.

Hockney, David. *Illustrations for Fourteen Poems from C. P. Cavafy*. 1966. Tate, www.tate.org.uk/art/artworks/hockney-illustrations-for-fourteen-poems-from-cp-cavafy-65477. Accessed 25 June 2024.

Hoffman, Eva. *Lost in Translation: A Life in a New Language*. Penguin Books, 1989.

Hölderlin, Friedrich. *Selected Poetry*. Translated by David Constantine, Bloodaxe Books, 2018.

Homer. *Homeri Ilias*. Edited by Helmut van Thiel, Georg Olms, 1966.

———. *The Iliad*. Translated by Robert Fagles, Viking, 1998.

———. *The Odyssey*. Translated by Robert Fagles, Viking, 1996.

Houston, Natalie M. "Newspaper Poems: Material Texts in the Public Sphere." *Victorian Studies*, vol. 50, no. 2, winter 2008, pp. 233–42.

Huysmans, Joris-Karl. *Against Nature*. Translated by Robert Baldick, Penguin Books, 2003.

Ilbert, Robert, and Ilios Yannakakis, editors. *Alexandria, 1860–1960: The Brief Life of a Cosmopolitan Community*. Harpocrates Publishing, 1997.

"Index." *Onassis Cavafy Archive*, Onassis Foundation, cavafy.onassis.org/index/. Accessed 20 Dec. 2020.

"'In the Month of Athyr' by Constantine Peter Cavafy and John Tavener, with Paul McCartney as Narrator." *YouTube*, uploaded by Lily Snape, 17 Mar. 2023, www.youtube.com/watch?v=f0ng3gijXLo.

Η παγκοσμιότητα του Κωνσταντίνου Καβάφη [*I pangkosmiotita tou Konstantinou Kavafi*; *Constantine Cavafy's Universalism*]. Directed by Tasos Psarras, ERT1, 2013. *YouTube*, uploaded by alter 45, 1 May 2013, youtube.com/watch?v=LXqGkLeWqUY.

إيقاع الحياة [*Iqaʿ al-haya*; *The Rhythm of Life*]. Directed by ʿAtiyyat al-Abnudi, Abnoud Film, 1988. *YouTube*, uploaded by Ateyyat El-Abnoudy, 15 Oct. 2019, www.youtube.com/watch?v=bEIwYmDti4E.

Εις το φως της ημέρας [*Is to fos tis imeras*; *In Broad Daylight*]. Directed by Takis Spetsiotis, 1987. *YouTube*, uploaded by Takis Spetsiotus, 18 Mar. 2019, www.youtube.com/watch?v=nruGBrMJJko.

"'Ithaca' by C. P. Cavafy (Read by Sean Connery)." *YouTube*, uploaded by STRYV, 11 June 2021, youtube.com/watch?v=-uoKzLGQiqo.

"'Ithaca,' by K. P. Kavafis, Read by Ellie Lambeti." *YouTube*, uploaded by Tom's Translations, 20 June 2023, www.youtube.com/watch?v=6nMTLfWjsxQ&t=47s.

Jeffreys, Peter. *Eastern Questions: Hellenism and Orientalism in the Writings of E. M. Forster and C. P. Cavafy*. ELT Press, 2005.

———, editor. *The Forster-Cavafy Letters: Friends at a Slight Angle*. American U in Cairo P, 2009.

———. *Reframing Decadence: C. P. Cavafy's Imaginary Portraits*. Cornell UP, 2015.

Jevons, W. S. *The Theory of Political Economy*. McMillan, 1871.

Julian. *Misopogon; or, Beard-Hater. Orations 6–8. Letters to Themistius, To the Senate and People of Athens, To a Priest. The Caesars. Misopogon*, translated by Wilmer C. Wright, Harvard UP, 1913, pp. 418–512. Loeb Classical Library 29.

Jusdanis, Gregory. "Introduction: Modern Greek! Why?" *Journal of Modern Greek Studies*, vol. 15, no. 2, 1997, pp. 167–74.

———. *The Poetics of Cavafy: Textuality, Eroticism, History*. Princeton UP, 1987.

Jusdanis, Gregory, and Peter Jeffreys. *Constantine Cavafy: A New Biography*. Farrar, Straus and Giroux, 2025.

Kahan, Benjamin. "Conjectures on the Sexual World-System." *GLQ: A Journal of Lesbian and Gay Studies*, vol. 23, no. 3, 2017, https://doi.org/10.1215/10642684-3818441.

Kalasaridou, Sotiria. "The Presence of C. P. Cavafy in Greek Education: Landmarks and Gaps." *Journal of Literary Education*, vol. 2, 2019, pp. 90–109.

Kaplan, Alice Yaeger. "Working in the Archives." *Yale French Studies*, no. 77, 1990, pp. 103–16.

Karagiannis, Vangelis. Σημειώσεις από την Γενεαλογία του Καβάφη [*Simiosis apo tin genealogia tou Kavafi; Notes from Cavafy's Genealogy*]. Greek Literary and Historical Archive, 1983.

Karalis, Vrasidas, and Michael Tsianikas, editors. *Pages on C. P. Cavafy*. Special issue of *Modern Greek Studies (Australia and New Zealand)*. Vols. 11–12, 2003–04.

Karambeti, Karyofillia. Κ.Π. Καβάφης - Η Πόλις - Απολείπειν ο Θεός Αντώνιον (Διαβάζει η Καρυοφυλλιά Καραμπέτη). ["K. P. Kavafis - I Polis - Apolipin o theos Antonion"; "C. P. Cavafy - The City - God Abandoning Antony"]. *YouTube*, uploaded by lekkaspiano, 2 Mar. 2021, www.youtube.com/watch?app=desktop&v=6X0b-y3Qb0s.

Karampini-Iatrou, Michaela, editor. Η Βιβλιοθήκη Κ.Π. Καβάφη [*I bibliothiki K. P. Kavafi; C. P. Cavafy's Library*]. Ermis, 2003.

Karaoglou, Ch. L. Η Αθηναϊκή Κριτική και Ο Καβάφης, 1918–1924 [*I Athinaiki kritiki kai o Kavafis, 1918–1924; Athenian Criticism and Cavafy, 1918–1924*]. University Studio Press, 1985.

———. Κ.Π. Καβάφη [Ριμάριο] ["K. P. Kavafi [Rimario]"; "C. P. Cavafy [A Dictionary of Rhymes]"]. Μολυβδοκονδυλοπελεκητής [*Molyvdo-Kondylo-Pelekitis; Lead-Pencil-Carver*], vol. 2, 1990, pp. 71–123.

"Καβάφεια—Cavafy Symposium" ["Kavafia—Cavafy Symposium"]. *Facebook*, face book.com/CavafySymposium.

Καβάφης [*Kavafis*; *Cavafy*]. Directed by Yannis Smaragdis. Alexandros Film, 1996.

Kayalis, Takis. *Cavafy's Hellenistic Antiquities: History, Archaeology, Empire*. Palgrave Macmillan, 2024.

———. "Cavafy's Historical Poetics in Context: 'Caesarion' as Palimpsest." *On the Intersections of Modern Greece with Greek History and the Past*, special issue of *The Journal of Modern Hellenism*, edited by Nektaria Klapaki and Eirini Kotsovili, vol. 34, 2019, pp. 43–69.

Kazamias, Alexander. "Cromer's Assault on 'Internationalism': British Colonialism and the Greeks of Egypt, 1882–1907." *The Long 1890s in Egypt: Colonial Quiescence, Subterranean Resistance*, edited by M. Booth and A. Gorman, Edinburgh UP, 2014, pp. 253–83.

Keeley, Edmund. *Cavafy's Alexandria: Study of a Myth in Progress*. 1976. Princeton UP, 1996.

———. "Cavafy's Voice and Context." *Grand Street*, vol. 2, no. 3, 1983, pp. 157–77.

———. "C. P. Cavafy's Biography." Ιθάκη [*Ithaki*; *Ithaka*], cavafis.compupress.gr/bio2.htm.

Kelly, Jacinta. "Of Archives and Architecture: Domestication, Digital Collections, and the Poetry of Mina Loy." *Australian Feminist Studies*, vol. 32, nos. 91–92, 2017, pp. 171–85.

Kenyon, F. G. *Classical Texts from Papyri in the British Museum, including the Newly Discovered Poems of Herodas*. Trustees of the British Museum, 1891.

Kern, Richard. "Literacy as a New Organizing Principle." *Reading between the Lines: Perspectives on Foreign Language Literacy*, edited by Peter Patrikis, Yale UP, 2008, pp. 40–59.

Kitroeff, Alexander. "The Alexandria We Have Lost." *Journal of the Hellenic Diaspora*, vol. 10, nos. 1–2, 1983, pp. 11–21.

———. *The Greeks and the Making of Modern Egypt*. American U in Cairo P, 2019.

Klooster, Jacqueline. "Between (Unbearable) Lightness and Darkness: Trends in Scholarship on Hellenistic Poetry." *L'antiquité lassique*, vol. 83, 2014, pp. 159–69. *JSTOR*, www.jstor.org/stable/90004716.

Knowles, James. "The Joke about the Elgin Marbles." *Nineteenth Century*, vol. 29, Mar. 1891, pp. 495–506.

Kolaitis, Memas. *Cavafy As I Knew Him: With Twelve Annotated Translations of His Poems and a Translation of the Golden Verses of Pythagoras*. Kolaitis Dictionaries, 1980.

Korsos, Demetrios I. Το ελληνικό προσώπο του Καβάφης ["To elliniko prosopo tou Kavafi"; "Cavafy's Greek Face"]. Κριτικά Φύλλα [*Kritika Fylla*; *Critical Sheets*], vol. 6, 1978, pp. 67–93.

Kourelis, Kostas. "Closing the Window on Cavafy: Foregrounding the Background in the Photographic Portraits." Papanikolaou and Papargyriou, *Pop Cavafy*, pp. 227–52.

Κ.Π. Καβάφης—50 Χρόνια από τον θάνατό του [K. P. Kavafis—50 xronia apo to thanato tou; C. P. Cavafy—Fifty Years after His Death]. 1983. *YouTube*, uploaded by beasilentman, 21 July 2011, youtube.com/watch?v=tkksWnnHxZ0&t=2264s.

Κ.Π. Καβάφης, Η Πόλις (Όπου Το Μάτι Μου Γυρίσω) [K. P. Kavafis, i polis (Opou to mati mou gyriso); C. P. Cavafy, The City (Wherever I Turn My Eye)]. Directed by Panayiotis Kountouras and Aristarchos Papadaniel. *YouTube*, uploaded by Syllipsis, 10 Feb. 2019, youtube.com/watch?v=JCog2bWWi5U.

Kramer, Lawrence. *Music and Poetry: The Nineteenth Century and After*. U of California P, 1984.

Kramsch, Claire. *The Multilingual Subject: What Foreign Language Learners Say about Their Experiences and Why It Matters*. Oxford UP, 2010.

Kruczkowska, Joanna. *Irish Poets and Modern Greece: Heaney, Mahon, Cavafy, Seferis*. Palgrave Macmillan, 2017.

Lambropoulos, Vassilis. *Literature as National Institution: Studies in the Politics of Modern Greek Criticism*. Princeton UP, 1988.

———. "'Modern as Opposed to What?' The C. P. Cavafy Professorship Inaugural Address." *Convivium*, Department of Classical Studies, U of Michigan, vol. 7, summer 2002, pp. 3–7. Newsletter.

———. Πώς ο Καβάφης έγινε από συγγραφέας πεδίο ["Pos o Kavafis egine apo syggrafeas pedio"; "How Cavafy the Author Became a Field"]. Αυγή [*Avgi; Dawn*], 5 Jan. 2014, p. 41.

———. "The Violent Power of Knowledge: The Struggle of Discourses for Power over C. P. Cavafy's 'Young Men of Sidon, A.D. 400.'" *Journal of the Hellenic Diaspora*, vol. 10, nos. 1–2, 1983, pp. 149–66.

Lanier, Jaron. *Ten Arguments for Deleting Your Social Media Accounts Right Now*. Henry Holt, 2018.

Larkin, Philip. *Required Writing: Miscellaneous Pieces, 1955–1982*. U of Michigan P, 1999.

Layoun, Mary N., editor. *Modernism in Greece? Essays on the Critical and Literary Margins of a Movement*. Pella Publishing, 1990.

Lee, Lawrence Lynn. "The Julian Poems of C. P. Cavafy." *CLA Journal*, vol. 10, no. 3, 1967, pp. 239–51.

Lefevere, André. *Translation, Rewriting, and the Manipulation of Literary Fame*. Routledge, 1992.

Lefkowitz, Mary R., and James S. Romm, editors. *The Greek Plays: Sixteen Plays by Aeschylus, Sophocles, and Euripides*. Modern Library, 2016.

Lehnus, Luigi. "Callimachus Rediscovered in Papyri." *Brill's Companion to Callimachus*, edited by Benjamin Acosta-Hughes et al., Brill, 2011, pp. 23–38.

Leontis, Artemis, et al., editors. *"What These Ithakas Mean": Readings in Cavafy*. Hellenic Literary and Historical Archive, 2002.

Liddell, Henry G., et al. *Greek-English Lexicon: A Supplement*. Clarendon Press, 1968.

Liddell, Robert. *Cavafy: A Critical Biography*. Reprint ed., Duckworth, 2000.

———. *Unreal City*. Peter Owen, 1952.

Lopez, Matthew. *The Inheritance*. Faber and Faber, 2018.
Love, Heather. *Feeling Backward: Loss and the Politics of Queer History*. Harvard UP, 2007.
Mackridge, Peter. Introduction. Cavafy, *Collected Poems: A New Translation*, pp. xi–xxxiii.
———. *Language and National Identity in Greece, 1766–1976*. Oxford UP, 2009.
Mahaffy, J. P. *Empire of the Ptolemies*. Macmillan, 1895.
Malanos, Timos. Ο ποιητής Κ.Π. Καβάφης [*O piitis K. P. Kavafis; The Poet C. P. Cavafy*]. Difros, 1957.
Maronitis, Dimitrios N. Κ.Π. Καβάφης: Μελετήματα [*K. P. Kavafis: Meletimata; C. P. Cavafy: Studies*]. Ekdoseis Pataki, 2007.
Martindale, Charles, and Richard F. Thomas, editors. *Classics and the Uses of Reception*. Blackwell, 2006.
McCann, Richard. *Nights of 1990*. Warm Spring Press, 1990.
McGann, Jerome. *A Critique of Modern Textual Studies*. U of Chicago P, 1983.
McKinsey, Martin. "The Aesthetics of Pleasure." Cavafy, *Clearing*, pp. 125–60.
———. "Cavafy on Shakespeare: Two Essays and a Poem." *In-Between: Essays and Studies in Literary Criticism*, vol. 6, no. 1, 1997, pp. 3–18.
———. *Hellenism and the Postcolonial Imagination: Yeats, Cavafy, Walcott*. Fairleigh Dickinson UP, 2010.
McNamee, Roger. *Zucked: Waking Up to the Facebook Catastrophe*. Penguin Books, 2019.
Meguid, Ibrahim Abdel. *No One Sleeps in Alexandria*. Translated by Farouk Abdel Wahab, American U in Cairo P, 2006.
Mendelsohn, Daniel. "The Right Poem." *The New Yorker*, 27 July 2015, www.newyorker.com/magazine/2015/07/27/the-right-poem.
———. "'Waiting for the Barbarians' and the Government Shutdown." *The New Yorker*, 1 Oct. 2013, newyorker.com/books/page-turner/waiting-for-the-barbarians-and-the-government-shutdown.
Menger, Carl. *Grundsätze der Volkswirtschaftslehre*. Wilhelm Braumüller, 1871.
Merrill, James. *Collected Poems*. Edited by J. D. McClatchey and Stephen Yenser, Alfred A. Knopf, 2001.
———. "Marvelous Poet." Review of *Cavafy: A Critical Biography*, by Robert Liddell, and *C. P. Cavafy: Collected Poems*, translated by Edmund Keeley and Philip Sherrard. *The New York Review of Books*, vol. 22, no. 12, July 1975, pp. 12–17.
Michals, Duane. *The Adventures of Constantine Cavafy*. Twin Palms Publishers, 2007.
———. *Homage to Cavafy*. Addison House, 1978.
Mishan, Freda. *Designing Authenticity into Language Learning Materials*. Intellect, 2005.
Mitchell, Eleanor, et al., editors. *Past or Portal? Enhancing Undergraduate Learning through Special Collections and Archives*. Association of College and Research Libraries, 2012.

Monsacré, Hélène. *Les larmes d'Achille: Le héros, la femme et la souffrance dans la poésie d'Homère*. A. Michel, 1984.

Moretti, Franco. "Conjectures on World Literature." *New Left Review*, vol. 1, 2000, pp. 54–68.

Moschos, E. N. Ιλίας Φ. Ιλίου ["Ilias F. Iliou"]. Νέα Εστία [*Nea Estia*; *New Home*], no. 1383, 1985, pp. 261–63.

Muldoon, Paul. *Selected Poems, 1968–2014*. Faber and Faber, 2016.

Muñoz, José Esteban. *Cruising Utopia: The Then and There of Queer Futurity*. New York UP, 2009.

Mursi, Ahmad. إسكندرية كافافي ["Iskandariyyat Kavafi"; "Cavafy's Alexandria"]. Introduction. كافافي شاعر الإسكندرية [*Kavafi: Sha'ir al-Iskandariyya*; *Cavafy: Poet of Alexandria*], by C. P. Cavafy, translated by Ahmad Mursi, Manshurat al-Khazindar, 1992, pp. 55–72.

Nagy, Gregory. *The Best of the Achaeans: Concepts of the Hero in Archaic Greek Poetry*. Rev. ed., Johns Hopkins UP, 1999.

"The New Cavafy Archive Building on Frynich Street in Plaka." *Onassis*, Onassis Foundation, www.onassis.org/initiatives/cavafy-archive/the-new-cavafy-archive-building-on-frynichou-street-in-plaka. Accessed 1 Apr. 2024.

"Newspaper *La Réforme*." *Onassis Cavafy Archive*, Onassis Foundation, https://doi.org/10.26256/ca-sf02-s02-f25-sf007-0038.

Nikolakopoulos, Ilias. Ηλίας Ηλίου: Πολιτική Βιογραφία [*Ilias Iliou: Politiki viografia*; *Ilias Iliou: Political Biography*]. Idryma tis Voulis ton Ellinon, 2017.

Nikolaou, Paschalis. *The Return of Pytheas: Scenes from British and Greek Poetry in Dialogue*. Shearsman Books, 2017.

Τη Νύχτα που ο Φερνάντο Πεσσόα συνάντησε τον Κωνσταντίνο Καβάφη [*Ti nychta pou o Fernando Pessoa synantise ton Konstantino Kavafi*; *The Night Fernando Pessoa Met Constantine Cavafy*]. Directed by Stelios Charalambopoulos, 2008. *Internet Archive*, archive.org/details/TheNightFernandoPessoaMetConstantineCavafy.

Oliver, Mary. *Devotions: The Selected Poems of Mary Oliver*. Penguin Books, 2017.

"Open Call: International Cavafy Summer School 2023." *Onassis Cavafy Archive*, Onassis Foundation, www.onassis.org/open-calls/open-call-international-cavafy-summer-school-2023.

Orphanos, Stathis. *My Cavafy: Chance Encounters*. Preface by Gore Vidal, Sylvester and Orphanos, 2006.

Osborne, Peter. *The Politics of Time: Modernity and Avant-Garde*. Verso, 1995.

Ó Searcaigh, Cathal. *Out in the Open*. Edited and translated by Frank Sewell, Cló Iar-Chonnachta, 1997.

———. *Out of the Wilderness*. Translated by Gabriel Rosenstock, Onslaught Press, 2016.

Pamuk, Orhan. "Other Countries, Other Shores." *Subterranean Histories: Constantine Cavafy and the Poetics of Memory*, special issue of *Studies in the Literary Imagination*, edited by Louis A. Ruprecht, vol. 48, no. 2, fall 2015, pp. 107–09.

Panagiotopoulos, I. M. Τα πρόσωπα και τα πράγματα [*Ta prosopa kai ta pragmata*; *The Faces and the Texts*]. Aetos, 1946. Vol. 4 of Κ.Π. Καβάφης [*K. P. Kavafis*; *C. P. Cavafy*].

Papadimitriou, Dimitris, composer. *C. P. Cavafy: An Alexandrian Writes on an Alexandrian*. Alexandria Publications, 2007. CD booklet.

Papadopoulou, Margarita A. Η διδακτική του Καβάφη: Διδακτική προσέγγιση ποιημάτων με βάση γλωσσοπαιδαγωγικά πρότυπα ανάλυσης [*I didaktiki tou Kavafi: Didaktiki proseggisi piimaton me basi glossopaidagogika protypa analysis*; *Methods of Teaching Cavafy: An Approach to the Poems Based on Glosso-Pedagogical Models Analysis*]. Midnight Editions, 2015.

Papaleontiou, Lefteris. Προσθήκες στη βιβλιογραφία Κ.Π. Καβάφη, 1907–2000 ["Prosthikes sti bibliografia K. P. Kavafi, 1907–2000"; "Supplements to the C. P. Cavafy Bibliography, 1907–2000"]. Μικρά φιλολογικά τετράδια [*Mikra filologika tetradia*; *Small Philological Notebooks*], vol. 22, no. 40, 2016.

Papanikolaou, Dimitris. "Days of Those Made Like Me: Retrospective Pleasure, Sexual Knowledge, and C. P. Cavafy's Homobiographics." *Byzantine and Modern Greek Studies*, vol. 37, no. 2, 2013, pp. 261–77.

———. "The Pensive Spectator, the Possessive Reader and the Archive of Queer Feelings: A Reading of Constantine Giannaris's *Trojans*." Papanikolaou and Papargyriou, *Pop Cavafy*, pp. 279–97.

———. Σαν κ' εμένα καμωμένοι: Ο ομοφυλόφιλος Καβάφης και η ποιητική της σεξουαλικότητας [*San k' emena kamomenoi: O omofylofilos Kavafis kai i piitiki tis sexoualikotitas*; *Created Like Me: Gay Cavafy and Sexual Poetics*]. Pataki, 2014.

———. "'Words That Tell and Hide': Revisiting C. P. Cavafy's Closets." *Journal of Modern Greek Studies*, vol. 23, 2005, pp. 235–60.

Papanikolaou, Dimitris, and Eleni Papargyriou. "Cavafy Pop: Popular Reception, Cultural Productivity and the Many Lives of Poems." Papanikolaou and Papargyriou, *Pop Cavafy*, pp. 183–90.

———, editors. *Pop Cavafy: Readings of C. P. Cavafy in Popular Culture*. Special issue of *Journal of Greek Media and Culture*. Vol. 1, no. 2, 2015.

Paparrigopoulos, K. Ιστορία του ελληνικού έθνους, από των αρχαιοτάτων χρόνων μέχρι των νεωτέρων, χάριν των πολλών [*Istoria tou ellinikou ethnous, apo ton archaiotaton chronon mechri ton neoteron, charin ton pollon*; *History of the Greek Nation, from Ancient Times to Modern, for the Sake of the Many*]. N. F. Passari, 1865–71. 4 vols.

Pappa, Amalia. Η γεύση του αρχείου, Το αρχείο του Κ.Π. Καβάφη ["*I geysi tou archiou, to archio tou K. P. Kavafi*"; "The Taste of the Archive: C. P. Cavafy's Archive"]. Αρχείο Καβάφη—Βέλτιστες Πρακτικές Οργάνωσης Αρχείων [*Archio Kavafi—Beltistes Praktikes Organosis Archion*; *The Cavafy Archive—Best Practices on Archival Organization*], special issue of Νέα Εστία [*Nea Estia*; *New Home*], edited by Takis Kayalis et al., vol. 185, no. 1885, Dec. 2020, pp. 378–93.

Paschalis, Michael. "Cavafy's 'Iliadic' Poems." Roilos, *Imagination*, pp. 153–72.

Patel, Geeta. *Lyrical Movements, Historical Hauntings: On Gender, Colonialism, and Desire in Miraji's Urdu Poetry*. Stanford UP, 2002.

Peridis, Michalis. Ο βίος και το έργο του Κωνσταντίνου Καβάφη [*O vios kai to ergo tou Konstantinou Kavafi; The Life and Work of Constantine Cavafy*]. Ikaros, 1948.

Philip, M. NourbeSe. *Zong*. Mercury Press, 2008.

Philippides, Dia M. L. *Check-list of English-Language Sources Useful in the Study of Modern Greek Literature, 1824–1987*. Modern Greek Studies Association, 1990.

Pieris, Michalis. Σημειώματα για τα τελευταία χρόνια και την αρρώστια της Χαρίκλειας Καβάφη (1899) ["Simiomata gia ta teleutaia chronia kai tin arostia tis Chariklias Kavafi (1899)"; "Notes on the Final Years and Illness of Haricleia Cavafy (1899)"]. Μολυβδοκονδυλοπελεκητής [*Molyvdo-Kondylo-Pelekitis; Lead-Pencil-Carver*], no. 3, 1991, pp. 171–210.

Pinchin, Jane Lagoudis. *Alexandria Still: Forster, Durrell, and Cavafy*. Princeton UP, 1977.

Plantzos, Dimitris. "Behold the Raking Geison: The New Acropolis Museum." *Antiquity*, vol. 85, no. 328, 2011, pp. 613–25.

———. "Perverse Fragments: Citing Cavafy in Crisis-Stricken Athens." Papanikolaou and Papargyriou, *Pop Cavafy*, pp. 191–205.

Plato. *Platonis Opera*. Edited by John Burnet, Oxford UP, 1903.

———. *The Republic*. Translated by Desmond Lee, Penguin Classics, 2007.

Poe, Edgar Allan. *The Selected Writing of Edgar Allan Poe*. Edited by G. R. Thompson, W. W. Norton, 2004.

Poggioli, Renato. "*Qualis Artifex Pereo!* or, Barbarism and Decadence." Harvey, pp. 127–56.

Politis, Linos. *A History of Modern Greek Literature*. Oxford UP, 1973.

"Pornostroika Dadaifi—Το Λυκόφως των Πορνοκρατόρων [2004]." *YouTube*, uploaded by Panos WakeUp, 16 Sept. 2021, www.youtube.com/watch?v=FfhmsJLP2vo&t=2589s.

Porter, James I. "What Is 'Classical' about Classical' Antiquity? Eight Propositions." *Arion*, vol. 13, no. 1, 2005, pp. 27–61.

Potolsky, Matthew. *The Decadent Republic of Letters: Taste, Politics, and Cosmopolitan Community from Baudelaire to Beardsley*. U of Pennsylvania P, 2013.

Rabel, Robert J. "Apollo as a Model for Achilles in the *Iliad*." *The American Journal of Philology*, vol. 111, no. 4, 1990, pp. 429–40.

Radt, Stefan, editor. *Aeschylus*. Vandenhoeck and Ruprecht, 1985. Vol. 3 of *Tragicorum graecorum fragmenta*.

Ramanujan, A. K. *The Collected Poems of A. K. Ramanujan*. Oxford UP, 2011.

Ramazani, Jahan. *The Hybrid Muse: Postcolonial Poetry in English*. U of Chicago P, 2001.

Reid, David Malcolm. *Contesting Antiquity in Egypt: Archaeology, Museums and the Struggle for Identities from World War I to Nasser*. American U in Cairo P, 2015.

———. *Whose Pharaohs? Archaeology, Museums, and Egyptian National Identity from Napoleon to World War I*. U of California P, 2002.

Reimer, Michael J. *Colonial Bridgehead: Government and Society in Alexandria, 1807–1882*. Westview, 1997.
Report from the Select Committee of the House of Commons on the Earl of Elgin's Sculptures Marbles &c. John Murray, 1816.
Reynolds, Matthew. *The Poetry of Translation*. Oxford UP, 2011.
Rhys, Jean. *Wide Sargasso Sea*. W. W. Norton, 1966.
Ricks, David. "Cavafy the Poet-Historian." *Byzantine and Modern Greek Studies*, vol. 12, 1988, pp. 169–83.
———. *The Shade of Homer: A Study in Modern Greek Poetry*. Cambridge UP, 1989.
Roberts, James A., and Meredith E. David. "The Social Media Party: Fear of Missing Out (FOMO), Social Media Intensity, Connection, and Well-Being." *International Journal of Human-Computer Interaction*, vol. 36, no. 4, 2020, pp. 386–92.
Robinson, Christopher. *C. P. Cavafy*. Aristide D. Caratzas, 1988.
Roilos, Panagiotis. *C. P. Cavafy: The Economics of Metonymy*. U of Illinois P, 2009.
———, editor. *Imagination and Logos: Essays on C. P. Cavafy*. Department of the Classics, Harvard U / Harvard UP, 2010.
Rowe, Christopher, editor and translator. *The Last Days of Socrates: Euthyphro, Apology, Crito, Phaedo*. Penguin Classics, 2011.
Ruprecht, Louis A., editor. *Subterranean Histories: Constantine Cavafy and the Poetics of Memory*. Special issue of *Studies in the Literary Imagination*. Vol. 48, no. 2, fall 2015.
Rushdie, Salman. "The Empire Writes Back with a Vengeance." *The Times*, 3 July 1982, p. 8.
Rutherford, W. G. Ἡρώνδου μιμίαβοι: Herondas [*Irondou mimiavi: Herondas*; *The Mimiambs of Herodas*]. Macmillan, 1891.
Said, Edward W. "Glimpses of Late Style." *On Late Style: Music and Literature against the Grain*, by Said, Vintage, 2006, pp. 134–48.
———. "Reflections on Ireland and Postcolonialism." Afterword. *Ireland and Postcolonial Theory*, edited by Patricia King and Clare Carroll, U of Notre Dame P, 2003, pp. 177–85.
———. "Yeats and Decolonization." *Nationalism, Colonialism, and Literature*, edited by Terry Eagleton et al., U of Minnesota P, 1990, pp. 69–98.
Sakallieros, Giorgos. *Dimitri Mitropoulos and His Works in the 1920s: The Introduction of Musical Modernism in Greece*. Hellenic Music Centre, 2016.
Savidis, George P. Το αρχείο Κ.Π. Καβάφη ["To archio K. P. Kavafi"; "The Archive of C. P. Cavafy"]. Μικρά Καβαφικά [*Mikra Kavafika*; *Small Cavafy Works*], vol. 1, edited by Savidis, Hermes, 1985, pp. 29–55.
———. Το αρχείο Κ.Π. Καβάφη: Πρώτη ενημερωτική έκθεση [*To archio tou Kavafi: Proti enimerotiki ekthesi*; *The Cavafy Archive: A Preliminary Enumerative Essay*]. 1964.
———. Οι Καβαφικές εκδόσεις, 1891–1932 [*I Kavafikes ekdosis, 1891–1932*; *Cavafian Editions, 1891–1932*]. Ikaros, 1992.

———. Μικρά Καβαφικά Α [*Mikra Kavafika A*; *Small Cavafy Works A*]. Vol. 1, Hermes, 1985.

———. Μικρά Καβαφικά Β [*Mikra Kavafika B*; *Small Cavafy Works B*]. Vol. 2, Hermes, 1987.

Savidis, Lena. Λεύκωμα Καβάφη, 1863–1910 [*Leykoma Kavafi, 1863–1910*; *Cavafy Album, 1863–1910*]. Stamou and Sons, 1983.

Savidis, Manolis. Κ.Π. Καβάφης: Κατάλογος εκθεμάτων [*K. P. Kavafis: Katalogos ekthematon*; *C. P. Cavafy: Exhibit Catalogue*]. Center for Neo-Hellenic Studies, 2008.

———. Κ.Π. Καβάφης: Ο ανθρωπος και η εποχή του [*K. P. Kavafis: O anthropos kai i epochi tou*; *C. P. Cavafy: The Man and His Epoch*]. Hermes, 2003. CD-ROM.

Schein, Seth L. "Cavafy and *Iliad* 24: A Modern Alexandrian Interprets Homer." *Homer*, edited by K. C. King, Garland, 1994, pp. 177–89.

———. *Homeric Epic and Its Reception: Interpretive Essays*. Oxford UP, 2016.

Schwarz, Roberto. *Misplaced Ideas: Essays on Brazilian Culture*. Translated by John Gledson, Verso, 1992.

Scodel, Ruth. "Apollo's Perfidy: Iliad ω 59–63." *Harvard Studies in Classical Philology*, vol. 81, 1977, pp. 55–57.

Sedgwick, Eve Kosofsky. *The Epistemology of the Closet*. U of California P, 1990.

———. *The Weather in Proust*. Duke UP, 2011.

Seferis, George. "Cavafy and Eliot—a Comparison." *On the Greek Style: Selected Essays in Poetry and Hellenism*, translated by Th. D. Frangopoulos and Rex Warner, Little, Brown, 1966.

———. *A Poet's Journal: Days of 1945–1951*. Translated by Athan Anagnostopoulos, Harvard UP, 1999.

Segal, Charles P. *The Theme of the Mutilation of the Corpse in the Iliad*. Brill, 1972.

Shakespeare, William. *Julius Caesar*. Edited by Arthur Humphreys, Oxford UP, 1994.

Shaw, George Bernard. *John Bull's Other Island*. Brentano's, 1916.

Shelley, Percy Bysshe. *A Defense of Poetry*. Edited by Albert S. Cook, Ginn, 1890.

Showalter, Elaine. *Daughters of Decadence: Women Writers of the Fin-de-Siècle*. Rutgers UP, 1993.

Sichani, Anna-Maria. "Cavafy's Web Legacy: C. P. Cavafy in the Public Sphere of the Web 2.0." Papanikolaou and Papargyriou, *Pop Cavafy*, pp. 321–37.

Σημειώματα ["Simeiomata"; "Notes"]. Αλεξανδρινή Τέχνη [*Alexandrini Techni*; *Alexandrian Art*], vol. 5, nos. 9–10, 1931, pp. 300–03.

Smith, Carrie, and Lisa Stead, editors. *The Boundaries of the Literary Archive: Reclamation and Representation*. Ashgate, 2013.

Sommer, Theo. "Griechenland nach den Kürzungen–ein Gedicht." *Zeit Online*, 17 Sept. 2013, zeit.de/wirtschaft/2013-09/griechenland-kavafis-austeritaet.

Sphaellou, Kalliope A. Καβάφης ό ελληνικός [*Kavafis o ellinikos*; *The Greek Cavafy*]. 1977.

Srinivasan, Ragini Tharoor. "South Asia from Postcolonial to World Anglophone." *Interventions*, vol. 20, nos. 3–4, 2018, pp. 309–16, https://doi.org/10.1080/1369801X.2018.1446840.

Srivastava, Aruna. "The Empire Writes Back: Language and History in 'Shame' and 'Midnight's Children.'" *Ariel: A Review of International English Literature*, vol. 20, no. 4, 1989, pp. 62–78.

Steiner, George. *Extraterritorial: Papers on Literature and the Language Revolution*. Atheneum, 1971.

Stilling, Robert. *Beginning at the End: Decadence, Modernism, and Postcolonial Poetry*. Harvard UP, 2018.

Stoddart, Anna. *John Stuart Blackie: A Biography*. 2nd ed., William Blackwood and Sons, 1896.

Stoler, Ann Laura. *Along the Archival Grain: Epistemic Anxieties and Colonial Common Sense*. Princeton UP, 2009.

Stroebel, William. "Some Assembly Required: Suspending and Extending the Book with Cavafy's Collections." *Book History*, vol. 21, 2018, pp. 278–318.

A Study Guide for C. P. Cavafy's "Ithaka." Gale Cengage Learning, 2017.

Suetonius. *The Lives of the Twelve Caesars: An English Translation, Augmented with the Biographies of Contemporary Statesmen, Orators, Poets, and Other Associates*. Edited by J. Eugene Reed, translated by Alexander Thomson, Philadelphia, 1889.

Sutton, David C. "The Destinies of Literary Manuscripts: Past, Present and Future." *Archives and Manuscripts*, vol. 42, no. 3, 2014, pp. 295–300.

"Teaching the Archive." *Modern Language Association*, 2023, apps.mla.org/conv_listings_detail?prog_id=291&year=2016.

Thucydides. *History of the Peloponnesian War*. Translated by Richard Crawley, Dover Publications, 2017.

Tiffin, Helen. "Post-colonial Literatures and Counter-discourse." *Kunapipi*, vol. 9, no. 3, 1987, pp. 17–38.

Tompkins, Jane P. *Reader-Response Criticism: From Formalism to Post-structuralism*. Johns Hopkins UP, 1980.

A Tribute to C. P. Cavafy. *YouTube*, uploaded by PEN America, 24 Jan. 2014, youtube.com/watch?v=lkaHlsPRiDM.

Trimi, Katerina, and Ilios Yannakakis. "The Greeks: The *Parikia* of Alexandria." *Alexandria, 1860–1960: The Brief Life of a Cosmopolitan Community*, edited by Robert Ilber and Yannakakis, translated by Colin Clement, Harpocrates, 1997, pp. 65–71.

Trojans Eng Version. *Vimeo*, uploaded by Constantine Giannaris, 8 Mar. 2018, vimeo.com/259110579.

Trojans / Τρώες New Greek Version 2013. *Vimeo*, uploaded by Constantine Giannaris, 10 Aug. 2016, vimeo.com/178348254.

Tsiastikas, Theseas. Ο Σχολικός Καβάφης [*O scholikos Kavafis*; *The Teaching Guide to Cavafy*]. Books for All, 1994.

Tsirkas, Stratis. Ο Καβάφης και η εποχή του [*O Kavafis kai i epochi tou*; *Cavafy and His Times*]. 1958. Kedros, 1995.

———. Ο πολιτικός Καβάφης [*O politikos Kavafis*; *The Political Cavafy*]. 1971. Kedros, 1984.

Turkle, Sherry. *Reclaiming Conversation: The Power of Talk in a Digital Age*. Penguin Books, 2015.

Turner, Frank M. *The Greek Heritage in Victorian Britain*. Yale UP, 1981.

Tziovas, Dimitris, editor. *Greek Modernism and Beyond*. Rowman and Littlefield, 1997.

Tzouvelis, Spyros. *The Greek Poet Cavafy and History*. Translated by Panos Karagiorgos, Cambridge Scholars, 2016.

Vagenas, Nasos, editor. Συνομιλώντας με τον Καβάφη: Ανθολογία ξένων καβαφογενών ποιημάτων [*Snomilontas me ton Kavafi: Anthologia xenon kavafogenon piimaton; Conversing with Cavafy: An Anthology of Foreign Cavafian Poems*]. Center for the Greek Language, 2000.

Valaoritis, Nanos, and Thanasis Maskaleris, editors. *An Anthology of Modern Greek Poetry*. Talisman House, 2003.

Vanderborght, Paul. Letter to C. P. Cavafy. 4 Dec. 1928. *Onassis Cavafy Archive*, Onassis Foundation, https://doi.org/10.26256/ca-sf02-s01-ss01-f18-sf003-0109.

———. Letter to C. P. Cavafy. 12 Apr. 1929. *Onassis Cavafy Archive*, Onassis Foundation, https://doi.org/10.26256/ca-sf02-s01-ss01-f18-sf003-0114.

Van Dijck, José. *The Culture of Connectivity: A Critical History of Social Media*. Oxford UP, 2013.

Van Vechten, Carl. *Spider Boy: A Scenario for a Moving Picture*. Alfred A. Knopf, 1928.

Verlaine, Paul. *Jadis et naguère*. Léon Vanier, 1884.

Ververis, Apostolos. Photograph of Cavafy's bedroom and study. 1933. *Onassis Cavafy Archive*, Onassis Foundation, https://doi.org/10.26256/sing-s01-f04-0009.

Voss, Paul, and Marta Werner. "Toward a Poetics of the Archive." *Studies in the Literary Imagination*, vol. 32, no. 1, 1999, pp. i–viii.

Walcott, Derek. *Omeros*. Faber and Faber, 1990.

———. *Selected Poems*. Edited by Edward Baugh, Farrar, Straus and Giroux, 2007.

Watson, J. L. "Bodies Out of Time: Sculpting Queer Poetics and Queering Classical Sculpture in the Poetry of C. P. Cavafy." *International Journal of the Classical Tradition*, vol. 29, no. 2, 2021, pp. 190–213.

"What Is a Modern Poet Doing in an Archaeological Museum?" *Cavafy's World*, Kelsey Museum of Archaeology / Foundation for Modern Greek Studies, exhibitions.kelsey.lsa.umich.edu/galleries/Exhibits/cavafy/intro.html.

Whibley, Charles. "The 'Mimes' of Herodas." *Nineteenth Century*, vol. 30, Nov. 1891, pp. 746–52.

White, Hayden. *Figural Realism: Studies in the Mimesis Effect*. Johns Hopkins UP, 1999.

———. *Tropics of Discourse: Essays in Cultural Criticism*. Johns Hopkins UP, 1985.

Wilde, Oscar. *Oscar Wilde: The Major Works*. Edited by Isobel Murray, Oxford UP, 1989.

———. "The Soul of Man under Socialism." *The Artist as Critic: Critical Writings of Oscar Wilde*, edited by Richard Ellmann, U of Chicago P, 1967, pp. 255–89.

"World-Readiness Standards for Learning Languages." *ACTFL*, www.actfl.org/educator-resources/world-readiness-standards-for-learning-languages.

Xenopoulos, Grigoris. Ένας ποιητής ["Enas piitis"; "A Poet"]. Παναθήναια [*Panathinea*; *Panathenian*], no. 7, 30 Nov. 1903, pp. 97–102.

Yatromanolakis, Dimitrios. *Sappho in the Making: The Early Reception*. Center for Hellenic Studies / Trustees for Harvard University, 2007.

Yatromanolakis, Dimitrios, and Panagiotis Roilos. *Towards a Ritual Poetics*. Foundation of the Hellenic World, 2003.

Yeros, Dimitris. *Shades of Love: Photographs Inspired by the Poems of C. P. Cavafy*. Insight, 2010.

Yourcenar, Marguerite. "A Critical Introduction to Cavafy." 1939. *"The Dark Brain of Piranesi" and Other Essays*, translated by Richard Howard, Farrar, Straus and Giroux, 1984, pp. 154–98.

Youssef, Saadi. *Nostalgia, My Enemy*. Translated by Sinan Antoon and Peter Money, Graywolf Press, 2012.

———. *Without an Alphabet, without a Face*. Translated by Khaled Mattawa, Graywolf Press, 2002.

Zacharia, Katerina, editor. *Hellenisms: Culture, Identity, and Ethnicity from Antiquity to Modernity*. Ashgate, 2008.

Zamarou, Eirene. Καβάφης και Πλάτων: Πλατωνικά Στοιχεία στην Καβαφική Ποίηση [*Kavafis kai Platon: Platonika stichia stin Kavafiki piisi*; *Cavafy and Plato: Platonic Elements in Cavafy's Poetry*]. Kedros, 2005.

Zerba, Michelle. *Modern Odysseys: Cavafy, Woolf, Césaire and a Poetics of Indirection*. Ohio State UP, 2021.